Interpretation of
BLOODSTAIN EVIDENCE
at Crime Scenes
Second Edition

CRC SERIES IN
**PRACTICAL ASPECTS OF CRIMINAL
AND FORENSIC INVESTIGATIONS**

VERNON J. GEBERTH, BBA, MPS, FBINA *Series Editor*

**Practical Homicide Investigation: Tactics, Procedures, and Forensic Techniques,
   Third Edition**
Vernon J. Geberth

The Counter-Terrorism Handbook: Tactics, Procedures, and Techniques
Frank Bolz, Jr., Kenneth J. Dudonis, and David P. Schulz

Forensic Pathology
Dominick J. Di Maio and Vincent J. M. Di Maio

Interpretation of Bloodstain Evidence at Crime Scenes, Second Edition
William G. Eckert and Stuart H. James

Tire Imprint Evidence
Peter McDonald

Practical Drug Enforcement: Procedures and Administration
Michael D. Lyman

Practical Aspects of Rape Investigation: A Multidisciplinary Approach
Robert R. Hazelwood and Ann Wolbert Burgess

**The Sexual Exploitation of Children: A Practical Guide to Assessment,
   Investigation, and Intervention, Second Edition**
Seth L. Goldstein

**Gunshot Wounds: Practical Aspects of Firearms, Ballistics, and Forensic
   Techniques, Second Edition**
Vincent J. M. Di Maio

Friction Ridge Skin: Comparison and Identification of Fingerprints
James F. Cowger

Footwear Impression Evidence, Second Edition
William J. Bodziak

Principles of Kinesic Interview and Interrogation
Stan Walters

Practical Fire and Arson Investigation, Second Edition
David R. Redsicker and John J. O'Connor

The Practical Methodology of Forensic Photography
David R. Redsicker

Practical Gambling Investigation Techniques
Kevin B. Kinnee

Practical Aspects of Interview and Interrogation
David E. Zulawski and Douglas E. Wicklander

Practical Investigation Techniques
Kevin B. Kinnee

Investigating Computer Crime
Franklin Clark and Ken Diliberto

Practical Homicide Investigation Checklist and Field Guide
Vernon J. Geberth

Bloodstain Pattern Analysis: With an Introduction to Crime Scene Reconstruction
Tom Bevel and Ross M. Gardner

Interpretation of
BLOODSTAIN EVIDENCE
at Crime Scenes
Second Edition

Stuart H. James
James and Associates
Forensic Consultants, Inc.
Fort Lauderdale, Florida

William G. Eckert, M.D.
Forensic Pathologist (Retired)
Terrytown, Louisiana

CRC Press
Boca Raton   Boston   London   New York   Washington, D.C.

Library of Congress Cataloging-in-Publication Data

James, Stuart H.
     Interpretation of bloodstain evidence at crime scenes / Stuart H.
James and William G. Eckert. — 2nd ed.
          p.   cm. — (CRC series in practical aspects of criminal and
forensic investigations)
     Rev. ed. of: Interpretation of bloodstain evidence at crime scenes /
William G. Eckert, Stuart H. James.   1993.
     Includes bibliographical references and index.
     ISBN 0-8493-8126-6 (alk. paper)
     1. Bloodstains—Analysis.   2. Forensic hematology.   I. Eckert,
William G., 1926–   .   II. Eckert, William G., 1926–   .
Interpretation of bloodstain evidence at crime scenes.   III. Title.
IV. Series.
RA1061.E26   1998
614´.1—dc21   98-13158
                                                                               CIP

This book contains information obtained from authentic and highly regarded sources. Reprinted material is quoted with permission, and sources are indicated. A wide variety of references are listed. Reasonable efforts have been made to publish reliable data and information, but the authors and the publisher cannot assume responsibility for the validity of all materials or for the consequences of their use.

Neither this book nor any part may be reproduced or transmitted in any form or by any means, electronic or mechanical, including photocopying, microfilming, and recording, or by any information storage or retrieval system, without prior permission in writing from the publisher.

The consent of CRC Press LLC does not extend to copying for general distribution, for promotion, for creating new works, or for resale. Specific permission must be obtained in writing from CRC Press LLC for such copying.

Direct all inquiries to CRC Press LLC, 2000 N.W. Corporate Blvd., Boca Raton, Florida 33431.

Trademark Notice: Product or corporate names may be trademarks or registered trademarks, and are used only for identification and explanation, without intent to infringe.

Visit the CRC Press Web site at www.crcpress.com

© 1998 by CRC Press LLC

No claim to original U.S. Government works
International Standard Book Number 0-8493-8126-6
Library of Congress Card Number 98-13158
Printed in the United States of America   2 3 4 5 6 7 8 9 0
Printed on acid-free paper

Table of Contents

Preface   ix
Editor's Note   xi
Acknowledgments   xiii

1   Introduction to Bloodstain Pattern Interpretation and Properties of Blood   1
Stuart H. James

General Considerations   1
Historical Development   3
Objectives of Bloodstain Pattern Interpretation   10
The Biological Properties of Blood   12
The Physical Properties of Blood   14
External Forces that Alter a Blood Source or Drop   15

2   Low-Velocity Impact and Angular Considerations of Bloodstains   19
Stuart H. James and T. Paulette Sutton

Free-Falling Drops of Blood onto Horizontal Surfaces   19
Free-Falling Drops of Blood onto Nonhorizontal
     Surfaces—Impact Angles   27
Determination of the Point or Area of Convergence   35
Determination of the Point or Area of Origin   36
Angular Impact Produced by Horizontal Motion   40
Splashed, Projected, and Cast-Off Blood   42
Other Bloodstain Patterns Associated
     with Low-Velocity Force   48

3   Medium- and High-Velocity Impact Blood Spatter   59
Stuart H. James and T. Paulette Sutton

Bloodstain Patterns Produced by Medium-Velocity Impact   59
Bloodstain Patterns Produced by High-Velocity Impact   67

Construction of a Simulated Head for High-Velocity
    Blood Spatter Experiments with Firearms   74
Detection of Blood in the Barrels of Firearms   80

**4   The Significance of Partially Dried, Clotted,
Aged, and Physically Altered Bloodstains   85**
Stuart H. James

Drying Time of Blood   85
Clotting of Blood   87
Blood Diffusion and Drying on Various Types
    of Cloth as a Function of Time   90
The Aging of Bloodstains   94
Blood Degradation Experiment   94
Other Alterations of Bloodstains   96

**5   Medical and Medicolegal Aspects
of Bloodshed at Crime Scenes   105**
William G. Eckert, M.D.

Age and Muscularity   105
General Health   105
Types of Wounds Associated with Blunt-Force Injuries   106
Types of Wounds Associated with Sharp-Force Injuries   106
Types of Wounds Associated with Gunshot Injuries   110
Wound Location and Major Vessel Disruption   112
Significance of Blood Loss Evidence   119
Estimation of Blood Volume at the Scene   122
Conclusion   122

**6   The Documentation, Collection,
and Evaluation of Bloodstain Evidence   125**
Stuart H. James

General Considerations   125
Methods for Conducting Crime Scene Searches   131
Crime Scene Diagrams   132
Collection and Preservation of Bloodstain Evidence   139
Examination of Bloodstained Clothing   142

7   The Detection of Blood Using Luminol   153
Dale L. Laux, M.S.

Introduction   153
Discovery   153

The Luminol Reaction   155
Preparation of Luminol   159
Interpretation of Luminescence   161
Use of Additional Presumptive Tests   162
Interpretation of Patterns   162
Effect of Substrates   163
Collection of Samples   164
Effects of Luminol on the Subsequent Analysis
    of Bloodstains   165
Photography   166
Report Writing   168
Testimony   169
Case Studies   169

**8   Case Studies in Bloodstain Pattern
      Interpretation   177**
      Stuart H. James

Gunshot Injuries   180
Blunt-Force Injuries   221
Cutting/Stabbing Injuries   281

Glossary   303

Appendix 1: Trigonometric Tables   309

**Appendix 2: Precautions for Infectious Diseases:
              AIDS and Hepatitis B and C   311**
              Henry C. Lee, Ph.D.

Index   317

Preface

It has been nine years since the first edition of the text entitled *Interpretation of Bloodstain Evidence at Crime Scenes* co-authored by Eckert and James was published in 1989. During that period of time the discipline of bloodstain pattern interpretation has continued to grow and mature as a branch of forensic science. Membership in the International Association of Bloodstain Pattern Analysts has increased and expert testimony on the subject has been accepted in most state, federal, and military courts. There has been an increase in the use of computers for determination of bloodstain origins and crime scene diagrams.

Scientific articles on the use of bloodstain pattern interpretation continue to be published in the forensic literature including the Journal of Forensic Sciences and the International Association of Bloodstain Pattern Analysts News. In 1997, the text entitled, *Bloodstain Pattern Analysis—With an Introduction to Crime Scene Reconstruction* authored by Tom Bevel and Ross Gardner was published. Also in 1997 Herbert Leon MacDonell revised his current text entitled *Bloodstain Patterns*.

This second edition of *Interpretation of Bloodstain Evidence at Crime Scenes* co-authored by Stuart H. James and William G. Eckert, is both revised and updated with improved quality of photographs and diagrams. This second edition represents an effort to provide a continuing resource and text for law enforcement officers, medicolegal personnel, prosecutors and defense attorneys involved with examination of bloodstain evidence, crime scene reconstruction and the ultimate presentation of this type of evidence in court.

The second edition introduces several new contributing authors. T. Paulette Sutton, MS has contributed her expertise and experience to Chapter 2, "Low-Velocity Impact and Angular Considerations of Bloodstains" and Chapter 3, "Medium- and High-Velocity Impact Blood Spatter." Dale L. Laux, MS has contributed Chapter 7, "The Detection of Blood with Luminol" which is supplemented with high quality color photographs of the luminol reaction.

Chapter 5, "Medical and Medicolegal Aspects of Bloodshed at Crime Scenes" written by Dr. William G. Eckert, MD has been revised and highlighted with many new photographs. David Redsicker and Craig Tomash have provided updated information on bloodstains at fire scenes.

Eight of the original case studies have been retained for their interpretative value with the addition of twelve new case studies. It is hoped that the reader will benefit from these updates and expansion of the text from the earlier book.

Stuart H. James
William G. Eckert

Editor's Note

This textbook is part of a series entitled "Practical Aspects of Criminal and Forensic Investigation". This series was created by Vernon J. Geberth, New York City Police Department Lieutenant Commander (Retired), who is an author, educator, and consultant on homicide and forensic investigations.

This series has been designed to provide contemporary, comprehensive, and pragmatic information to the practitioner involved in criminal and forensic investigations by authors who are nationally recognized experts in their respective fields.

Acknowledgments

The authors appreciate the efforts of the contributing authors, Dale L. Laux, MS of the Ohio Bureau of Criminal Identification and Investigation in Richfield, Ohio, and T. Paulette Sutton, MS of the University of Tennessee School of Medicine Pathology Department in Memphis, Tennessee for their assistance with the revisions and additions to the text, photographs and diagrams. The authors also acknowledge Charles F. Edel of the Broward County Sheriff's Office in Fort Lauderdale, Florida for his valuable assistance, photos, and diagrams.

The authors also would like to thank the following individuals and organizations for their support and contributions to this second edition of *Interpretation of Bloodstain Evidence at Crime Scenes.*

- William Best, Forensic Analytical Services, Gastonia, North Carolina
- Scott Croswell, Attorney at Law, Cincinnati, Ohio
- William Davis, Attorney at Law, Orlando, Florida
- Jan Ewanow, Detective, Binghamton, New York
- Gary Eldridge, Private Investigator, New Orleans, Louisiana
- Victoria Wendy Hilt, RN, Fort Lauderdale, Florida
- Paul Kish, Laboratory of Forensic Science, Corning, New York
- James Lohman, Attorney at Law, Tallahassee, Florida
- Erik Joyce, Welleby Photographics, Sunrise, Florida
- Fred Leatherman, Attorney at Law, Seattle, Washington
- Henry C. Lee, PhD, Connecticut State Police Laboratory, Meriden, Connecticut
- Herbert Leon MacDonell, Laboratory of Forensic Science, Corning, New York
- D.D. Maddox, Attorney at Law, Huntington, Tennessee
- Krista Pickens, Private Investigator, Salt Lake City, Utah
- David Redsicker, Peter Vallas Associates, Endicott, New York
- Gregory Shubert, Attorney at Law, Springfield, Massachusetts
- John Thompson, Attorney at Law, Springfield, Massachusetts
- Linda Thompson, Attorney at Law, Springfield, Massachusetts
- Craig Tomash, R.C.M.P. Forensic Laboratory, Halifax, Nova Scotia
- Ronald Yengich, Attorney at Law, Salt Lake City, Utah
- Binghamton Police Department, Binghamton, New York

- Boca Raton Police Department, Boca Raton, Florida
- Broward County Public Defender's Office, Fort Lauderdale, Florida
- Broward County Sheriff's Office, Fort Lauderdale, Florida
- Broward County State Attorney's Office, Fort Lauderdale, Florida
- Dade County Public Defender's Office, Miami, Florida
- Dauphin County District Attorney's Office, Harrisburg, Pennsylvania
- Davie Police Department, Davie, Florida
- Delray Beach Police Department, Delray Beach, Florida
- Florida Department of Law Enforcement, Tallahassee, Florida
- Harrisburg Police Department, Harrisburg, Pennsylvania
- Lycoming County District Attorney's Office, Lock Haven, Pennsylvania
- Martin County Sheriff's Office, Stuart, Florida
- Monroe County State Attorney's Office, Key West, Florida
- Oakland County Sheriff's Office, Pontiac, Michigan
- Palm Beach County Sheriff's Office, West Palm Beach, Florida
- Palm Beach County State Attorney's Office, West Palm Beach, Florida
- Palm Beach Police Department, Palm Beach, Florida
- Pinellas County Sheriff's Office, Clearwater, Florida
- United States Attorneys Office, Washington, DC

Introduction to Bloodstain Pattern Interpretation and Properties of Blood

1

STUART H. JAMES

General Considerations

Blood is one of the most significant and frequently encountered types of physical evidence associated with the forensic investigation of death and violent crime. The identification of human blood and its classification within the blood group systems such as ABO and Rh, the characterization of the red cell isoenzymes and serum genetic markers, and more recently, DNA profiling, have permitted a high degree of individualization of human blood in many cases.

The circumstances and nature of violent crimes frequently produce a variety of bloodstains that, when carefully studied and evaluated with respect to their geometry and distribution, may provide information of considerable value to assist the investigator with the reconstruction of the scene. The use of serological techniques to associate bloodstains with particular individuals, in concert with the reconstruction of events based upon bloodstain patterns, provides mutually valuable sources of physical evidence based upon the study of blood. The proper interpretation of bloodstain evidence has proved crucial in numerous cases where the manner of death is questioned and the issue of homicide, suicide, accident, or natural death must be resolved in a criminal or civil litigation or proceeding.

In cases of violent death, the external examination of the victim prior to autopsy by the forensic pathologist can reveal bloodstain patterns and changes within the body. Blunt trauma will often produce external bruising or contusions which may be characterized as fresh or old. It is not uncommon to find bruises on the skin that are a patterned signature of the object that struck the victim such as a hammer, chain, threaded pipe, or other blunt instrument (Figure 1.1). Minute hemorrhages or petechiae on the skin or within the eye are often present in asphyxial deaths (Figure 1.2). Postmortem lividity or livor mortis is the settling and accumulation of blood in the small

1

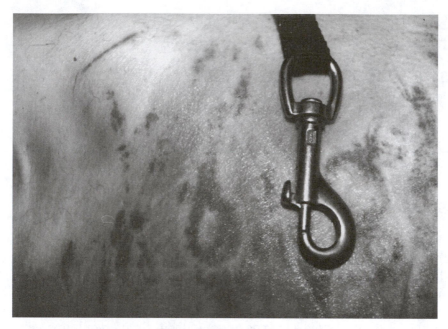

Figure 1.1 Patterned contusion, produced by metal clasp on dog leash, on back of elderly male victim of spousal abuse.

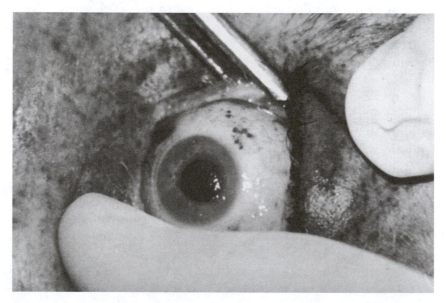

Figure 1.2 Petechial hemorrhages in eye of victim of manual strangulation.

vessels of the dependent areas of the body due to gravity. The degree of reddish to purple discoloration of the skin after death may assist with the approximation of the time of death in conjunction with the degree of rigor mortis, body temperature, and other postmortem chemical changes in the blood and body fluids. The location of livor mortis on the body can also indicate postmortem movement of the victim when the location of the settled blood is not consistent with the position in which the body was found at a scene (Figure 1.3).

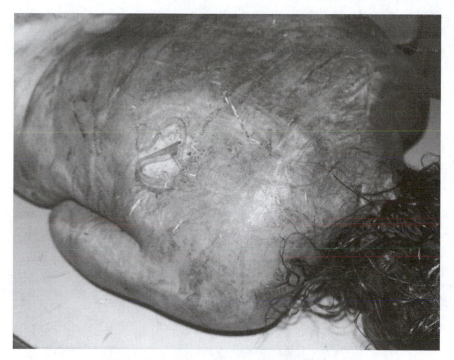

Figure 1.3 Distribution of postmortem lividity on back of victim.

Historical Development

The study of bloodstain patterns and the consideration of the physical processes in the distribution of these patterns to reconstruct details of activities at scenes of death and violent crime have recently emerged as a recognized forensic skill. Historically, bloodstain interpretation has suffered through a long period of neglect and, as a result, investigators in death cases frequently have not appreciated the very obvious information available from this source. The earliest known significant study in bloodstain interpretation that has been documented and preserved was done by Dr. Eduard Piotrowski, assistant at the Institute for Forensic Medicine in Krakow, Poland. This work, entitled, *Uber Entstehung, Form, Richtung und Ausbreitung der Blutspuren nach Hiebwunden des Kopfes,* was published in Vienna in 1895. Through the efforts of Herbert Leon MacDonell of Corning, New York, the historian for the International Association of Bloodstain Pattern Analysts, this work has been translated from the German text and reprinted in German and English as *Concerning the Origin, Shape, Direction and Distribution of the Bloodstains Following Head Wounds Caused by Blows.* This work is complete with reproduced color plates of the extensive bloodstain experiments performed by Dr. Piotrowski (Figures 1.4 and 1.5). According to MacDonell, "No one preceded Piotrowski in designing meaningful scientific experiments to show blood dynamics with such imagination, methodology, and thoroughness. He had an excellent knowledge of the scientific method and a good understanding of its practical application to bloodstain pattern interpretation".

Figure 1.4 The 1895 publication of Dr. Eduard Piotrowski, *Concerning the Origin, Shape, Direction and Distribution of the Bloodstains Following Head Wounds Caused by Blows.*

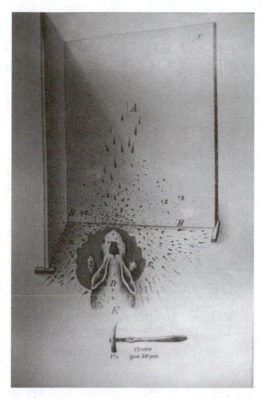

Figure 1.5 An example of an illustration in Dr. Eduard Piotrowski's publication showing radiating blood spatter from blows with a hammer onto a target surface.

Subsequent, significant work involving the study of bloodstain patterns at a crime scene is documented by Dr. Paul Jeserich, a forensic chemist in Berlin who examined homicide scenes during the first decade of the twentieth century.

The French scientist, Dr. Victor Balthazard and his associates conducted original research and experimentation with bloodstain trajectories and patterns and presented a paper at the 22nd Congress of Forensic Medicine in 1939 entitled *Étude des Gouttes de Sang Projeté* (Figures 1.6 and 1.7). This was translated from French to English as *Research on Blood Spatter*. There were individual cases involving bloodstain pattern interpretation in later years including the 1949 Setty case in London, England reviewed by the late Dr. Francis Camps.

In 1955, Dr. Paul Kirk of the University of California at Berkeley prepared an affidavit regarding his findings based upon bloodstain evidence to the Court of Common Pleas in the case of the *State of Ohio v. Samuel Sheppard*. This was a significant milestone in the recognition of bloodstain evidence by

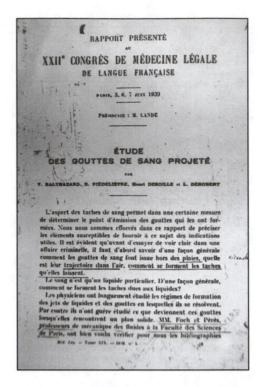

Figure 1.6 Research paper on blood spatter by Victor Balthazard and his associates presented at the 22nd Congress of Forensic Medicine in Paris, in 1939.

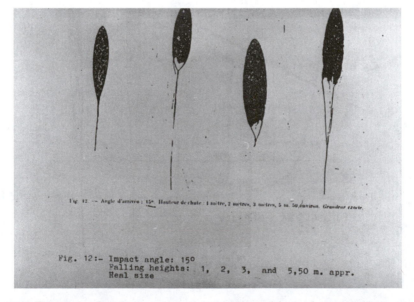

Figure 1.7 Angle of impact studies performed by Balthazard as part of his research.

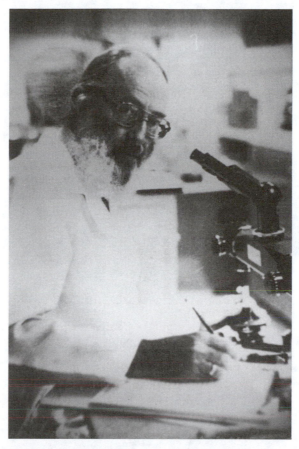

Figure 1.8 Professor Herbert Leon MacDonell at the Laboratory of Forensic Science in Corning, NY.

the legal system. Dr. Kirk was able to establish the relative position of the attacker and victim at the time of the administration of the beating. He was also able to determine that the attacker administered blows with a left hand, which was significant in that Dr. Sheppard was right-handed.

The further growth of interest and use of the significance of bloodstain evidence is a direct result of the scientific research and practical applications of bloodstain theory by Herbert Leon MacDonell (Figure 1.8). Through the assistance of a Law Enforcement Assistance Administration (LEAA) grant, MacDonell conducted research and performed experiments to re-create and duplicate bloodstain patterns observed at crime scenes. This resulted in his 1971 publication of the first modern treatise on bloodstain interpretation, entitled *Flight Characteristics of Human Blood and Stain Patterns* (Figure 1.9). This was followed in 1973 by a second publication, *Laboratory Manual on the Geometric Interpretation of Human Bloodstain Evidence* (Figure 1.10).

Figure 1.9 The original version of *Flight Characteristics of Human Blood and Stain Patterns* by Herbert Leon MacDonell published in 1971 by the U.S. Department of Justice.

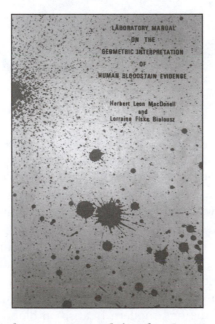

Figure 1.10 The *Laboratory Manual for the Geometric Interpretation of Human Bloodstain Evidence* used in classes in the Basic Bloodstain Institutes taught by Herbert Leon MacDonell.

Figure 1.11 The updated, revised edition of *Bloodstain Patterns* published by Herbert Leon MacDonell in 1997.

In 1982, MacDonell expanded his original work in a publication entitled *Bloodstain Pattern Interpretation* which was further updated in 1993 with the title, *Bloodstain Patterns* which underwent a revision in 1997 (Figure 1.11).

MacDonell organized formal instruction for investigators in bloodstain interpretation through bloodstain institutes conducted throughout the United States and abroad and has trained hundreds of police investigators, forensic scientists, and crime laboratory personnel at these institutes. As a direct result of MacDonell's efforts, the state of the art of bloodstain interpretation in forensic science has increased considerably and others continue to make contributions to the field in crime scene reconstruction, teaching, and publications.

In 1983, Terry L. Laber and Barton P. Epstein produced a laboratory manual entitled *Experiments and Practical Exercises in Bloodstain Pattern Analysis.*

The textbook, *Interpretation of Bloodstain Evidence at Crime Scenes*, co-authored by Dr. William G. Eckert and Stuart H. James was published in 1989. This work included numerous case studies involving bloodstain pattern interpretation. In 1990, Ross Gardner and Tom Bevel co-authored a laboratory manual entitled, *Bloodstain Pattern Analysis—Theory and Practice.*

T. Paulette Sutton at the University of Tennessee in Memphis produced a comprehensive manual in 1993, entitled *Bloodstain Pattern Analysis in Violent Crimes.* Tom Bevel and Ross M. Gardner co-authored the text entitled *Bloodstain Analysis With An Introduction to Crime Scene Reconstruction* in 1997. Scientific articles pertaining to aspects of bloodstain pattern interpretation are gaining increasing visability in well-known publications including the *Journal of Forensic Sciences,* the *American Journal of Forensic Medicine and Pathology,* the *Journal of the Canadian Society of Forensic Science,* and the *Journal of Forensic Identification.*

At the first Advanced Bloodstain Institute held in Corning, New York in 1983, the International Association of Bloodstain Pattern Analysts (IABPA) was founded by Herbert Leon MacDonell and those individuals in attendance at that Institute. As of 1998, this organization consisted of more than 350 members from throughout the United States and Canada as well as countries throughout the world including Great Britain, Denmark, Finland, Sweden, Norway, New Zealand, Australia, Taiwan, Guam, and Colombia. IABPA publishes a newsletter on current bloodstain topics and schedules of training courses and explores such issues as the curriculum for basic instructional courses in bloodstain interpretation, uniformity in bloodstain terminology and research in the field. The yearly IABPA conference agenda includes numerous case presentations and research topics by members and guest lecturers.

Objectives of Bloodstain Pattern Interpretation

Bloodstain pattern interpretation is a discipline which utilizes the sciences of biology, physics, and mathematics. Bloodstain interpretation may be accomplished by direct scene evaluation and/or careful study of scene photographs (preferably color photographs with measuring device in view) in conjunction with detailed examination of clothing, weapons, and other objects regarded as physical evidence. Details of hospital records, postmortem examination, and autopsy photographs also provide useful information and should be included for evaluation and study. In cases where on-scene investigation is not possible and photographs must be relied upon, detailed sketches, diagrams, reports of crime scene investigators, and laboratory reports should be available for review.

Relative to the reconstruction of a crime scene, bloodstain interpretation may provide information to the investigator in many areas:

1. Origin(s) of the bloodstains.
2. Distances between impact areas of blood spatter and origin at time of bloodshed.

3. Type and direction of impact that produced bloodstains or spatter.
4. Object(s) that produced particular bloodstain patterns.
5. Number of blows, shots, etc. that occurred.
6. Position of victim, assailant, or objects at the scene during bloodshed.
7. Movement and direction of victim, assailant or objects at scene after bloodshed.
8. Support or contradiction of statements given by suspect or witnesses.
9. Additional criteria for estimation of postmortem interval.
10. Correlation with other laboratory and pathology findings relevant to the investigation.

The goal of the reconstruction of the crime scene utilizing bloodstain pattern interpretation is to assist the overall forensic investigation with the ultimate questions that must be addressed which include, but are not limited to the following:

1. What events occurred?
2. When and in what sequence did they occur?
3. Who was there during each event?
4. Who was not there during each event?
5. What did not occur?

A combination of training through formal instruction, personal experimentation, and experience with actual case work is necessary before an individual acquires proficiency in the correct interpretation of bloodstain patterns to answer these types of questions. Contemporaneous experiments to duplicate specific patterns should be considered relative to a given case to support an interpretation or conclusion. Some conservative speculation is permissible during the initial investigative stages of a case. However, final opinions, contents of the written report, and ultimate court testimony must be based on scientific fact with no speculation. Alternate conclusions should be explored thoroughly, recognized and acknowledged by the analyst. Interpretation of bloodstains should be correlated with postmortem and laboratory findings in an investigation. For example, when an arterial spurt pattern is observed, the autopsy report should indicate a cut or breached artery in the victim. In cases where an assailant, as well as the victim, produces bloodshed, or where there are multiple victims, the individualization of the bloodstains by the forensic laboratory is critical. It is important to be conservative and not to over-interpret bloodstain evidence, especially when the number of bloodstains is limited and are only subjected to a presumptive test for blood. A single or few small bloodstains rarely lend themselves to useful, valid interpretations. Conclusions based upon crime scene photographs should be conservative when the investigator has not had the opportunity to examine the crime scene personally and must rely upon the photographic expertise of others.

The Biological Properties of Blood

Blood can be characterized as a fluid mixture, consisting of cellular components and plasma that circulates throughout the body via the arterial, venous, and capillary systems. Blood accounts for approximately 8% of the total human body weight. For a normal adult, the total blood volume may range from 4.5 to 6 liters. The cellular components of blood comprise approximately 45% of the total blood volume (Figure 1.12). There are three categories of cellular components of the blood:

1. **Red blood cells (RBCs)**—also referred to as erythrocytes, contain hemoglobin which transports oxygen from the lungs throughout the body via the arterial system and returns carbon dioxide to the lungs for expiration through the venous system. The oxygen-rich blood within the arteries is due to the oxyhemoglobin complexing which imparts a bright-red color to the blood whereupon the blood within the venous system is somewhat darker in color since it is oxygen-deficient. Oxygen can also be released from the hemoglobin by exposure to the atmosphere. This causes blood, which has been shed, to become progressively darker as it loses its oxygen to the surrounding environment.
2. **White blood cells (WBCs)**—also referred to as leukocytes, perform vital functions relative to the immunological response of the body to foreign substances and infection.
3. **Platelets**—an integral part of the clotting mechanism of the blood.
4. **Plasma**—the liquid portion of blood constitutes approximately 55% of the total blood volume. Plasma is approximately 9% water in which numerous chemical compounds, both solids and gases are dissolved. It is a medium for the circulation of blood cells, and carries nutritive substances, hormones, electrolytes, and antibodies throughout the body and assists with the removal of the waste products of metabolism from the body. The term plasma describes the liquid portion of the blood which has not clotted. Once blood has clotted, the liquid portion is referred to as serum. It is the pale, yellow liquid which appears around an exposed blood clot which has jelled and retracted and is often observed at crime scenes.

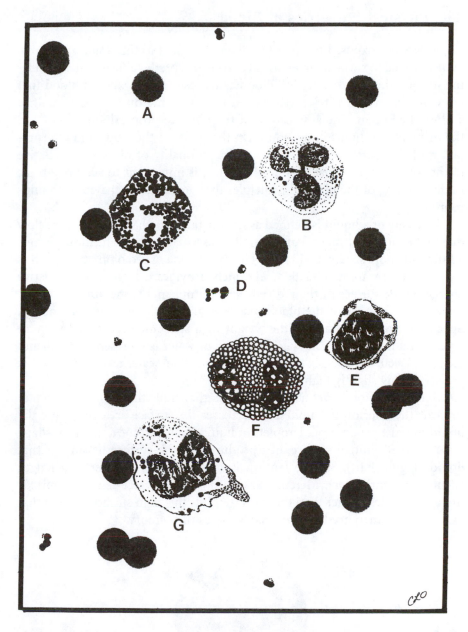

Figure 1.12   Normal cellular components of human blood as viewed microscopically. **(A)** Red cell (erythrocyte); **(B)** white cell (leukocyte—neutrophil); **(C)** white cell (leukocyte—basophil); **(D)** platelet (thrombocyte); **(E)** white cell (leukocyte—lymphocyte); **(F)** white cell (leukocyte—eosinophil); **(G)** white cell (leukocyte—monocyte).

The Physical Properties of Blood

When blood is exposed to the external environment as the result of trauma, and subjected to various forces, it will behave in a predictable manner according to the principles of physics. Bloodstains result from exposed blood that has come in contact with external surfaces in the environment as a result of a bloodshed event. The application of the physical properties of blood and the principles of fluids in motion form the basis for the study and interpretation of the location, shape, size, and directionality of bloodstains relative to the force or forces that produced them. It is important to acquire a basic understanding of the physical principles that govern the behavior of liquids in motion.

Viscosity of a liquid is defined as its resistance to change of form or flow due to the mutual attraction of the molecules to each other. The more viscous a fluid, the more slowly it will flow. The membrane of red blood cells possess a high concentration of sialic acid which provides a large electronegative charge on the surface of the red cells which implements the viscosity of the blood. The viscosity of the blood increases greatly as the result of clotting. Specific gravity is defined as the weight of a substance compared with an equal volume of water. The specific gravity of water is represented 1.000 and blood as 1.060. Blood is six times more viscous than water though its specific gravity is only slightly higher.

Surface tension is defined as the force that pulls the surface molecules towards the interior of a fluid and decreases the surface area and cause the liquid to resist penetration. Droplets of liquid in air assume a spherical shape which is the minimal surface area produced by the surface tension of that liquid (Figure 1.13). Surface tension is measured in force per unit length (dynes per centimeter). Mercury has a very high surface tension approximately 6.5 times greater than that of water. It is this high surface tension that causes spilled mercury to form small spheres of mercury.

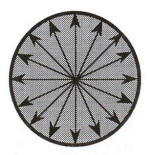

Figure 1.13 Diagram representing surface tension forces on the surface of a liquid droplet that tend to decrease its surface area and resist penetration.

The established surface tension of common fluids (measured in dynes per centimeter at 20°C) is represented as follows:

soap	25.0
ethyl alcohol	22.3
mercury	465.0
blood	50.0
water	72.5
olive oil	32.0
glycerine	63.1

External Forces that Alter a Blood Source or Drop

The physical properties of blood, including specific gravity, viscosity, and surface tension, tend to maintain the stability of exposed blood or blood drops and cause them to be resistant to alteration or breaking up. External forces can act upon exposed blood, overcome these physical properties, and create a variety of blood formations, droplets, and spatters. This results in the production of numerous types of bloodstains that will exhibit directionality and observable differences in their size and distribution on the surfaces they contact or impact. When a source of exposed blood is subjected to an external force, energy is transferred to the blood which causes the blood to break up into smaller droplets referred to as spatter. Weaker external forces result in larger droplets while stronger external forces result in smaller droplets. The larger droplets or spatters due to their mass will travel further from the source than the smaller ones which are more affected by air resistance.

Traditionally, bloodstains have been classified into three major categories based upon the amount of external force required to produce them, as well as, their relative size. It should be appreciated that the forces applied to the blood source as well as the size of the resultant bloodstains and spatters are expressed in ranges. As would be expected, there is a degree of overlapping of these criteria. Interpretations should be based upon the preponderance of bloodstains of a certain category. The three general categories are described as follows:

1. **Low-velocity impact** is characterized by external force applied to the blood source of up to 5 feet/second. This includes the normal gravitational force. The typical size of bloodstains produced is 3 mm or greater in diameter. A variety of directionalities may be produced. Examples of activities producing bloodstains in this category are:

- Free-falling drops of blood affected only by gravity.
- Blood dripping into blood.
- Single drops falling through air with horizontal motion (walking or running).
- Splashed and projected blood.
- Stepping into blood.
- Blood flow patterns on horizontal or vertical surfaces.
- Blood transfer patterns (hair swipes, hand, foot, or bloody object impressions).
- Cast-off blood.

2. **Medium-velocity impact** is characterized by external force applied to the blood source between 5 and 25 feet/second although forces up to 100 feet/second can be exerted with whips, golf clubs, and some martial arts weapons. The typical size of bloodstains produced is 1 to 3 mm in diameter although larger and smaller stains may be present. A variety of directionalities may be produced. Examples of activities producing bloodstains in this category are:

- Blunt force trauma (beating with fists, bats, bricks, hammers, etc.).
- Cutting and stabbing trauma.

3. **High-velocity impact** is characterized by external force applied to the blood source of greater than 100 feet/second. The typical size of bloodstains produced is less than 1 mm diameter although larger and smaller stains may be present. A variety of directionalities may be produced. Examples of activities producing bloodstains in this category are:

- Gunshot trauma.
- Explosions.
- High-speed machinery trauma.

There are types of projected blood patterns that are easily recognized that do not totally fit into one of the three described categories. The bloodstains may be in the size range of low- to medium-velocity impact. Examples of activities producing bloodstains in this category are:

- Arterial spurting or gushing.
- Running through exposed blood.
- Stamping or slapping exposed blood.

Other activities such as the flicking of fingers wet with blood, and exhaling or expirating blood from the nose or mouth may produce bloodstains in the medium- to high-velocity size range. The interrelationships of the forces involved in bloodshed events are summarized in the following flow chart (Figure 1.14).

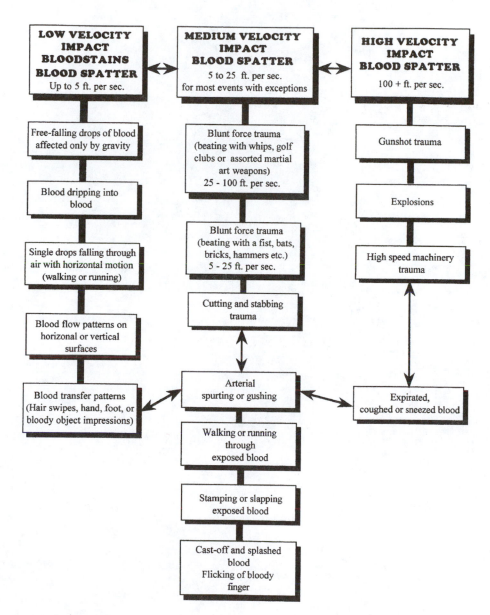

Figure 1.14 Flow chart summarizing the interrelationship of forces acting upon a source of blood.

Low-Velocity Impact and Angular Considerations of Bloodstains

2

STUART H. JAMES
T. PAULETTE SUTTON

Free-Falling Drops of Blood on Horizontal Surfaces

Blood can drip from an open wound, saturated clothing, hair, weapons, or any object having a sufficient volume of blood to permit the formation of free-falling drops of blood. Prior to the drop breaking free from the primary source, this downward pull of gravity, along with the accumulating weight of the forming drop, are countered by surface tension forces that are trying to reduce the exposed surface and push the drop back to its original source. The separation of these drops from the primary source of blood is caused by the constant gravitational forces exceeding the cohesive forces of the surface tension (Figure 2.1). A free-falling drop of blood is considered to be spherical in shape due to the effects of surface tension. When the drop initially breaks free, it is very slightly elongated. As the drop continues to fall, it will flatten slightly and essentially assume the shape of a sphere or ball. This is contrary to the teardrop shape as often characterized by artists in numerous media productions. The spherical drop will not break up in air unless acted upon by a force other than gravity. It may, however, oscillate due to the effects of air friction or resistance. The larger a drop, the more it will tend to oscillate. Studies by Peterson have shown that droplets 0.5 mm in diameter exhibit little if any oscillations, whereas drops 5 mm in diameter displayed distinctive oscillations. The length of time that a blood drop will oscillate in air prior to resuming its spherical shape is referred to in physics as damping time. Damping time is inversely proportional to the viscosity of the fluid. Since viscosity of blood is approximately six times greater than that of water, the oscillations are dampened quickly (98% in 0.8 seconds for large drops) and the spherical or ball shape is re-established.

The volume of a single drop of free-falling blood was studied by MacDonell in 1971, Laber in 1985, and White in 1986. The original experiments conducted by MacDonell measured the average volume of a drop of

19

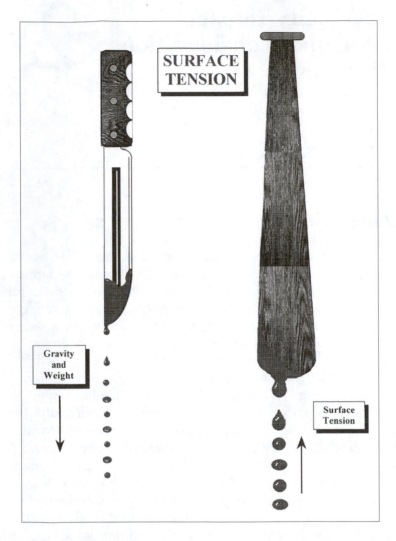

Figure 2.1 Diagrammatic representation of the spherical shape of free-falling drops of blood from objects.

blood to be approximately 0.05 ml which corresponds to a widely accepted standard of 20 drops of blood per milliliter. Laber demonstrated variations in blood drop volumes between 0.013 and 0.16 ml of blood drops falling from different sources including fingertip, knife blade, screwdriver tip and cloth. As surface tension increases, more blood volume (weight) is required for it to break free. The greater the surface area of a blood drop the greater will be the effects of surface tension. In actual practice, drops of blood of different volumes may be produced from a variety of surfaces. Differences in the volume of a drop of blood falling from a wound site, clothing, fingers, or hair would be expected due to differences in surface area and surface tension of the primary source of blood.

The terminal velocity of a free-falling drop of blood is the maximum speed that the drop can reach in air. A blood drop as well as any other particle or object falling through air will increase its velocity until the force of air resistance opposing the falling drop is equal to the downward gravitational pull. At this point, the falling drop is in equilibrium and will maintain a constant velocity. MacDonell established that for a typical free-falling blood drop size of 0.05 ml, the maximum terminal velocity is 25.1 feet/second plus or minus 0.5 feet/second. This would be achieved in a maximum falling distance of approximately 20 to 25 feet though most of the velocity is achieved at approximately 4 feet. The smaller the drop volume, the faster it will achieve maximum terminal velocity and the lower this terminal velocity will be compared to the larger free-falling blood drops which attain higher maximum terminal velocities.

The resulting diameter of the bloodstain produced by a free-falling drop of blood is a function of the volume of the drop, the distance fallen and the surface texture upon which it impacts. Experimentally, it is easily demonstrated that free-falling drops of blood with a typical volume of 0.05 ml will produce bloodstains of increasing diameters when allowed to drop from increasing increments of height onto smooth, hard cardboard. The measured diameters range from 13 to 21.5 mm over a dropping range of 6 inches to 7 feet. In excess of 6 to 7 feet there is no appreciable increase in diameter (Figures 2.2 and 2.3). Larger blood drops will produce bloodstains with a greater diameter at less falling distance.

A blood drop will not break up in air regardless of the distance fallen unless acted upon by forces other than gravity. The surface upon which a

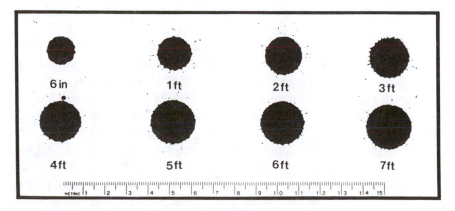

Figure 2.2 Increasing diameter of bloodstains as a function of increasing distance fallen by single drops of blood from fingertips onto smooth cardboard.

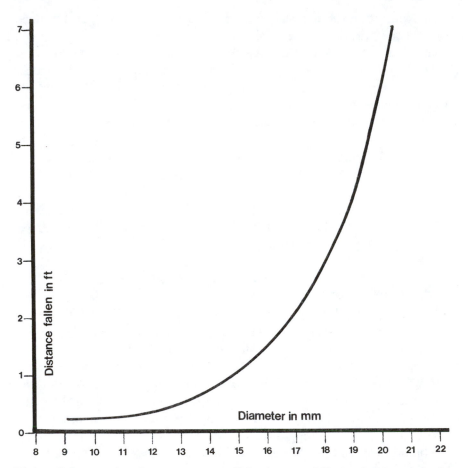

Figure 2.3 Graphical representation of the distance fallen in feet by single drops of blood from fingertips versus diameter, in millimeters, of bloodstains produced on smooth cardboard.

drop of blood falls will however, affect the distortion of the stain and the degree of spattering that may occur. When a free-falling drop of blood strikes or impacts a horizontal surface it will produce a more or less circular bloodstain depending upon the nature of the surface. Upon impact with smooth, hard surfaces, the surface tension will resist rupture and a uniformly circular stain will be produced independent of the falling distance. Conversely, a rough-textured or porous surface will overcome the surface tension of a blood drop and cause it to rupture upon impact. The resultant bloodstain will exhibit distortion, irregular shape and spiny edges. Spines are the pointed edge characteristics of a bloodstain that radiate away from the central area of the stain. In addition to spiny edges, the bloodstain may exhibit some peripheral spatter. It is important to understand that the degree of distortion and spattering of a bloodstain resulting from a free-falling drop is a function of the surface texture of the target rather than the distance fallen. Concrete, unpolished wood, and fabric material are considered to be rough surfaces. Newspaper and tissue paper though not considered rough surfaces, often produce very irregular and distorted bloodstains. Clean glass, porcelain and tile as well as hard smooth cardboard exhibit the least distortion with respect to impacted bloodstains on their surfaces (Figure 2.4 A through H). Unless the volume of the original free-falling drop is known and the effect of the target surface taken into consideration, extreme caution must be exercised

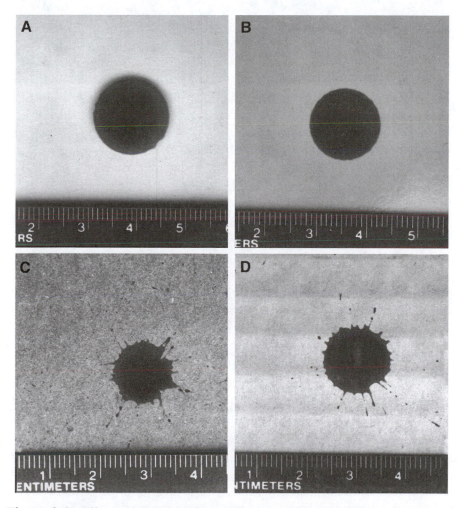

Figure 2.4 Effects of target surface textures on bloodstain characteristics and degree of spatter produced from single drops of blood falling 30 inches onto (**A**) glass; (**B**) smooth, polished tile; (**C**) cardboard; (**D**) corrugated cardboard; (**E**) wood paneling; (**F**) newspaper; (**G**) concrete; (**H**) denim material.

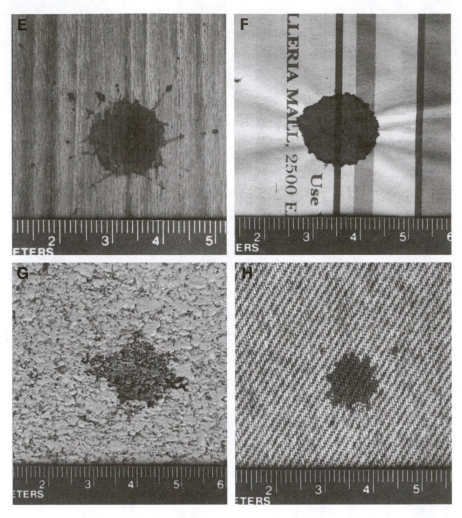

Figure 2.4 (continued)

when estimating the height from which a blood drop has fallen based upon the diameter of the resultant stain. Conservative estimates should be based upon experiments conducted by the investigator that utilize similar target surfaces as well as the various possible primary sources of blood to establish the range of possible blood drop volumes. It must be determined how and from what source the drop originated. In actual practice this variable would be difficult to establish. Bloodshed at a crime scene may produce many drops of different volumes that have created stains on different surfaces. To estimate the distance a drop of blood has fallen as merely a function of the diameter of the resultant stain can result in gross error in interpretation and is not recommended.

When there are multiple free-falling drops of blood produced from a stationary source onto a horizontal surface, drip patterns will result from blood drops falling into previously deposited wet bloodstains or a small pool of blood. These drip patterns will be large and irregular in shape with small (0.1 to 1.0 mm) circular to oval satellite spatters around the periphery of the central stain on the horizontal as well as nearby vertical surfaces. Satellite spatters are the result of smaller droplets of blood that have detached from the main blood volume at the moment of impact (Figures 2.5 and 2.6).

Paul Kish of the Laboratory of Forensic Science in Corning, NY conducted research on the topic of "Satellite Spatter Resulting from Single Drops of Blood and the Factors Affecting their Interpretation" and presented his preliminary findings at the Annual Meeting of the American Academy of Forensic Sciences in February, 1996. He demonstrated the maximum height that satellite spatters of human blood would impact on a vertical surface. Factors affecting this are blood drop volume, freshness of blood, surface texture, and the distance of the vertical target from the impact site. He concluded that rough surfaces such as concrete produce substantial satellite blood spatter from a single drop impact as well as blood dripping into blood. The vertical height achievable within 3 inches of a vertical target with a single drop impacting on concrete can be as high as 12 inches. He observed a greater concentration of spatter on the horizontal and vertical surfaces with blood dripping into blood on concrete (Figure 2.7). Investigators often interpret

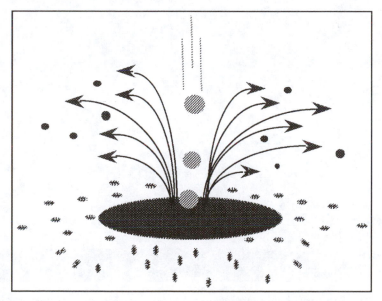

Figure 2.5 Diagrammatic representation of blood dripping into blood and the resultant satellite spatter.

Figure 2.6 Drip pattern of blood onto concrete with a large quantity of satellite spatter.

Figure 2.7 Satellite blood spatters produced on a vertical surface within 3 inches of blood dripping into blood on concrete. These can be mistaken for medium-velocity impact blood spatters on footwear, lower trouser legs, and other surfaces.

small spatters of blood on suspects trouser legs, socks, and shoes as medium- or high-velocity impact blood spatter associated with a beating or shooting due to their small diameters. The mechanism of satellite blood spatter causing these stains should be thoroughly explored before reaching a final interpretation and conclusion.

From a practical point of view it is important that the investigator be able to recognize the types of bloodstains and patterns resulting from free-falling drops based upon their size, shape, and distribution and to document their locations. These bloodstains should be categorized relative to the low-velocity events that produced them. The stains should be related to the possible sources and movement of these sources through the recognition of trails and drip patterns.

Free-Falling Drops of Blood onto Nonhorizontal Surfaces—Impact Angles

The angle of impact is the acute or internal angle formed between the direction of a blood drop and the plane of the surface it strikes. Free-falling blood drops that fall vertically onto a horizontal surface impact at 90 degrees. The resultant bloodstains are essentially circular in shape on a smooth hard surface. They are more irregular in shape often exhibiting spinelike projections and peripheral spatter on the rougher and more porous surfaces as previously described.

When a spherical, free-falling drop of blood traveling through the air strikes a nonhorizontal surface, the resultant bloodstain is more oval or elliptical and elongated relative to the angle of impact. The elongation is produced by the blood drop contacting and wiping or skidding against the target surface. The more acute the angle of impact, the greater the elongation of the bloodstain as the width decreases and the length increases. The widest point of the stain corresponds to the center or widest point of the sphere. The narrowest end of an elongated bloodstain produced from a free-falling drop striking a nonhorizontal surface points in the direction of travel. Depending upon the type of surface impacted, the characteristics at the leading edge of the bloodstain may exhibit tapering, spiny projections, a small dot-like spatter or a tadpole shaped wave cast-off which has flipped from the parent stain. Whereas the tail of the parent drop points in its direction of travel, the tail of the wave cast off points back to the parent bloodstain (Figure 2.8).

A mathematical or trigonometric relationship exists between the angle of impact of a blood droplet or sphere on a flat surface and the width and length of the resultant bloodstain. This relationship is demonstrated with the use of mathematical models (Figures 2.9 and 2.10). Considering Figure 2.9,

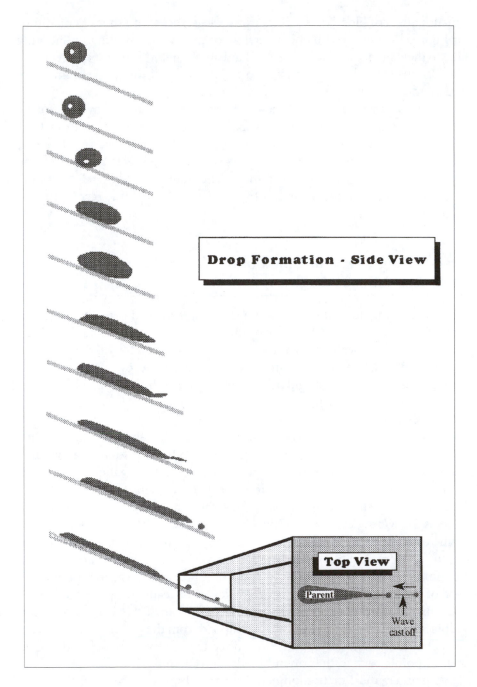

Figure 2.8 Diagrammatic representation of the dynamics of blood droplet and stain formation on a nonhorizontal surface. Note production of wave cast-off with the tail pointing back to the direction of the parent bloodstain.

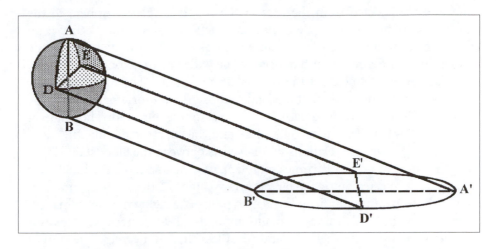

Figure 2.9 Spherical blood droplet projected to a resultant elliptical or elongated bloodstain at an angular impact.

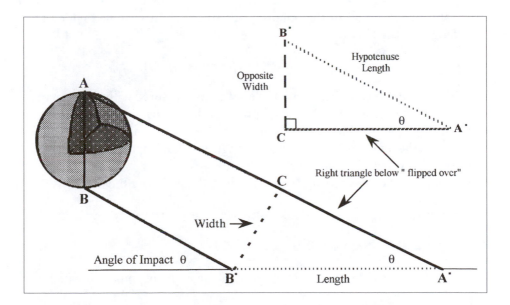

Figure 2.10 Trigonometric relationship existing between the bloodstain ellipse and the angle of impact of the blood droplet.

lines are constructed from the axes of the blood droplet or sphere to the target surface at a given angle of impact. The four points, A,B,D, and E on the surface of the sphere are projected as A', B', D', and E' forming the dimensions of the resultant bloodstain. The width of the bloodstain ellipse, D'E' is also the diameter of the bloodstain in air, DE. The line A'B' corresponds to the length of the bloodstain ellipse. In the original sphere, the width, DE is equal to the length, AB since a sphere is round. The angle of impact, θ lies between the target surface and the constructed line, BB'.

The trigonometric relationship that exists between the bloodstain ellipse and the angle of impact becomes more apparent with a cross sectional view of a sphere projected onto a flat target surface (Figure 2.10). If a perpendicular line is drawn from point C on line AA' to point B' a right triangle is formed. A right triangle by definition contains an angle of 90 degrees (C) plus two smaller or more acute angles (A and B) of less than 90 degrees. The sum of A, B, and C equals 180 degrees. By mathematical convention, the side of the triangle opposite the 90 degree angle C is referred to as the hypotenuse. The side opposite the acute angle A' or θ in the model is referred to as the opposite and the side opposite the acute angle B' is referred to as the adjacent.

The length of the resultant bloodstain is equal to the hypotenuse of the right triangle and its width is equal to the adjacent side of the right triangle. The angle θ of this right triangle represents the angle of impact of the blood droplet or sphere. Trigonometrically, the sine of the angle A' or θ is equal to the ratio of the length of the opposite side of the right triangle divided by the length of the hypotenuse.

$$\text{Sine } \theta = \text{opposite} / \text{hµypotenuse} = W/L$$

Referring again to Figure 2.10, the angle A' or θ is measured with a protractor to be 26.0 degrees. Line B'C which represents the opposite side of the right triangle and the width of a bloodstain measures 31.5 mm. Line A'B' which represents the hypotenuse of the right triangle and the length of a bloodstain measures 72.0 mm.

Applying the above formula and dividing the width by the length W/L:

$$\text{Sine } \theta = \text{opposite} / \text{hypotenuse} = W/L = 31.5 / 72.0 = 0.4375$$

$$\theta = 25.9 \text{ degrees}$$

The figure 0.4375 represents the sine of the angle of impact θ which is 25.9 degrees.

In actual practice the angle of impact of a bloodstain is determined by accurate measurements of the width and length of the bloodstain through the central axis of each dimension. The width of a bloodstain is measured across the center of the stain perpendicular to the long axis. The length of a bloodstain is measured along the long axis of the stain. For bloodstains striking a surface at 90 degrees, the width and length will be equal. Bloodstains which result from striking a surface at extremely acute angles (30 to 10 degrees) will exhibit lengths much greater than their widths (Figure 2.11). Care must be exercised with these measurements especially when there is distortion due to the particular surface texture upon which the bloodstain has impacted. The actual width and length of the distorted stain can be determined by rounding the stain to an elliptical shape when making the measurements. The selection of well-formed bloodstains for measurements improves accuracy considerably (Figure 2.12).

The calculation of the angle of impact may be determined in several ways with the use of the width and length data:

1. Determine length to width ratio (L/W). The angle of impact is determined from graphical representation of the L/W ratio versus known angles of impact from prepared standards of bloodstains (Figure 2.13).
2. Determine width to length ratio (W/L). The angle of impact is determined from graphical representation of the W/L ratio versus known angles of impact from prepared standards of bloodstains (Figure 2.14).
3. Determine width to length ratio (W/L). This ratio value is utilized in the formula:

$$\text{Angle of impact} = \text{arc sin } W/L$$

The arc sin value may be determined by use of the trigonometric tables or with the use of a scientific calculator which has the arc sin function. For a stain which has the width equal to its length, the ratio is 1.0 and the angle of impact is 90 degrees. The W/L ratio for a bloodstain on a surface produced by a blood drop striking at less than 90 degrees must be less than 1.0. For example, a stain measured to have a width of 5 mm and a length of 10 mm, the W/L ration is calculated to be 0.5. The arc sin of 0.5 is 30 degrees. With a 30 degree impact the length of the bloodstain is always twice its width.

Changes in the overall appearance of a bloodstain resulting from various surface textures may alter the proportional relationship that exists between the width and length of the stain. An example of this would be a case where a bloodstain is overlapping two adjoining dissimilar surfaces such as an area of painted and unpainted wood. In this instance the width to length ratio relationship will be altered and the angle of impact calculation would not be accurate. An excellent example of a distorted angular bloodstain was produced by a single drop of blood striking a screen, passing through, and impacting on a section of wood (Figure 2.15 A and B).

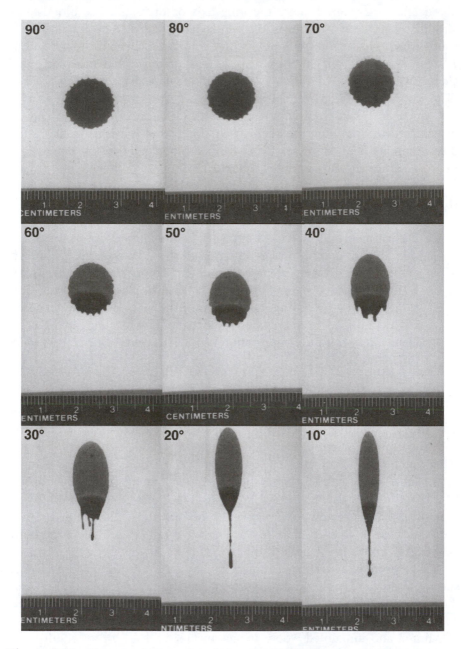

Figure 2.11 Shape and increasing elongation of bloodstains relative to decreasing angles of impact of single drops of blood falling 30 inches onto smooth cardboard.

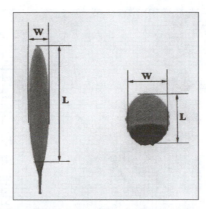

Figure 2.12   Measurement of the width and length of a bloodstain.

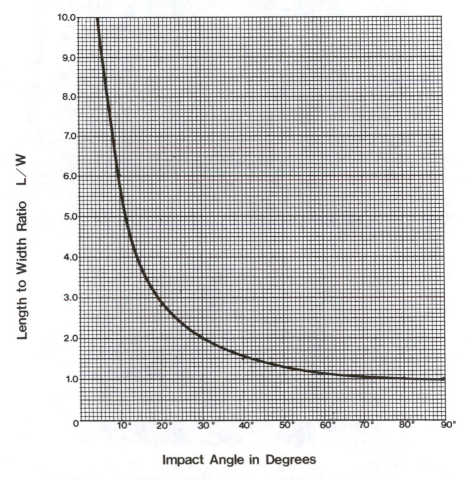

Impact Angle in Degrees

Figure 2.13   Impact angle of a bloodstain as a function of its length to width ratio.

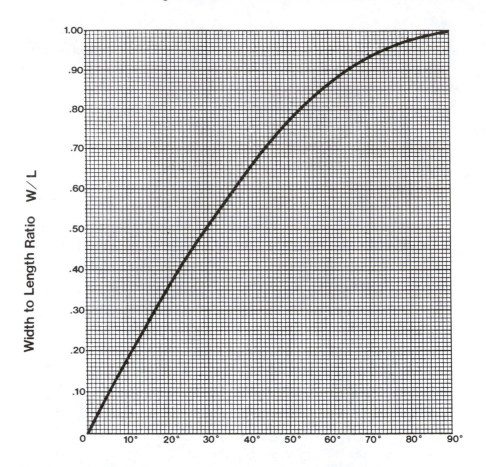

Figure 2.14 Impact angle of a bloodstain as a function of its width to length ratio (sine function).

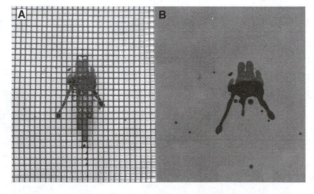

Figure 2.15 **(A)** Bloodstain produced by a single drop of blood falling 30 inches onto screen-covered wood at approximately 60 degrees. **(B)** Same bloodstain with screen removed.

Determination of the Point or Area of Convergence

When a blood source is subjected to a force or impact, the resultant blood droplets may strike a target surface at various impact angles and directionalities. The area or point of convergence is a point or area to which a bloodstain pattern can be projected. This point is determined by tracing the long axis of well-defined bloodstains within the pattern back to a common point or source. The point or area of convergence on a surface is a two-dimensional representation (Figure 2.16). These intersecting lines will define the direction of travel of each blood droplet prior to its striking that surface. The point or area of convergence can be established at the scene with the use of strings taped to the target surface extending through the long axis of the individual bloodstains. Do not tape over the actual bloodstains but below them. Graphical representation of the area or point of convergence is determined by measuring the location of the bloodstains relative to a known set of points such as the distance above the floor and the distance from the corner of a wall along with the angle of directionality on the vertical surface of the wall.

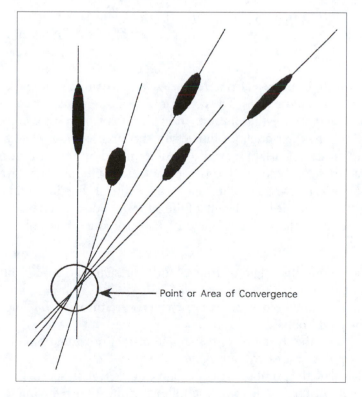

Figure 2.16   Determination of the point or area of convergence of bloodstains.

The convergence is then plotted on graph paper. This type of reference point is often referred to in terms of the X and the Y axis and provides the two-dimensional representation. The determination of several points of convergence may represent multiple impact sites and movement at the source of blood. The actual origin of the blood droplets or the height or distance of the source of blood from that surface requires the determination of the angle of impact of the blood droplets to provide a three-dimensional representation. This is often referred to as the Z axis (Figure 2.17 A and B).

Determination of the Point or Area of Origin

The point or area of origin of a bloodstain is the location from which the blood that produced the bloodstain originated. This is determined by projecting angles of impact of well-defined bloodstains back to an axis constructed through the established point or area of convergence.

The point or area of origin is the combination of the point of convergence with the information provided by the measurement of the angle of impact which relates to the Z axis or third dimension in space. The addition of the angle of impact provides the distance from the surface that the lines of convergence were established defining the origin of the bloodstain. At the scene, strings can be projected with the use of a protractor from each measured bloodstain at its angle of impact, back to an axis perpendicular to the plane on which the bloodstains were located, and passing through their point of convergence (Figure 2.18). The point or area of origin may be constructed graphically by plotting the distance from the point of convergence of the bloodstains with their angle of impact on the target surface (Figure 2.19). The point or area of origin may also be determined by the tangent method which has proven easy to use and is popular among bloodstain analysts. The tangent method is based on the trigonometric principle that in a right triangle the tangent of an angle is the length of the opposite side divided by the length of the adjacent side (Figure 2.20 A and B). The procedure is described in steps as follows:

1. Determine the angle of impact for representative bloodstains on a surface.
2. Determine the point or area of convergence through the long axes of the bloodstains.
3. Measure the distance from the base of the individual bloodstains to the point or area of convergence.
4. Calculate the point or area of origin or elevation in space which is the length of the Z axis using the following equation referring to Figure 2.20 B as an example:

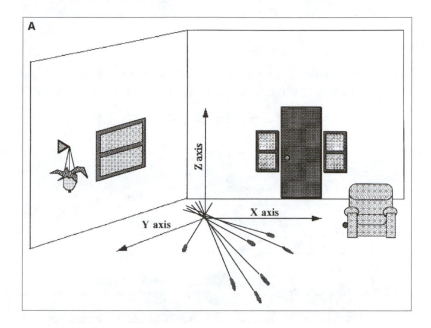

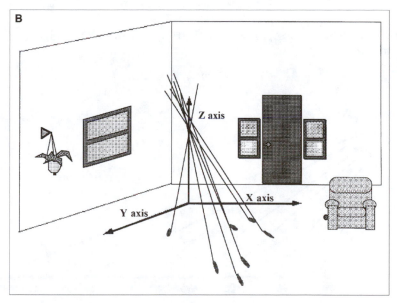

Figure 2.17 (A) Determination of point or area of convergence of bloodstains on the floor of a room with the X and the Y axis; (B) determination of the point or area of origin in space of bloodstains on the floor of a room with the use of the angle of impact of the bloodstains and the Z axis.

Tangent of angle of impact = opposite / adjacent or Z/Y
Solve for Z by multiplying each side of the equation by Y

Therefore:

Point or area of origin or Z = tangent of angle of impact ×
distance of stain from area or point or area of convergence or Y

Z = Tan of angle of impact × Y
Z = Tan of 30 degrees × 15
Z = 0.5773 × 15 = 8.66

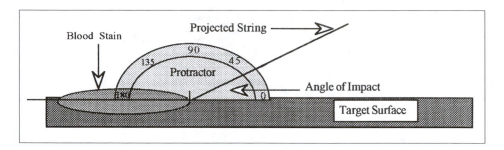

Figure 2.18 The use of a protractor and string to represent the angle of impact of bloodstains.

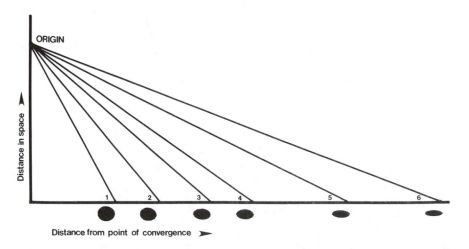

Figure 2.19 Graphical representation of the point of origin of bloodstains by projection of impact angles from distance of bloodstains from the point of convergence.

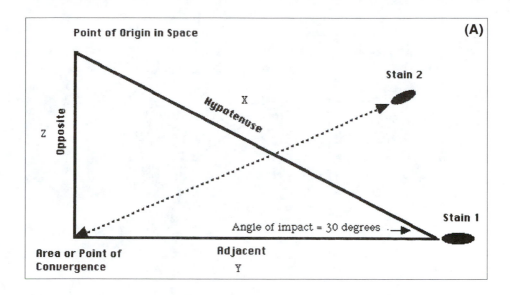

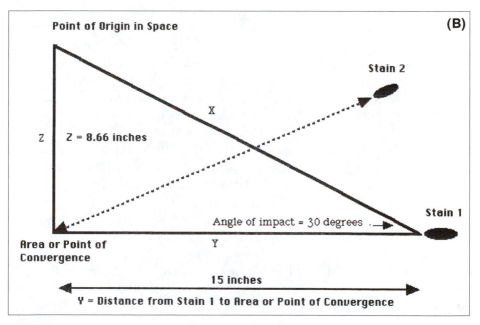

Figure 2.20 (A) Formation of a right triangle and the tangent of the angle of impact. (B) The use of a right triangle using angle of impact and distance from the point or area of convergence of bloodstains to determine the point of origin (Z).

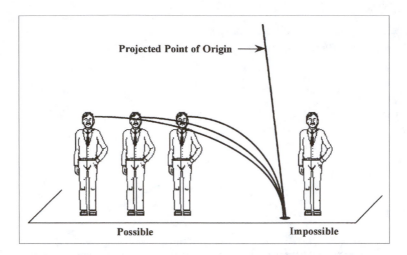

Figure 2.21 Diagrammatic representation of the projected point of origin of a bloodstain and possible and impossible locations of the source of the blood droplet.

The determined point or area of origin by either method could represent the height above a floor or the distance from a wall, ceiling or other object to the source of blood or impact site. When conclusions are drawn, a range of possible impact sites should be expressed. Blood droplets have their individual trajectories traveling from impact site to target surface depending upon velocity and distance traveled. When points of origin are determined a range of possible flight paths should be considered that could produce the same angle of impact. The projected point of origin represents the maximum height for the actual point of origin which is either at or below this point. Shorter travel distances and higher velocities of blood droplets tend to produce straighter lines of trajectory and more accurately reflect the actual point of origin and limit the possibilities. The point or area of origin may show whether a victim was standing, sitting or lying down at the time the blows were struck. Multiple points of origin may indicate different positions of the victim during bloodshed. Impossible points of origin can also be established which may assist with the reconstruction of the scene and either confirm or refute the version of events given by a suspect (Figure 2.21).

Angular Impact Produced by Horizontal Motion

When free-falling blood drops are subjected to a force producing horizontal motion as well as the downward pull of gravity, they may have angular impact on vertical or horizontal surfaces. The angle of impact may be established by the width to length ratio on both surfaces by the methods previously described. Directionality may usually be established by the stain shape and edge characteristics. A bleeding person in a fast walk or run would provide the source of blood with sufficient horizontal motion to allow the free-falling drops to impact a horizontal surface, such as a floor, at an impact angle of less than 90 degrees. A series of bloodstains resulting from free-falling blood drops traveling in a particular direction with sufficient horizontal motion may exhibit scalloped edges on the leading edge indicating the direction of travel of the source (Figure 2.22). A bleeding person in a slow walk may produce nearly circular bloodstains and directionality based upon leading edge characteristics of the bloodstains may not be obvious. Vertical surfaces such as walls may receive angular impact when the surface is in proximity to the free-falling drops. If the source of blood is not an active bleeding site, the quantity of blood available for dripping may be limited and the distance of the trail pattern may be short. This applies to bloody weapons or objects carried around or from a scene by an assailant. A falling blood drop may rupture upon impact and project smaller droplets. The resultant spatters or stains appear as long narrow streaks which will point in the direction of the parent drop rather than the direction of their travel. The edge characteristics of the parent drop will show the direction of travel.

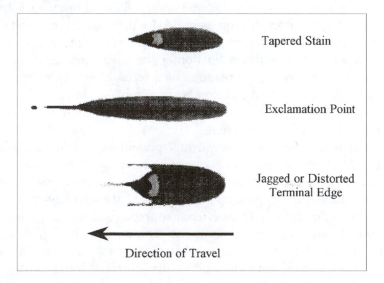

Figure 2.22 Bloodstains resulting from individual drops of blood falling to the surface with a right to left horizontal motion.

Splashed, Projected, and Cast-Off Blood

When a quantity of blood in excess of 1.0 ml is subjected to minor or low velocity forces or impact is allowed to fall to a surface, a splashed bloodstain pattern will be produced. Splashed bloodstain patterns usually have a large central area with peripheral spatter appearing as elongated bloodstains (Figure 2.23).

Secondary blood splashing or ricochetting may occur as a result of the deflection of large volumes of blood after impact from one surface to another. When sufficient bleeding has occurred, splash patterns may be produced by the movement of the victim or assailant. These patterns are often produced when pools of blood are disturbed by objects such as a shoe stepping into the blood pool or by large volumes of blood falling from a source such as a victim's wound. Larger quantities of splashed blood will create more spatters.

A projected bloodstain pattern is produced when blood is projected or released as the result of force. When blood of sufficient volume is projected horizontally or downward exceeding the pull of gravity, the edges of the resultant bloodstains exhibit numerous spine-like projections with narrow streaking of the secondary spatters (Figure 2.24). The vomiting of blood is an example of projected blood in large volume. Blood may also be projected by rapid movement or running a source or pool of blood.

Blood exiting the body under pressure as the result of a cut or breached artery is a form of projected blood and is referred to as arterial gushing or spurting. The resultant bloodstains on floors, walls, and other surfaces and objects are very characteristic and identified by their appearance and shape. Frequently, arterial spurt patterns appear as clusters of large stains and flow patterns depending upon the inclination of the target surface (Figures 2.25 and 2.26). In some cases, fluctuations of arterial blood pressure may be identified within the pattern and may bear resemblance to an electrocardiogram tracing. Observation of the distinct bright-red color of oxygenated arterial blood may also be apparent.

Arterial spurt patterns are frequently present at violent scenes where cutting and stabbing trauma has occurred and may also occur as a result of blunt force or gunshot trauma. Depending upon the relative position of the victim and assailant, the clothing and person of the assailant may receive considerable bloodstaining from arterial sources. In death cases where an accidental fall has occurred, the scene may be extremely bloody due to the spurting of blood from a cut temporal artery. The resulting bloodstain patterns may arouse suspicion of foul play unless correctly interpreted.

Cast-off bloodstain patterns occur when blood is released or thrown onto a surface from a bloody source or object in motion such as beating instruments, (bat, crowbar, hammer, etc.) owing to a whip-like action (Figures 2.27 and 2.28).

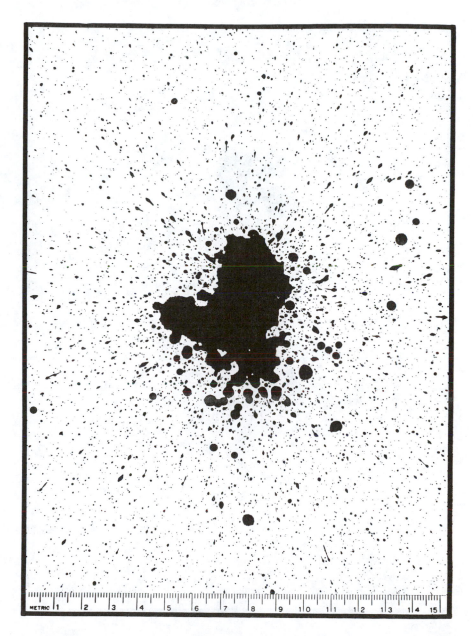

Figure 2.23 Bloodstain pattern produced by 1 ml of blood falling 72 inches onto smooth cardboard.

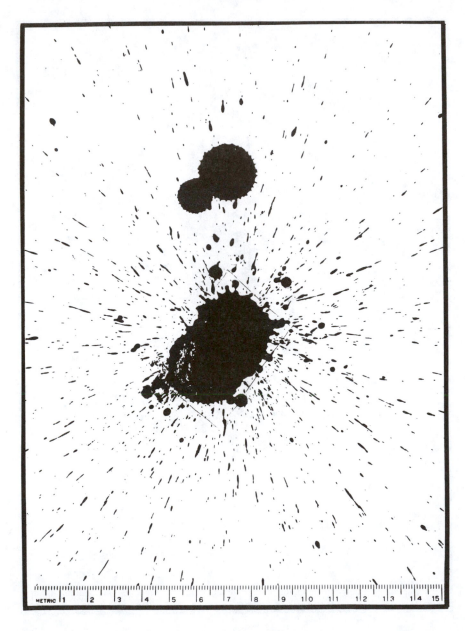

Figure 2.24 Bloodstain pattern produced by 1 ml of blood that was projected downward 36 inches onto smooth cardboard.

Figure 2.25 Arterial spurt pattern produced on the side of a clothes dryer by victim who sustained stab wounds to the chest.

Figure 2.26 Arterial spurt pattern produced on bathroom wall and tub by a postoperative patient who purposely tore out his arterial graft in a suicide attempt.

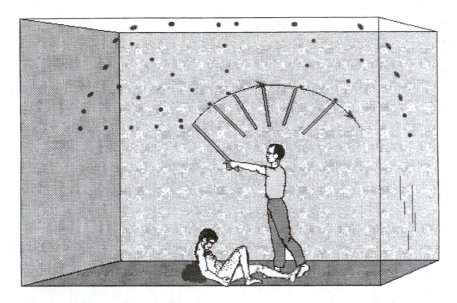

Figure 2.27 Diagrammatic representation of the mechanics of cast-off bloodstain patterns produced by the back- and forward swing of a blunt weapon during a beating.

Figure 2.28 Cast-off bloodstain pattern produced on the ceiling as the result of the back swing of a blunt weapon during a beating.

A distinction should be made between these cast-off patterns and the wave cast-off bloodstains originating from a parent drop as previously discussed.

In many cases of blunt trauma, the weapon is swung repeatedly at the victim. Once blood has been produced or exposed, it will adhere to the weapon in varying degrees depending upon the type of weapon and the quantity of blood at the site of injury. During the back swing away from the victim, the blood adhering to the weapon will be thrown off and travel tangentially to the arc of the swing and the droplets will impact on nearby surfaces such as walls, ceilings, floors, and other objects in their path. Less blood is cast off during the course of the downward or return swing of the weapon when the back swing arc is complete. The initial blood that is cast off from a weapon during the arc of the back swing may strike a target surface and produce circular bloodstains of 90 degree impact such as a ceiling or nearby wall depending upon the plane of the arc.

As the back swing continues the remainder of the blood is cast off a greater distance and will produce more oval-shaped bloodstains due to the angular impact. The size of cast-off bloodstains is generally in the range of 4–8 mm although they may be larger or smaller depending upon the type of weapon, amount of available blood, and the forcefulness and the length of the arc of the swing. Cast-off bloodstains are often seen as uniformly distributed trails on the impacting surfaces with the more elongated bloodstains most distant from the source. Determination of the angle of impact and convergence of the cast-off bloodstains will permit projection back to the source relative to the position of the victim and the assailant during the administration of the blows.

When there are multiple cast-off patterns present, an estimation of the minimum number of blows struck may be determined. The number of distinct patterns or trails of cast-off bloodstains would equal the minimum number of blows struck plus one since the initial blow generally does not produce sufficient exposed blood on the weapon to produce cast-off bloodstains. If multiple blows were struck on the same plane, the cast-off patterns or trails may overlap which is a reason why only a minimum number of blows struck may be estimated.

Sometimes the location of bloodstain patterns may indicate in which hand a weapon was held while being swung. This interpretation should be made with caution with the possibility of a two-handed or backhanded delivery kept in mind. Cast-off bloodstains on the back of an individual's shirt or the back of the trouser legs may be produced while swinging the weapon overhead while in a leaning or kneeling position. Cast-off bloodstains on the front of an individual's clothing may indicate proximity to a bloodshed event (Figure 2.29).

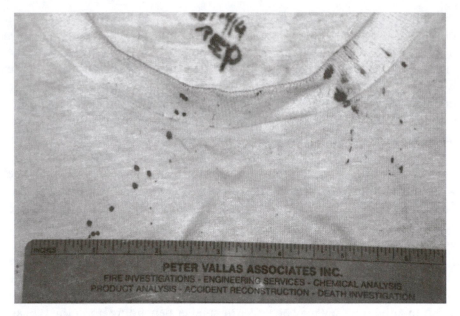

Figure 2.29 Cast-off bloodstain pattern on the front of the shirt worn by a bystander in close proximity to a victim of a beating.

Other Bloodstain Patterns Associated with Low-Velocity Force

A flow pattern is the change in shape and direction of a wet bloodstain due to the influence of gravity or movement of an object. Flow patterns may terminate in a larger quantity of blood referred to as a pool. Flow patterns and pools of blood are important to recognize for they may yield important information such as movement of a victim during bloodshed as well as postmortem movement or disturbance of the body and alteration of the scene of the death. Flow patterns may be observed on the body or clothing of the victim as well as the surface upon which the victim is found (floor, bed, chair, etc.). The directionality of flow patterns is governed by gravity and the angle of the surface upon which it is flowing (Figures 2.30 and 2.31). Obstructions in the path of a flow pattern may result in the blood flowing around the obstructing object. The quantity of blood within flow patterns and pooling of blood, or lack thereof, should be observed with respect to the injuries sustained by the victim to help determine whether the victim received the injuries at the present scene or moved from another location after injury or death.

A smudge is a bloodstain that has been altered or distorted by contact with a nonbloody surface so that further classification of the bloodstain is

Figure 2.30 Downward flow patterns of blood on a doorway.

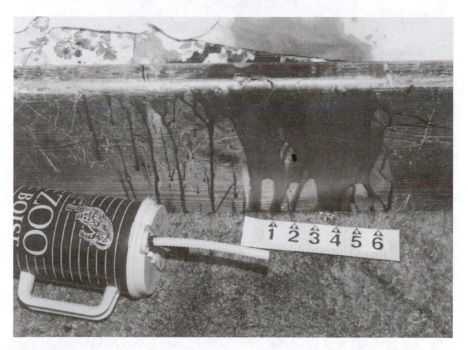

Figure 2.31 Blood llow patterns from the victim of a gunshot wound to the head contacting side of bed.

not possible. However, recognition of smudges of blood may indicate movement of the victim or assailant.

A wipe pattern is characterized as a bloodstain created when an object moves through an existing wet bloodstain thereby removing blood from the original stain and altering its appearance. The nature of the object producing wipe patterns may sometimes be determined by careful observation as having been produced by a hand, finger, fabric, etc. (Figure 2.32). A drag pattern is a type of wipe which is created when an existing pool of blood is altered by the movement of a victim on a surface such as a floor. The feathering of the leading edge of the pattern indicates the direction of the movement (Figure 2.33 A and B).

Figure 2.32 Alteration of partial footwear impressions on tile by wiping a second surface through the wet impressions.

The two types of bloodstain patterns which may indicate the presence or location of an object are transfer bloodstain patterns and void areas. A transfer bloodstain pattern is a contact bloodstain created when a surface wet with blood contacts a second surface as the result of compression or lateral movement. A recognizable mirror image of the original surface or at least a recognizable portion of the original surface may be transferred to the second surface. Common examples of transfer bloodstain patterns on surfaces are palm, finger, foot, or shoe impressions as well as fabric and weapon impressions (Figures 2.34 and 2.35). In some cases, class and/or individual characteristics may be determined from the bloody transfer impressions. Bloody hair swipes are a frequently observed type of blood transfer pattern (Figure 2.36).

Figure 2.33 (A) Drag pattern showing movement across existing blood pooling on concrete carport floor. (B) Continuation of the drag pattern across the floor. Victim was shot in the back and wrapped in tarpaulin prior to being dragged to the rear of the house. The tarpaulin leaked blood through a tear creating the thin continuation of the drag pattern.

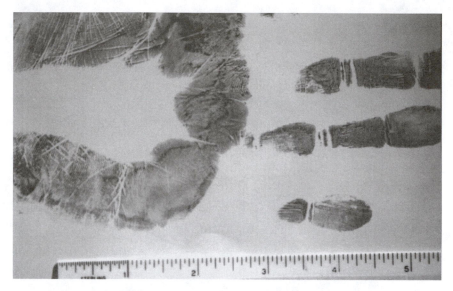

Figure 2.34 Right handprint transfer in blood produced on smooth cardboard.

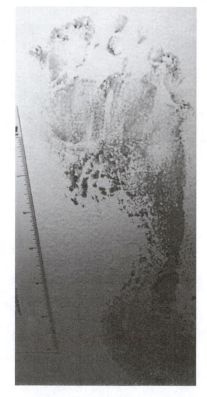

Figure 2.35 Foot transfer impression in blood on floor.

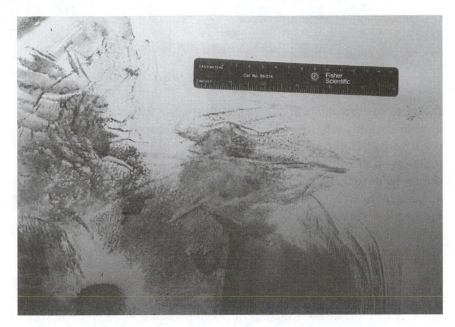

Figure 2.36 Hair transfer bloodstain pattern on wall.

A void, or shadow pattern, is the absence of bloodstain in an otherwise continuous bloodstain. The void is due to the presence of intervening objects or persons. If the object or person is shifted in position or completely removed, the resultant unstained void pattern remains. The void may be the recognizable outline of an object or may just show that someone or something interrupted the bloodstain pattern. Frequently, the position of a victim can be reconstructed by observation of a complete or partial outline of the victim or assailant within a bloodstained area (Figure 2.37). Void areas may be present on the clothing of victims that may indicate folding or position of arms or hands or legs at the time of bloodshed. An example of a void pattern created by a shoe within the area of blood spatter is shown in Figure 2.38.

It is possible in some cases to sequence bloodstains at a scene or reposition objects that have been moved after bloodshed has occurred. Sequencing may be demonstrated by the observation of overlapping stain patterns such as spatters of blood on top of a palm-, shoe-, or footprint at a scene. In a recent beating case, a partial bloody palmprint consistent with the victim's blood and matching a suspect was found on a wall above the head of the victim. The suspect stated that he was indeed at the scene, but after the victim was dead. He must have touched the victim and transferred the print in that manner. However, medium-velocity impact blood spatters were clearly on top of the ridge detail of the print indicating that the suspect deposited the

Figure 2.37 Void area created by victim of shooting while sitting on edge of bed while bleeding from head wound. Note V-shaped heavy bloodstaining in crotch area.

Figure 2.38 Void pattern around footwear in area of medium-velocity impact blood spatters on floor.

bloody print at an earlier time than stated. Physical activity that produced the blood spatters occurred afterward consistent with the suspect's presence at the scene during the beating of the victim (Figure 2.39). Experimentation by Hurley and Pex in 1990 has shown that the differentiation of blood spatter that has dried prior to being stepped on from a dried bloodprint with blood spatter on the top is not always possible. Caution should be exercised especially if this is attempted from photographs.

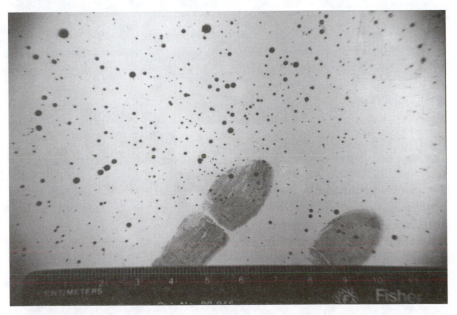

Figure 2.39 Blood spatter over a fingerprint transfer in blood indicating that the print transfer occurred before the production of spatter.

The repositioning of bloodstained objects to their original location that have been moved after bloodshed in a clean-up attempt by the assailant can be demonstrated by a case involving the gunshot death of a young woman. It was determined that the woman was not shot in the location where she was found. The woman's boyfriend denied knowledge of the shooting and permitted police to search the house he shared with the victim. Initial examination of the living room of the residence did not reveal apparent bloodstains until the throw rugs near the coffee table were removed (Figure 2.40 A and B). A bloodstained hassock was found hidden in the garage. Based upon the location of dried pools of blood on the living room carpet and flow patterns on the sides of the hassock, the hassock (was able to be) positioned in its original position. This area was partially covered by the coffee table (Figure 2.41 A and B). The victim originally was lying across the hassock while bleeding. The boyfriend finally admitted to an argument with his girlfriend

Figure 2.40 (A) Throw rugs covering bloodstains on carpet; (B) appearance of bloodstains on carpet after removal of throw rugs.

which resulted in the shooting as they struggled over a shotgun. He eventually pled guilty to manslaughter.

Smudges, wipes, and transfer patterns of victim's blood are frequently produced on and within an assailant's vehicle while leaving the scene. Door handles, steering wheel, gearshift apparatus, console, and floor pedals should be examined carefully for these types of bloodstains (Figure 2.42).

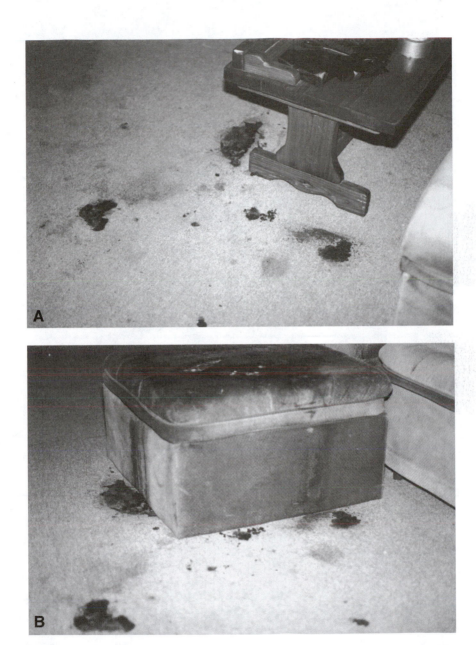

Figure 2.41 (A) Location of bloodstains on carpet prior to positioning of hassock; (B) hassock returned to its original position.

Figure 2.42 Blood transfer on top of gear-shift apparatus in vehicle.

Medium- and High-Velocity Impact Blood Spatter

3

STUART H. JAMES
T. PAULETTE SUTTON

Bloodstain Patterns Produced by Medium-Velocity Impact

When a strong force impacts upon an exposed source of blood, surface tension is overcome and the blood is broken up into many small droplets as a result of being subjected to this increased force. The velocity of the force refers to the impacting object rather than to the speed of the blood droplets in motion that are produced from the impact. When these droplets strike a target surface they produce bloodstain patterns that are distinguishable from patterns produced by dripped, projected, splashed, and cast-off bloodstain patterns, all of which are associated with low-velocity force or impact. Medium-velocity impact blood spatter consists of stains produced on a surface when the blood source has been subjected to a force at a velocity between approximately 5 and 25 feet per second (Figures 3.1, 3.2, and 3.3). Impact velocities associated with beatings and stabbings fall within this range. This convention, accepted by most bloodstain analysts distinguishes this type of blood spatter from the low-velocity category where the force applied to the exposed blood is up to 5 feet per second. The third conventional category to be discussed later in this chapter is high-velocity impact blood spatter where the force applied to the blood source exceeds 100 feet per second.

For years, the gray area of velocity between 25 to 100 feet per second was not addressed by bloodstain analysts. MacDonell noted in his 1993 edition of *Bloodstain Patterns* that a golf club may be swung at a velocity of over 75 feet per second. Whips and some martial arts weapons can also achieve similar velocities when swung. The size of the individual bloodstains produced is usually within the range of 1 to 3 mm in diameter although smaller and larger bloodstains are not uncommon. The highest beating velocities do not approach the velocities of projectiles fired from weapons that typically produce high-velocity impact blood spatter. Blows administered to a victim with blunt instruments (fists, club, hammer, rock, golf club), as well as sharp objects such as knives and axes, will produce medium-velocity blood spatter that may be

59

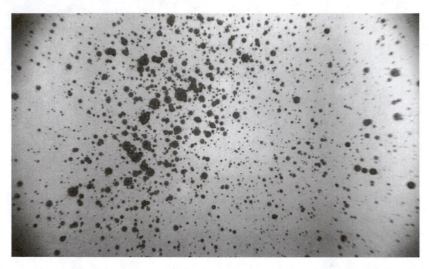

Figure 3.1 Medium-velocity impact blood spatter that has impacted onto a vertical smooth cardboard surface at 90 degrees.

Figure 3.2 Medium-velocity impact blood spatter that has impacted onto horizontal smooth cardboard surfaces creating angular bloodstains.

differentiated from high-velocity events. It is important to remember that a single blow usually is not sufficient to produce significant blood spatter except perhaps in the case of massive crushing injury. The source of blood must be exposed when receiving the impact in order to create spatter. The directionality, convergence, angle of impact, and origin of these bloodstains are determined by the location and geometry of the stains within the patterns produced.

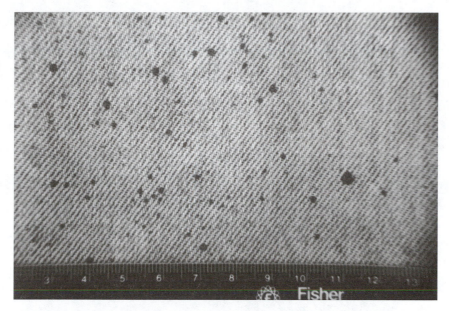

Figure 3.3 Medium-velocity impact blood spatter that has impacted onto denim blue jean material.

Multiple blows to the head with a blunt instrument typically create considerable amounts of medium-velocity impact blood spatter (Figure 3.4). However, there are occasions where the victim's head is covered with bedding, towels, or other materials prior to or during a beating which will lessen the amount of blood spatter produced.

The study of the distribution of medium-velocity bloodstain patterns and determination of the directionality and origin of the individual blood-stains may determine the relative position of the assailant and victim at the time the blows were delivered. Radial patterns of blood spatter produced by medium-velocity impact are common and are distributed in a fashion not unlike the spokes of a wheel. If the victim is on a floor or other surface during the course of a beating, the spatter may be observed radiating away from the area of impact producing streaking patterns on the victim and floor and impacting at a low level on nearby walls or other objects within range. Sometimes a sector or portion of the radial pattern will appear free of blood. This void area may represent interception of the blood spatter by the assailant. During events of this type the assailant may receive significant blood spatter on shoes, trouser, shirt, and other garments. The quantity and location of blood spatter deposited on an assailant depends on the relative position of the assailant and the victim, the angle of the force, and the number and location of blows struck. For example, an assailant delivering blows with overhead swings to a prone victim would likely receive blood spatter on his

Figure 3.4 Medium-velocity impact bloodstain pattern on wall. The head of the victim which was severely beaten repeatedly with a blunt object was located close to the floor at the apex of the V-pattern.

lower legs as well as the hand and arm that wielded the weapon (Figure 3.5). On the other hand, when blows are struck to a victim at an angle with the direction of force away from the assailant such as side swings, little if any spatter may impact upon the assailant. An assailant may also wear protective garments, change clothes prior to apprehension or not be wearing any clothing during the attack on the victim. It should be recognized that the absence of blood spatter on the clothing of a suspect does not necessarily exonerate the accused. The issue of the significance of the lack of blood on a suspect was effectively addressed by Paul Kish and Herbert MacDonell of the Laboratory of Forensic Science in Corning, New York. They combined to write an excellent editorial in the *Journal of Forensic Identification* entitled, "Absence

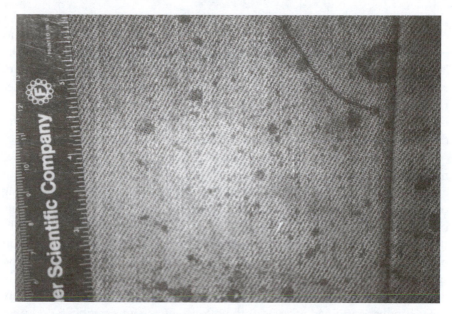

Figure 3.5 Medium-velocity impact blood spatter on the lower jean leg of assailant who struck prone victim on the head multiple times with a hammer.

of Evidence is Not Evidence of Absence" in 1996. They state that "the complete absence of bloodstains on a defendant or his clothing is frequently assumed by many to be definitive evidence that the defendant did not directly participate in a violent act. This is a misconception fostered and exploited by those who have insufficient knowledge and experience in bloodstain pattern interpretation or by those who hope that such an opinion would aid in their client's defense. Explanations for the lack of bloodstaining on an individual who has actively participated in a violent act are innumerable." The authors stress that conclusions should be drawn based upon the presence of bloodstains whereas the absence of bloodstains on clothing should neither implicate nor exonerate the accused.

Experience has shown that other objects worn by an assailant may contain blood spatter that may not be apparent to a person attempting to wash bloody clothing to obscure involvement in a homicide. Examples of this are socks, belts, hats, glasses, watches, and other jewelry items. Weapons should also be carefully examined for evidence of medium-velocity blood spatter.

Blood spatter on clothing should be examined thoroughly especially with respect to estimation of impact angle and spot size. Fabrics can alter the appearance and size of bloodstains. R.B. White researched bloodstain patterns on fabrics and published an article in 1986 entitled "The Effect of Drop Volume, Dropping Height, and Impact Angle". Evaluation of bloodstain patterns on clothing is enhanced by dressing the clothing on a mannequin for proper orientation and directionality. Blood spatter on clothing may be obscured by the presence of other blood patterns. Also, dark fabrics, such as blue jeans denim, may hinder evaluation of small blood spots, due to the lack of contrast. The use of a stereomicroscope is helpful in many cases especially when small blood droplets have penetrated the weave of the material. Diagrams of clothing and shoes that indicate the location of bloodstains is useful for documentation purposes especially when the small stains are difficult to visualize without the aid of magnification.

It should be recognized that events other than beatings can produce medium- to high-velocity sized blood spatter at a crime scene. Nonviolent events such as the slapping of a hand or other object in a blood source, flicking of bloody fingers, blood dripping into blood can produce small blood spatters in the 1 to 3 mm diameter size range or less (Figures 3.6 and 3.7). Additionally, there are instances where minor arterial spurt patterns and small cast off bloodstains may exhibit similarities to medium- to high-velocity impact blood spatter. The investigator should be alerted for the presence of bloodstain patterns resulting from coughing and exhalation of blood in those cases where the victim has sustained injuries of the mouth, nose, sinus cavities, and lungs. In these instances, exhaled or expired bloodstain patterns can result from simple exhalation of blood and air through the nose or mouth, sneezes, coughs, gurgling, sucking, chest wounds, or even paramedic activity such as CPR on the victim (Figure 3.8). The resultant bloodstain patterns can be confused with medium- or high-velocity impact spatter associated with blunt force trauma or gunshot injury due to their small size. There are criteria that may assist with the recognition of bloodstain patterns that have resulted from expired blood. Some of the bloodstains may appear diluted having been mixed with saliva or nasal secretions. The mixture of blood and air that is exhaled may produce bloodstains with characteristic air bubbles or vacuoles within them. These can be visualized with a hand or stereo microscope. The occurrence of these events can often be recognized and distinguished appropriately during careful examination of the entire scene, the victim's injuries, and clothing. If there is no evidence of blood in the nose, mouth, or airway passages then the bloodstains could not have been produced by exhaled or expired blood. Conversely, the presence of blood in these areas should alert the investigator to the possibility of expired bloodstain patterns.

The activity of flies at the scene where blood has been shed is another possible source of small stains of blood that may be confused with medium- to high-velocity impact blood spatter (Figures 3.9 and 3.10). An understanding of the mechanics of flies feeding on blood and decomposing bodies is essential for proper interpretation of these bloodstains. The horse fly is characterized as a biter, while the common house fly is specialized as a lapper and sucker. Flies ingest blood and regurgitate it onto a surface to allow enzymes to break

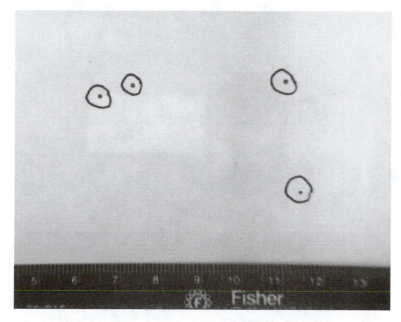

Figure 3.6 Blood spatter on a vertical surface created by the flicking of blood from the fingers. The spatter has been circled for documentation purposes.

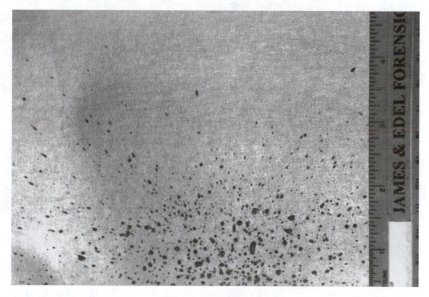

Figure 3.7 Blood spatter on a vertical surface created by blood dripping into blood.

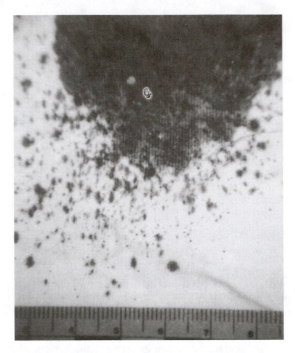

Figure 3.8   Exhaled or expired bloodstain pattern on the left front upper shirt of victim originating from the nose.

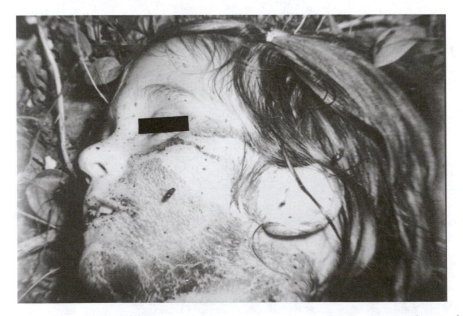

Figure 3.9   Victim found in wooded outdoor environment showing evidence of fly activity. Note small apparent blood spatters on lips, nose, and left cheek which are the result of fly deposits.

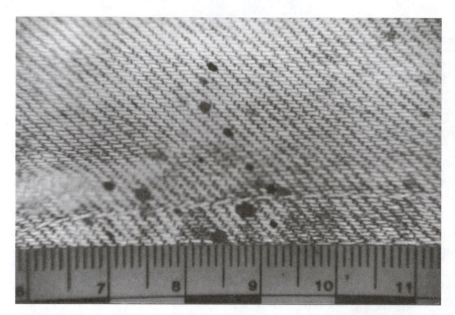

Figure 3.10 Fly deposits similar to blood spatter on left thigh area of denim jeans of victim who received single gunshot wound to the head.

down the blood. At a later time, the flies return to the areas of regurgitated blood and consume a portion of the blood. The surfaces upon which these activities have taken place will contain small spots of blood material which are often a millimeter or less in diameter with no definite point of convergence or origin. Some of the stains will exhibit dome shaped craters due to the sucking process and others may show swiping due to defecation. These stains may be observed on many surfaces at the scene especially lamp shades, blinds and ceilings as well as on the victim and clothing. Their locations may be inconsistent with blood spatter associated with injuries sustained by the victim.

It is critical to evaluate an entire bloodstain pattern when evaluating the origin of blood spatters. Conclusions should be considered carefully when there are a limited number of small bloodstains available for evaluation. There are instances where the mechanism that produced small blood spatters cannot be determined with certainty or lend itself to alternative explanations. This concept can be applied to many stains and patterns that are characterized as low-, medium-, or high-velocity type bloodstains.

Bloodstain Patterns Produced by High-Velocity Impact

A bloodstain pattern produced by high-velocity impact is characterized by the presence of high-velocity blood spatter. A high-velocity impact is

considered to be approximately 100 feet per second or greater. Many of the
blood droplets produced by this type of impact are extremely small and create
a mist-like dispersion. Because of their low mass these droplets will travel
only a short distance (up to 4 feet) through the air. Individual bloodstains
within a high-velocity pattern are usually 0.1 mm or smaller in diameter but
are frequently seen in association with larger bloodstains in the medium-
velocity size range (Figures 3.11 and 3.12). The larger droplets of course will
travel greater distances owing to their greater mass and may be present without the characteristic mist-like dispersion of minute droplets (Figures 3.13
and 3.14). Therefore the resultant impact spatter size may be predominantly
in the medium-velocity size range. Because of their relatively small size, care
must be taken when observing and measuring medium- and high-velocity
blood spatters for directionality and impact angles. A pocket microscope or
other magnifying device with a scale in tenths of millimeters is very useful.

At crime scenes, evidence of high-velocity impact blood spatter is most
frequently associated with gunshot injury but is seen also in cases involving
explosions, power tool and machinery injuries as well as in some automobile
accidents (Figures 3.15, 3.16, and 3.17). When a victim has sustained gunshot
injury there may be evidence of back spatter from the entrance wound and
forward spatter associated with the exit wound if one exists. Back spatter
results from blood droplets directed back towards the source of energy which

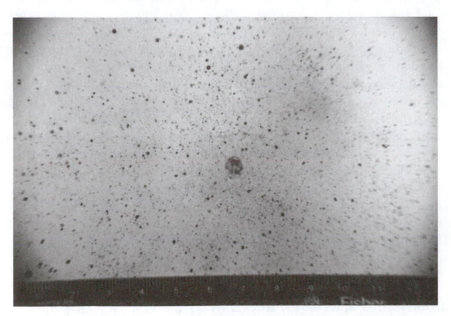

Figure 3.11 High-velocity impact blood spatter that has impacted on a vertical
smooth cardboard surface at 90 degrees.

Figure 3.12 High-velocity impact blood spatter from exit wound surrounding projectile hole on wall. Victim received a through and through gunshot wound to the head while sitting on bed near wall.

Figure 3.13 High-velocity impact blood spatter produced by high speed blade at distance of 1 foot on horizontal surface.

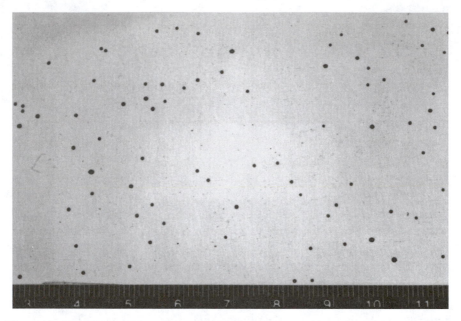

Figure 3.14 High-velocity impact blood spatter produced by high-speed blade at distance of 6 feet on horizontal surface.

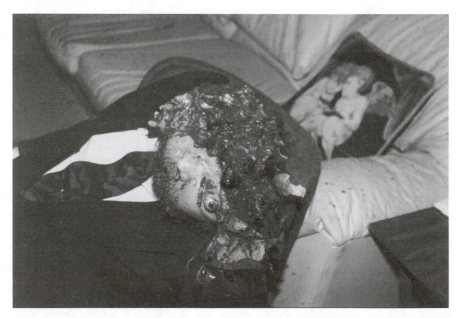

Figure 3.15 View of victim who sustained a self-inflicted contact gunshot wound to the head.

Figure 3.16 Wooden support constructed by victim to position rifle. The string attachment to trigger permitted him to fire the weapon with his right hand while sitting.

Figure 3.17 High-velocity impact blood spatter on the wall surrounding the projectile hole in the wall directly behind the seated victim. Hair fragments are also deposited on the wall within the blood spatter pattern.

would be the weapon. It may be deposited on skin, clothing, or any object or surface near the entrance wound relative to the position of the victim at the time of discharge of the firearm (Figure 3.18). Back spatter may also be deposited on the firearm and the exposed hand, shirt cuff, or arm of an assailant holding the weapon if it is discharged at contact or close range (Figure 3.19).If there is an exposed source of blood such as may be the case with multiple gunshot wounds, muzzle to target distances of up to 6 inches may produce significant back spatter. Shooting into exposed blood will increase the quantity of back spatter but the distance it will travel will still be limited to up to 4 feet for the minute droplets. In cases of possible self-inflicted gunshot injury, the hands and arms of the victim, and the weapon should be carefully examined for evidence of high-velocity blood spatter that may indicate the position of the hands on the weapon at the time of discharge of the firearm.

Forward spatter is produced by blood droplets traveling in the same direction as the source of energy and in gunshot cases is usually associated with the exit wound. An exception to this would be a shoring or furrowing projectile path on a peripheral area of the body where a true exit wound is not apparent. The demonstration of the presence of high velocity forward spatter will assist in the location of the victim at the time of discharge of the weapon. When a projectile has reentered a body after passing through a hand or arm, there will likely be high-velocity forward spatter around the periphery

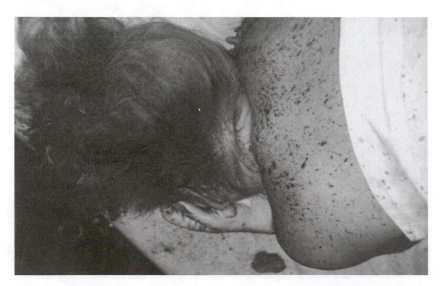

Figure 3.18 High-velocity impact back spatter on the skin of the upper back of the victim who sustained a close-range gunshot wound to the back of the head.

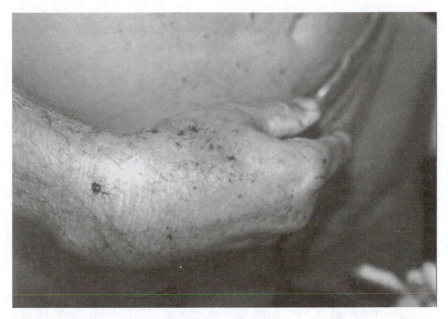

Figure 3.19 High-velocity impact back spatter on right-hand held around muzzle of weapon by victim in self-inflicted contact gunshot wound to the head.

of the reentry wound, and its presence will help reconstruct the position of the victim at the time of weapon discharge.

The quantity and distribution of high-velocity blood spatter whether it be forward or back spatter varies considerably depending upon many factors. Usually, when there is an exit wound the amount of forward spatter will exceed that of back spatter. The amount of back spatter is affected by the type of weapon and ammunition, muzzle to target distance, and anatomic features of the wound site. In 1983, Stephens and Allen documented factors affecting the amount of back spatter experimentally. They noted that back spatter may be completely absent with considerable muzzle to target distances. With respect to shotguns and high-powered firearms, a greater quantity of high-velocity blood spatter would be expected especially when the weapon is discharged at close or contact range (Figure 3.20). The quantity of back- and forward high-velocity blood spatter is also reduced by the blocking effect of hair and clothing including hats and or other headgear worn by a victim. In 1987, Pex and Vaughan conducted further experiments with back spatter and applied their findings to actual case investigation where back spatter was identified on the sleeve of suspects. Their work also corroborated the work of Stephens and others.

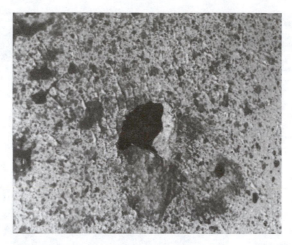

Figure 3.20 Large quantity of high-velocity impact blood spatter produced on ceiling with projectile hole as result of suicidal contact shotgun wound to the head.

Construction of a Simulated Head for High-Velocity Blood Spatter Experiments with Firearms

A basic course in bloodstain interpretation includes laboratory exercises to create bloodstains of various patterns that are studied in relation to actual bloodstains found at crime scenes.

During the reconstruction of crime scenes utilizing bloodstain interpretation, it is often desirable to conduct experiments under known conditions for comparison to and verification of conclusions drawn from the actual bloodstain patterns at the scene.

The investigation of gunshot injuries of the head often produces significant bloodstain patterns of high-velocity blood spatter usually more prevalent in the form of forward spatter from the exit wound. In conjunction with the angle of entry and exit of the projectile and wound characteristics, the quantity and distribution of this blood spatter can assist with the reconstruction of the shooting and the distinction between homicide, suicide, or accident. Laboratory experiments in basic bloodstain courses have utilized the principle of shooting through blood-soaked polyurethane sponges to demonstrate forward and back spatter. This creates an amount of high-velocity blood spatter in excess of that produced at many crime scenes since the blood source is fully exposed and not covered by headgear, clothing, hair, skin, tissue, or bone. The following described construction of simulated human heads was devised to study experimentally the distribution of high-velocity forward blood spatter and has been related effectively to actual case work.

This procedure for construction of the heads was a modification of a technique developed by MacDonell and Brooks for their research of the drawback effect of blood into the muzzle of firearms, which is described later in this chapter. Styrofoam wig supports were chosen for the head structures (Figure 3.21) and were sawed longitudinally into left and right halves. A propane torch was utilized to hollow out a "brain cavity" (Figure 3.22). The halves were then reunited and taped together (Figure 3.23). Gelatin was used to simulate brain material, and it was poured into the head cavities through the existing opening in the necks. The heads were then refrigerated overnight to allow the gelatin to solidify.

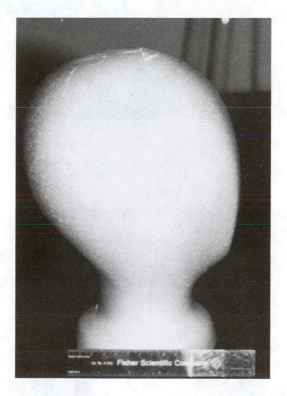

Figure 3.21 Styrofoam wig head prior to head construction.

With the use of a heated putty knife, 3 1/2 × 3 1/2 × 1/2 inch depressions were created in the Styrofoam surface in areas approximating the entrance and exit wounds that existed on the victim (Figure 3.24 A and B). Cut sections of skull that were available for this purpose (Figure 3.25 A and B) were placed within these depressions. For comparative purposes, hard plastic sections were substituted for bone in some of the heads.

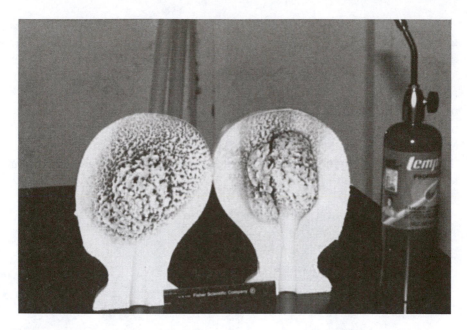

Figure 3.22 Styrofoam head halved with saw and cavities hollowed out with propane torch.

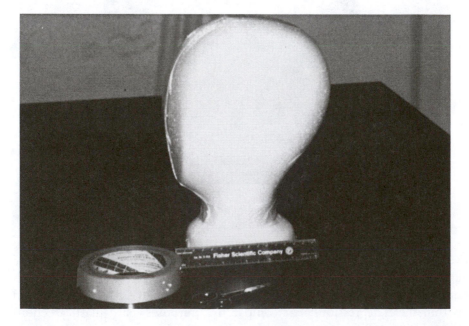

Figure 3.23 Reassembled styrofoam head and cavity filled with gelatin to simulate brain tissue.

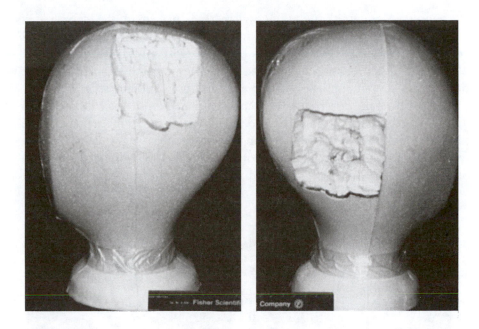

Figure 3.24 **(A)** Entrance wound area formed with hot putty knife. **(B)** Exit wound area formed with hot putty knife.

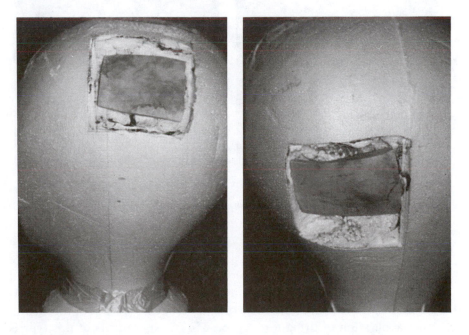

Figure 3.25 **(A)** Bone or plastic inserted into entrance wound site. **(B)** Bone or plastic inserted into exit wound site.

Pieces of polyurethane sponge were then placed in the depressions over the bone or plastic previously inserted to act as a matrix for blood (Figure 3.26 A and B). Fresh pigskin, obtained from a local slaughterhouse, was cleaned, shaved, and cut into sections. They were then taped over the depressions containing the bone or plastic and polyurethane sponge to simulate human skin. Fresh, anticoagulated human blood was obtained and approximately 20 ml was injected into the polyurethane sponges through the pigskin to simulate the blood supply in the wound areas (Figure 3.27). Finally, wig hair was placed over the exit wound site and the completed prepared Styrofoam head was then positioned in the appropriate location and held with clamps (Figure 3.28).

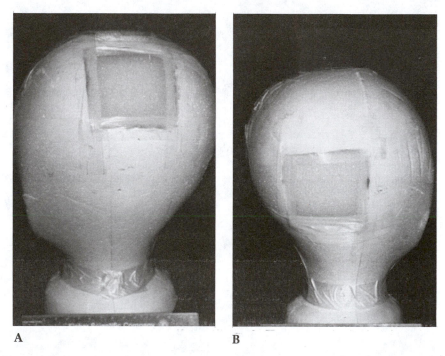

A   **B**

Figure 3.26 (A) Polyurethane sponge inserted into entrance wound site. (B) Polyurethane sponge inserted into exit wound site.

The areas expected to receive the blood spatter were covered with white sheets to enhance visibility of the bloodstains (Figure 3.29). The identical weapon and similar ammunition was utilized for test firings through the simulated heads approximating the angle of entry and exit wounds of the victim. Another application of firing through pigskin in experiments of this type is the determination of estimations of the distance from muzzle to target based upon distribution and amount of observed gunpowder tattooing (Figure 3.30).

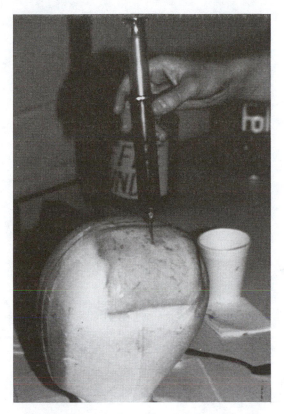

Figure 3.27 Human blood injected into entrance wound site through pigskin covering.

This form of head simulation has been used with success and the quantities and distribution of high-velocity blood spatter were found to be more realistic than those seen when uncovered blood-soaked polyurethane sponge is fired through. Quantities of forward and back spatter are decreased due to the blocking effect of hair, skin, simulated tissue, and bone. To date, this experimental head simulation has been utilized in gunshot cases where the distances from muzzle to target have been within 6 inches and the emphasis has been on the distribution of the quantity and location of the forward high-velocity blood spatter. However, it is anticipated that this type of head simulation will be useful in studying further the extent of back spatter especially related to increased distances from muzzle to target as described by Stephens.

Another phenomenon associated with contact and close-range gunshot injury is the drawback effect. This is the presence in the barrel of the firearm of blood that has been drawn backward due to the effect of the discharged gases accompanying the projectile. Original research in this area was conducted by MacDonell and Brooks in 1977 and it was demonstrated that the

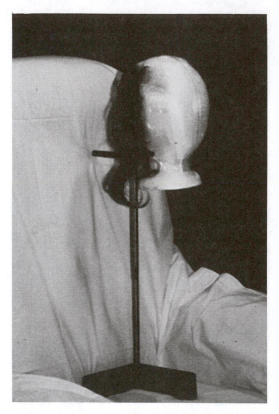

Figure 3.28 Hair placed over exit wound site and head placed into target area.

depth of penetration of blood into the muzzle of a firearm was a function of the caliber of the weapon and the discharge distance.

It should be obvious that the examination of firearms for blood both on the outside surface and within the barrel should be conducted prior to handling and test firing of the weapon in question.

Detection of Blood in the Barrels of Firearms

In 1977, MacDonell and Brooks published in the *Legal Medicine Annual* an article entitled "Detection and Significance of Blood in Firearms". Their research determined that a relationship existed between discharge distance and the distance to which blood is drawn back into the barrel of the firearm. Maximum discharge distances at which traces of blood were detected to a depth of 5 mm or greater inside the weapon's muzzle ranged from 1 to 1 1/2 inches for 22-caliber revolvers to 5 inches for 12-, 16-, or 20-gauge standard shotguns. Several general observations were made as a result of their research:

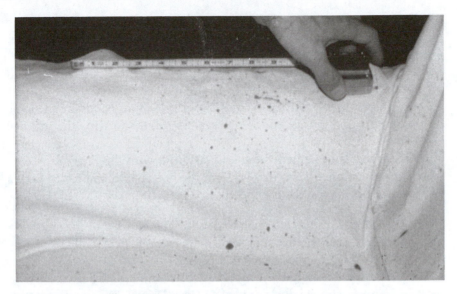

Figure 3.29 Documentation of high-velocity impact forward blood spatter from exit wound on white sheet covering hair.

1. The larger the caliber or gauge, the greater the depth of penetration into the barrel.
2. Recoil-operated autoloading weapons will produce less depth of blood penetration than a weapon whose barrel does not recoil.
3. The use of magnum or similar higher-energy loads will produce more depth of blood penetration than standard ammunition in the barrel of a given firearm.
4. When a double-barreled shotgun is discharged at contact, considerable back spatter occurs (up to 12 cm) in the dormant barrel.

The MacDonell and Brooks procedure for detection of blood in the barrel of handguns is detailed in Figure 3.31.

1. A straw is cut about 1 inch longer than the barrel of the weapon. A piece of pipe cleaner is cut about 2 inches longer than the straw.
2. The pipe cleaner is first saturated with water and then inserted into the barrel of the weapon until it extends about 1/2 inch from both breech and muzzle. If possible, insertion should be made from the breech end. This is not possible with solid-frame revolvers. It is important that the insertion of the straw be accomplished without scraping the inside of the barrel. Such contact could result in possible contamination farther down the barrel and would suggest greater depth of blood penetration. Naturally, this applies only when the straw has been inserted from the muzzle end.

3. The plastic straw is pulled back flush with the breech by holding the pipe cleaner about 1 inch from the muzzle and sliding the straw over the pipe cleaner.
4. The exposed pipe cleaner in the breech is bent over and firmly held while the straw is withdrawn from the muzzle end.
5. A "crank" is formed by making two right-angle bends in the pipe cleaner at the muzzle end. This crank is rotated to wipe the internal surface of the barrel.
6. The crank is straightened out and cut flush with the muzzle.
7. The pipe cleaner is withdrawn from the breech end and tested with a catalytic color test for the presence of blood.

The procedure for rifles is similar to that for handguns with the exception that the length of the straws and pipe cleaners must be extended by splicing the straws and attaching pipe cleaners together.

The procedure for shotguns is modified to accommodate barrel size with the use of 3/8 inch wooden dowels of appropriate length. The wooden dowels

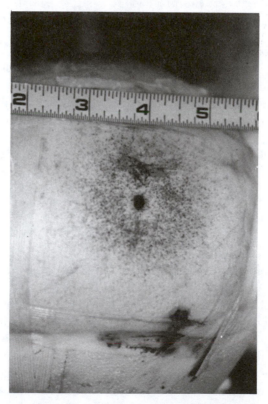

Figure 3.30 View of entrance wound site of simulated head after discharge of weapon at muzzle to target distance of approximately 4 inches.

are securely wrapped with moist filter paper both with double-sided Scotch tape and spiral wrapping with thread. The dowel is then inserted into the breech end of the shotgun barrel avoiding contact with the sides of the barrel. The use of wooden blocks is suggested to guide the dowel in order to avoid accidental contact and contamination. The barrel is then wiped in a fashion similar to handguns, removed, and tested.

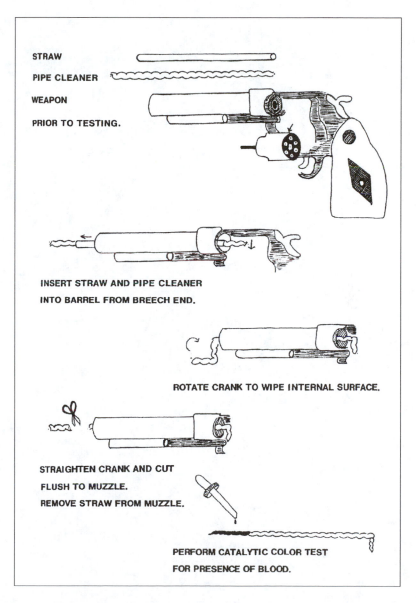

Figure 3.31 Procedure for the detection of blood in the barrel of a firearm.

The Significance of Partially Dried, Clotted, Aged, and Physically Altered Bloodstains

4

STUART H. JAMES

Drying Time of Blood

When blood is exposed to an external environment the drying process on various surfaces is initiated. The drying time of blood is a function of the bloodstain size and volume, the nature of the target surface and the influences or effects of the external environment. Small impact spatters, light transfer stains, and thin flow patterns of blood dry within a few minutes at normal conditions of temperature, humidity, and air flow on nonporous surfaces. Bloodstains of greater size and volume require longer periods of time to dry under similar conditions. The drying time of blood in general is decreased by increased temperature and decreased humidity, the presence of significant air currents such as wind and the effect of a fan. It follows that humid environments, lower temperatures and minimal air flow will produce longer drying times. Surfaces which permit the soaking of blood into the material may produce significantly longer drying times.

Research by Epstein and Laber in their manual, *Experiments and Practical Exercises in Bloodstain Pattern Analysis* published in 1983, contains significant data on the drying time of blood. They studied the effect of temperature, humidity, air flow and surface texture on the drying time of blood utilizing a single drop, 1 ml, 5 ml, and 10 ml volumes of blood to create the bloodstains. Their study can be used as a general guideline. However, when drying times are to be estimated in case work they should be very conservative. When comparative experiments are considered, the bloodstain size should be estimated and the surface texture and environmental conditions duplicated as closely as possible.

Figure 4.1 Flaking of the central portion of a dried bloodstain produces a skeletonized stain.

The drying of bloodstains is observed initially around the edges or periphery and proceeds inward to the central portion of the stain. Occasionally the dried central area of a dried bloodstain will flake away leaving an intact circular rim. This is referred to as a skeletonized bloodstain (Figure 4.1). Another type of skeletonized bloodstain occurs when the central area of a partially dried bloodstain is altered by contact or a swiping motion leaving the peripheral rim intact. It can be interpreted as a sequence of activity occurring after the bloodstain began to dry (Figure 4.2). This could involve a significant amount of time with importance to the overall bloodstain reconstruction of the scene.

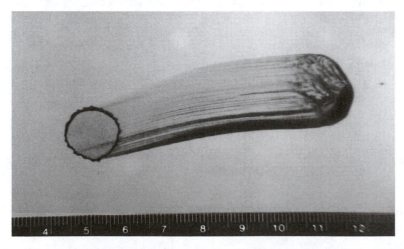

Figure 4.2 Wiping alteration of a partially dried bloodstain indicating activity occurring shortly after the blood was deposited. This is also referred to as a skeletonized bloodstain.

A useful observation of bloodstains on surfaces other than horizontal is the recognition of the dense zone. When a blood droplet of sufficient volume strikes a nonhorizontal surface, gravitational forces continue to act upon the liquid portion of the bloodstain. The lower area or base of the bloodstain will be more dense due to the continued accumulation of blood. After the bloodstain has dried sufficiently on the surface, this dense zone cannot be altered (Figure 4.3). Bloodstains on objects or surfaces which have been moved after the blood has dried may show dense zones inconsistent with their observed positions. This observation would indicate an alteration of the scene.

Figure 4.3 Accumulation of blood due to gravity at the lowest area of the bloodstain referred to as the dense zone.

Clotting of Blood

A blood clot is formed by a complex mechanism involving the plasma protein fibrinogen, platelets, and other clotting factors. It is observed visually as a network of fibrous material (fibrin and red blood cells). Subsequently, the blood clot begins to retract causing a separation of the remaining liquid portion which is referred to as serum (Figure 4.4). Blood clots and serum stains surrounding them as well as the degree of observed drying of blood should be recognized as important information at crime scenes. Occasionally, events take place after blood has been shed and has begun the clotting process. Bloodstain patterns produced by partially clotted or clotted blood indicate a time interval between the bloodshed and the activity producing the pattern. This interval may be short or extended depending upon the degree of clotting, source and quantity of blood, and environmental conditions existing at the time. An average time of 3 to 15 minutes for blood to commence clotting outside the body may be used as a guideline for a minimal interval.

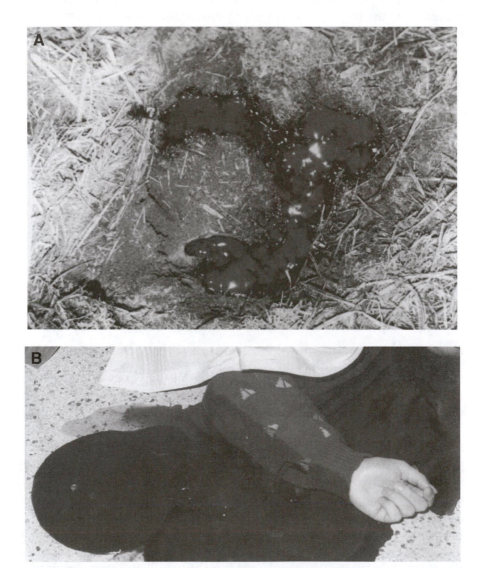

Figure 4.4 (**A**) Appearance of clotted blood on the ground. Note the shiny appearance of serum, retraction of central blood clot, and drying bloodstain around edges; (**B**) Serum separation and clot retraction on tile floor.

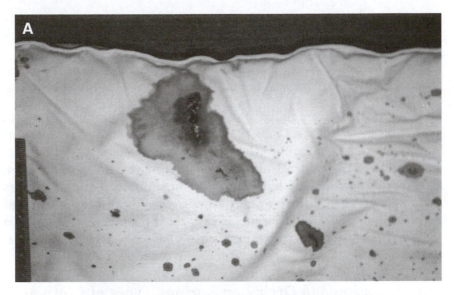

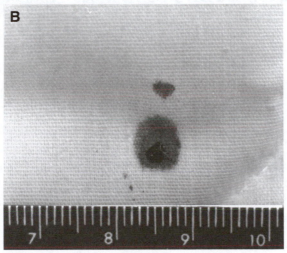

Figure 4.5 (**A**) Clotted medium-velocity impact blood spatter on pillow indicating time interval between initial bloodshed and final blows struck to victim on bed. Note darkened centers of the stains which represent clot. (**B**) Close up view of clotted spatter.

Examples of the significance of partially clotted or clotted bloodstain patterns are:

1. Clotted blood spatter on victim's clothing and/or surrounding surfaces associated with a beating death may indicate a significant interval between blows administered and possibly postmortem infliction of injury (Figure 4.5 A and B).

2. Clotted bloodstain patterns associated with a pedestrian victim on a roadway may indicate an interval between impacts associated with more than a single vehicle.
3. Coughing or exhalation of clotted blood by victim may be associated with post injury survival time.

An estimation of the degree of blood clotting and drying of pools of blood associated with a victim, when used in conjunction with other signs of postmortem change, may be helpful in the determination of the postmortem interval or in substantiating postmortem movement of the victim. Estimation of degree of clotting and drying time of blood at crime scenes should be reproduced experimentally using freshly drawn human blood of similar volume placed on an identical surface with similar environmental conditions existing during the experiment as were observed at the scene. Estimates of this interval should be made with caution.

Blood Diffusion and Drying on Various Types of Cloth as a Function of Time

Purpose
The purpose of this experiment is to observe and record the diffusion activity of fresh blood on cloth of various types and the changes that occur due to the effects of capillary action and the clotting and drying of blood over a period of time on cloth surfaces.

Method
Strips of the following cloth materials were prepared and suspended over glass petri dishes so that the lower ends of the cloth were immersed in fresh blood when it was added to the dishes. Laboratory conditions were at a temperature of 72°F with an approximate relative humidity of 55%.

- 100% cotton
- 100% polyester
- 50% cotton/50% polyester

Sixty milliliters of fresh blood was drawn from the antecubital vein of a volunteer using standard Vacutainer apparatus at 9:30 AM which was used as zero time for the experiment. Fifteen milliliters of this freshly drawn blood was placed into each of the three petri dishes and allowed to diffuse up the cloth strips. Each petri dish contained two strips of cloth of the respective type with one oriented with a vertical weave and the second a horizontal weave orientation. For control purposes, 2.5 and 5.0 ml of blood were placed into two separate petri dishes to observe for the appearance of clot retraction and serum production. Additionally, the remainder of the fresh blood which was approximately 7.5 ml was placed on a 50% cotton/50% polyester cloth and wrapped around my arm for the purpose of observing the drying time of blood under these conditions.

At the conclusion of the first diffusion experiment, the procedure was repeated using the remaining serum in the petri dishes and cloth strips of 100% cotton and 50% cotton/50% polyester with a vertical weave orientation.

The two diffusion experiments were observed and photographed at timed intervals and the clot retraction and drying time controls were observed over timed intervals.

Results

Run #1   (Height in Inches)

Time (in min)	Cotton (100%)		Polyester (100%)		Cotton/Poly (50%/50%)	
0	V	H	V	H	V	H
5	1.0	.50	.25	.25	1.25	1.25
10	1.0	.75	.50	.50	1.50	1.50
15	1.0	1.0	.50	.50	1.50	1.50
20	1.25	1.0	.75	.50	1.75	1.75
25	1.25	1.0	1.0	.75	1.75	2.0
30	1.25	1.0	1.0	.75	1.75	2.0
40	1.50	1.25	1.25	1.0	2.25	2.25
50	1.50	1.25	1.25	1.25	2.50	2.25
60	1.50	1.25	1.75	1.50	2.75	2.50
90	1.50	1.25	2.25	1.75	2.75	2.50
120	1.50	1.25	2.25	1.75	2.75	2.50
150	1.75	1.50	2.25	1.75	2.75	2.50

Note: Cloth strips were removed and allowed to dry. Drying complete at 300 minutes (5 hours).

Run #2   (Height in Inches)

Time (in min)	Cotton (100%)		Cotton/Poly (50%/50%)	
0	V	H	V	H
5	1.25	1.50	2.0	1.75
10	1.50	1.75	2.50	2.25
15	1.75	2.0	2.75	2.50
20	2.0	2.0	3.25	3.0
25	2.0	2.0	3.50	3.25
30	2.0	2.0	3.50	3.25
60	2.0	2.0	3.50	3.25
120	2.0	2.0	3.50	3.25

Note: Cloth strips removed and allowed to dry. Drying complete at 260 minutes (4 hours, 20 minutes).

Discussion

The dynamics of blood and serum diffusion and migration on cloth is a chromatographic function of the ability of the liquid components of the blood (mobile phase) to travel by capillary action on a porous surface (stationary phase). It is apparent that the chromatographic separation of blood components on cotton or polyester cloth is not a rapid nor efficient chromatographic procedure. The most rapid capillary diffusion is seen to occur during the initial 5 minutes of exposure due to the wetting action of the blood with a slow but measurable rise thereafter. The distance traveled by the mobile phase is also a function of the equilibrium in the system. Within a closed chromatographic system, the ultimate height of diffusion is considerably higher.

In this experiment, the initial appearance of serum was seen at approximately 60 minutes with significant clot retraction at approximately 90 minutes. The presence of serum promotes the height of diffusion and was seen to maintain the wetness of the clot in the chromatographic system. The appearance of the red upper band at the top of the diffusion becomes distinctive on the 100% cotton cloth between 60 and 90 minutes and on the 50% cotton/50% polyester cloth between 50 and 60 minutes. In each case the red band became very distinct on the cloth strips between 120 and 150 minutes from time of immersion. This observation may also be due to the presence of serum.

At the end of 150 minutes, there was no perceptible drying on any of the cloths. This is likely due to the continuous supply of serum within the fibers of the cloth which would delay the drying time of the blood and serum on the cloth counteracting air drying. When the cloth strips were removed from the blood serum at the end of 150 minutes an additional 150 minutes were required for the cloth strips to become dry. At this time, the red bands were considerably darker and very distinct due to the drying effect (Figures 4.6 and 4.7).

The second experiment utilizing already produced bloody serum showed an increase in the height of migration in the 100% cotton cloth and the 50% cotton/50% polyester cloth as compared to the experiment done with freshly drawn blood. The red band at the top of the 100% cotton cloth initially appeared between 15 and 20 minutes and on the 50% cotton/50% polyester cloth between 25 and 30 minutes. This is considered to be the result of the immediate availability of serum. Between 60 and 120 minutes the red band at the top of each clot became very distinct. After removal from the bloody serum, each cloth required approximately 140 minutes for drying.

The cloth control soaked with 7.5 ml of fresh blood which was wrapped around my arm was dry in approximately 110 minutes. Clot retraction occurred with the 2.5 ml of blood in approximately 65 minutes and 80 minutes for the 5.0 ml quantity.

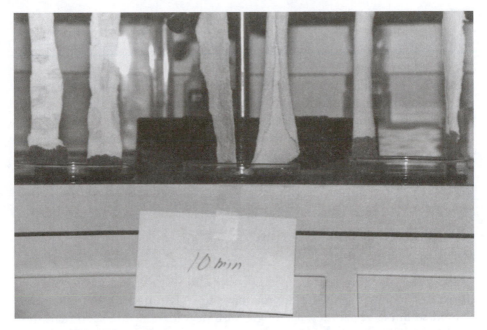

Figure 4.6 Appearance of diffusion of blood at 10 minutes.

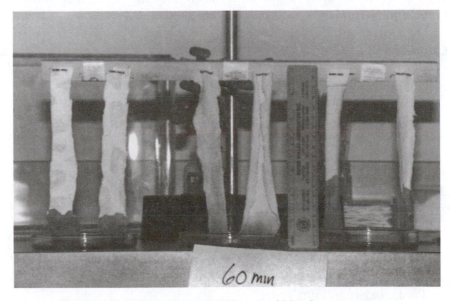

Figure 4.7 Appearance of diffusion of blood at 60 minutes.

The Aging of Bloodstains

As bloodstains increase in age, they progress through a series of color changes from red to reddish brown to green and eventually to dark brown and black. This change of color is attributable to alterations in the hemoglobin of the blood. A particular environment and especially the presence of bacteria and other microorganisms will affect the sequence and duration of color changes in bloodstains. Therefore, estimations of the age of bloodstains based upon their color at the scene should be very conservative. An example of an experiment is illustrated as follows.

Blood Degradation Experiment

Purpose

In order to investigate the approximate time required for fresh human blood/serum to reach the stage of greenish degradation, an experiment was devised for this estimation.

Sections of the clean area of the floral patterned fitted sheet and the underlying white sheet were obtained as well as a comparison section of a greenish area on the floral patterned sheet. Fresh blood was drawn and applied to sections of clean sheet areas taken from the originals and allowed to dry and age under four different parameters.

Conditions

Outdoor temperature at scene 68°F at 2:00 PM
Temperature 87 to 71°F
Humidity 92 to 84%
Indoor temperature 78°F
Heating pad temperature 98.7°F

Apparatus

Vented plastic bags (1 gallon size)
Sections of floral printed fitted sheet
Sections of white fitted sheet
Heating pad
Plastic bag containing water
Fresh human blood, approximately 60 ml

Procedure

- Test 1
  20 ml of fresh human blood was applied to layered sheet sections and placed into a plastic bag. A plastic bag of water and heating pad was placed over bag containing sheet sections and blood.
- Test 2
  20 ml of fresh human blood was applied to layered sheet sections and placed into a plastic bag and exposed to room temperature.
- Test 3
  10 ml of fresh human blood was applied to layered sheet sections and exposed to room temperature.
- Test 4
  10 ml of fresh human blood was applied to layered sheet sections and placed into a plastic bag and exposed to outdoor temperature.

Results

Time	Test 1	Test 2	Test 3	Test 4
12:40 PM	Begin	Begin	Begin	Begin
2:20 PM	Wet, red	Wet, red	Edges dry, red	Wet, red
3:05 PM	Wet, red	Wet, red	Dry, red	Wet, red
4:35 PM	Wet, red	Wet, red	Dry, red	Wet, red
6:10 PM	Wet, red	Wet, red	Dry, red	Wet, red
7:40 PM	Wet, red	Wet, red	Dry, red	Wet, red
9:05 PM	Wet, red	Wet, red	Dry, red	Wet, red
10:55 PM	Wet, red	Wet, red	Dry, red	Wet, red
12:45 AM	Wet, red	Edges dry, red	Dry, red	Wet, red
7:15 AM	Edges dry, red brown	Almost dry, red	Dry, red	Wet, red
9:10 AM	Edges dry, red brown, decomp. odor	Dry, red	Dry, red	Wet, red
10:00 AM	More dry, red brown, decomp. odor	Dry, red	Dry, red	Wet, red
11:20 AM	More dry, red brown, decomp. odor	Dry, red decomp. odor	Dry, red	Edges dry, red
1:05 PM	More dry, slt. green edges, decomp. odor	Dry, red	Dry, red	Edges dry, red, decomp. odor
3:40 PM	More dry, greener edges, decomp. odor	Dry, red	Dry, red	Edges dry, red, decomp. odor
5:45 PM	Dry, greener, decomp odor	Dry, red	Dry, red	More dry, red, decomp. odor

Conclusions

The significant test was Test 1 which showed observable greenish changes of the blood/serum at approximately 24 hours which became more pronounced at 28 hours under the described conditions. This would be a minimum time for comparison to the bloodstains at the scene. It is not known how long the greenish stains on the sheets and mattress were dry before the officers arrived at the scene. It should be noted that the color of dried bloodstains that have soaked into fabric does not appreciably change after they have dried. Therefore, the bloodstains could have been deposited on the sheet and mattress considerably earlier than 24 to 28 hours prior to the body being discovered.

This information can be utilized with the age of the fly eggs on the face of the victim and the quantity and type of food in his stomach (breakfast, lunch, or dinner) to assist with further estimation of the time of death in a case.

Other Alterations of Bloodstains

The deposition of bloodstains at crime scenes occurs under many environmental and physical conditions that may alter their appearance either initially or thereafter.

Diluted bloodstains may be present at scenes where excessive moisture is present such as external environments involving rain or snow and the characteristics of the original stains may be altered to the point where interpretation is difficult or impossible. Diluted bloodstains may be encountered at crime scenes due to mixture with water or other fluids. A feature of a diluted bloodstain is a prominent outer rim with a lighter center area (Figure 4.8). In extremely cold environments, bloodstain patterns deposited on snow or ice are frequently recognizable and should be preserved photographically as soon as possible. Homicides have occurred in walk-in freezers and resultant bloodstains have not presented problems with interpretation. In those types of cases the bloodstains may freeze to the surface even before they would have dried and their characteristics may be less likely altered.

Another form of diluted bloodstains occurs occasionally with massive head trauma involving the combination of blood and spinal fluid. In a recent suicide, a young man sat on a bed and discharged a shotgun into his forehead. Brain tissue and blood were projected and spattered throughout the small room. On the ceiling tiles above and forward of the victim were seen numerous areas of blood tinged and clear high-velocity spatters of spinal fluid which were easily interpreted (Figure 4.9).

The alteration of bloodstains as the result of the effects of heat, fire, and smoke is another consideration for interpretation. In some cases bloodstains may be covered by soot and be missed entirely at the scene of a homicide that preceded a fire. In many cases where soot is deposited over bloodstains on a surface such as a wall, the bloodstains may appear darker than the

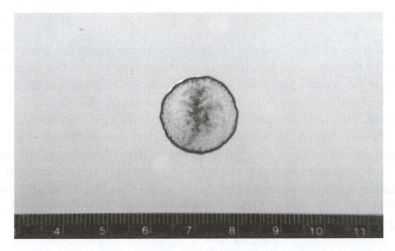

Figure 4.8 Appearance of dried bloodstain produced by a drop of blood, diluted 50/50 with water, falling onto a smooth cardboard. Note the darker outer rim.

surrounding soot covered surface and lend themselves to interpretation. MacDonell, in his 1997 publication entitled *Bloodstain Patterns*, demonstrated that the outer layer of soot is easily removed with lifting tape. The distinction of soot over bloodstains or conversely bloodstains over soot is helpful to determine the sequence of events. This is demonstrated in a case

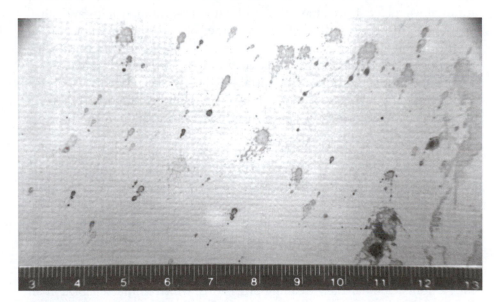

Figure 4.9 Appearance of high-velocity spinal fluid both clear and tinged with blood on ceiling of room.

described later in the book involving gunshot soot over bloodstains on a couch surface.

The study of the effects of heat and fire on bloodstains has been studied by David Redsicker and published in *Interpretation of Bloodstains at Crime Scenes* by Eckert and James in 1989. More recently, Redsicker addresses this subject in conjunction with Sgt. Craig Tomash of the Royal Canadian Mounted Police in Halifax, Nova Scotia in the text *Fire Investigation* published in 1996. As would be expected, bloodstains undergo a variety of physical changes depending upon their proximity to sources of heat, fire, and smoke. Bloodstains may darken, fade (ghosting effect) or be totally destroyed depending upon the intensity and duration of a fire (Figure 4.10 A and B, and Figure 4.11 A and B). It is also important to recognize alterations to bloodstains at fire scenes that may occur due to effects of water and the activities of fire fighting personnel.

Attempts to eliminate bloodstain evidence at a scene and/or the washing of bloodstained clothing is often encountered during the course of an investigation. Attempts have been made to clean or obliterate bloodstains from surfaces at the scene and clothing by various methods which result in alteration, partial or complete removal of the stained areas. These procedures include the use of detergent and water, bleach, pool acid (HCl), paint, fire, and even gouging. As experience has shown, the cleaning procedures utilized often do not completely eliminate the presence of bloodstains. The use of luminol will detect trace quantities of blood. Cast-off bloodstains and small spatters on furniture, walls, ceilings and other objects often are not noticed by the person attempting to clean up the scene. There is usually compelling evidence of the use of bleach and caustic agents. In a particular case, an assailant attempted to remove bloodstains from a brown carpet with bleach which was very obvious. The same individual attempted to gouge out small impact blood spatters from a painted sheetrock wall but abandoned this effort due to the large number of blood spatters.

Blood has been successfully removed from clothing by washing but this depends upon the quantity and age of the bloodstains and the type of fabric involved as well as the washing procedure utilized. Fresh bloodstains are more easily removed by washing in cold water. However, experiments have shown that cold water wash and rinse with detergent do not completely remove drips and transfers of blood on denim material when the bloodstains have been allowed to dry for 72 hours. However, small spatters of blood on denim were in fact more effectively removed by this washing procedure after drying for 72 hours. Standard dry cleaning procedures which immerse fabric in an organic solvent are not effective for the removal of bloodstains. William Best, a forensic scientist from North Carolina demonstrated this in a case where a serologist testified that dry cleaning likely removed blood from a jacket that

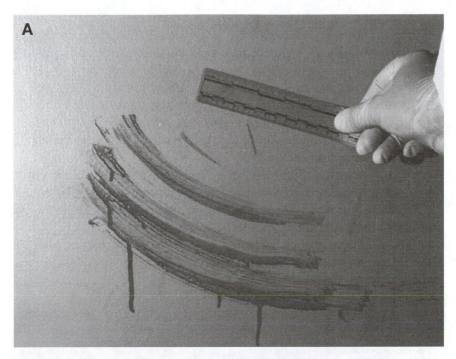

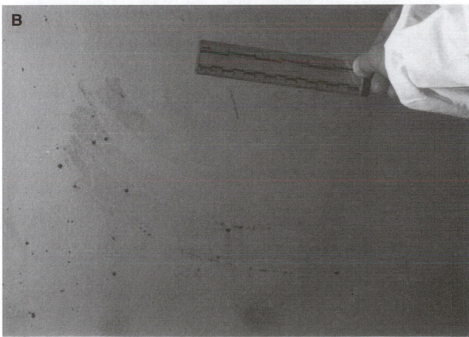

Figure 4.10 **(A)** Swiping transfer of blood on wall prior to fire. **(B)** Post-fire appearance of same area of swiping transfer of blood on wall close to fire.

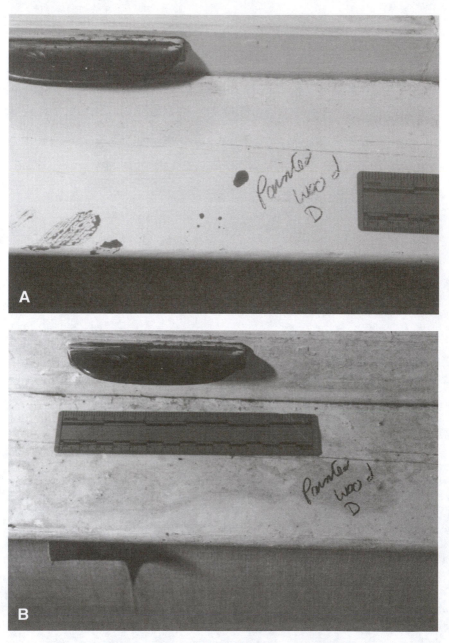

Figure 4.11 (A) Transfer and circular low-velocity bloodstains on window sill prior to fire. (B) Post-fire appearance of same area of transfer and circular low-velocity bloodstains on window sill close to fire.

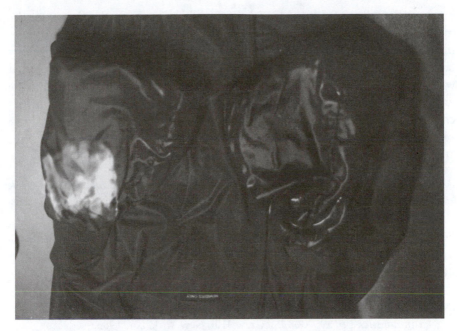

Figure 4.12 Blood on jacket visualized with luminol after jacket was subjected to dry cleaning.

was negative upon examination. Best applied his blood to a similar jacket and detected the blood on the jacket with luminol after the dry cleaning was completed (Figures 4.12).

The issue of diluted bloodstains in the form of small spatters on the sleeves of a husband's jacket accused of fatally beating and stabbing his three children and stabbing his wife to death became important evidence for the defense during his trial. The presence of blood spatters on the sleeves of the jacket were not apparent until a prosecution expert sprayed the jacket with luminol to identify the spatters of blood. The expert testified that the presence of these spatters was consistent with the defendant administering blows or stab wounds to the members of his family. The husband claimed that he had returned to his residence and found the bodies of his wife and children. He admitted carrying one of his children who was barely alive from a bathroom to the living room floor before calling for help. After police and medical personnel arrived the husband who had visible blood on his hands began washing his hands under the faucet at the kitchen sink. A police officer testified that he observed this and directed the husband to stop washing his hands. The scene photographs clearly showed diluted blood in the sink and some blood transfer on a roll of paper towels near the sink. The force of the tap water on the bloodstained hands of the husband certainly could have produced spatters of diluted blood that would deposit on the sleeves of the husband and not be apparent to the naked eye on the jacket. This was presented to the jury in addition to other bloodstain and forensic pathology testimony which resulted in the acquittal of the husband on all charges. It was the position of the defense and convincing evidence to show that the wife had beaten and stabbed her children and then stabbed herself in the chest resulting in a triple homicide and suicide.

References for Chapters 1 to 4

Balthazard, V., Piedelievre, R., DeSoille, H., and DeRobert, L., *Etude des Gouttes de Sang Projecte.* Presented at the 22nd Congress of Forensic Medicine, Paris, France. 1939.

Bevel, Tom. 1983 Geometric Bloodstain Interpretation. *FBI Law Enforcement Bulletin.* Office of Congressional and Public Affairs, Vol. 52, No. 5, pp. 7–10, May, 1983.

Bevel, Tom and Gardner, Ross, M., *Bloodstain Pattern Analysis—With An Introduction to Crime Scene Reconstruction.*, CRC Press, Boca Raton, FL, 1997.

DeForest, P.R., Gaensslen, R.E., and Lee, H.C., *Forensic Science—An Introduction to Criminalistics*, pp. 295–308, McGraw-Hill, New York, NY, 1983.

Eckert, W. G. and James S.H., *Interpretation of Bloodstain Evidence at Crime Scenes*, CRC Press, Boca Raton, FL, 1989.

Hurley, M. and Pex, J., *Sequencing of Bloody Shoe Impressions by Blood Spatter and Blood Droplet Drying Times*, I.A.B.P.A. News, Dec., 1990.

James, S.H. and Edel, C.F., *Bloodstain Pattern Interpretation, Introduction to Forensic Sciences*, W.E. Eckert, Ed., CRC Press, Boca Raton, FL, 1997.

Kirk, P.L., *Blood—A Neglected Criminalistics Research Area, Law Enforcement Science and Technology.* Vol. 1, pp. 267–272, Academic Press, London, 1967.

Kirk, P.L., *Crime Investigation*, 2nd Edition, pp. 167–181, John Wiley & Sons, New York, NY, 1974.

Kish, P.E. and MacDonell, H.L., *Absence of Evidence is Not Evidence of Absence, Journal of Forensic Identification*, 46, No. 2, pp. 160–164, March/April, 1996.

Laber, T.L., Diameter of a Bloodstain as a Function of Origin, Distance Fallen and Volume of Drop., *I.A.B.P.A. News*, Vol. 2, No.1, pp. 12–16, 1985.

Laber, T.L. and Epstein, B.P., *Bloodstain Pattern Analysis*, Callen Publishing Company, Minneapolis, MN, 1983.

Lee, H.C., Gaensslen, R.E., and Pagliaro, E.M., *Bloodstain Volume Estimation*, I.A.B.P.A. News, Vol.3, No. 2, pp. 47–54, 1986.

LeRoy, H.A., *Bloodstain Pattern Interpretation*, Identification Newsletter of the Canadian Identification Society, January, 1983.

MacDonell, H.L., Interpretation of Bloodstains—Physical Considerations, *Legal Medicine Annual*, Cyril Wecht, Ed., pp. 91–136, Appleton-Century-Crofts, New York, NY, 1971.

MacDonell, H.L., *Preserving Bloodstain Evidence at Crime Scenes, Law and Order,* Vol.25, pp. 66–69, April, 1977.

MacDonell, H.L., *Reconstruction of a Homicide, Law and Order,* pp. 26–31, July, 1977.

MacDonell, H.L., *Criminalistics, Bloodstain Examination, Forensic Sciences,* Vol.3, Cyril Wecht, Ed. 37.1–37.26, Matthew Bender, New York, NY, 1981.

MacDonell, H.L., *Bloodstain Pattern Interpretation,* Laboratory of Forensic Science, Corning, NY, 1982.

MacDonell, H.L., *Bloodstain Patterns,* Laboratory of Forensic Science, Corning, NY, 1993.

MacDonell, H.L., *Bloodstain Patterns—Revised,* Laboratory of Forensic Science, Corning, NY, 1997.

MacDonell, H.L. and Bialousz, L., *Flight Characteristics and Stain Patterns of Human Blood,* United States Department of Justice, Law Enforcement Assistance Administration, Washington, DC, 1971.

MacDonell, H.L. and Bialousz, L., *Laboratory Manual on the Geometric Interpretation of Human Bloodstain Evidence,* Laboratory of Forensic Science, Corning, NY, 1973.

MacDonell, H.L. and Brooks, B., *Detection and Significance of Blood in Firearms, Legal Medicine Annual,* Cyril Wecht, Ed. pp. 185–199, Appleton-Century-Crofts, New York, NY, 1977.

MacDonell, H.L. and Panchou, C., *Bloodstain Pattern Interpretation, Identification News,* Vol. 29, pp. 3–5, Feb., 1979.

MacDonell, H.L. and Panchou, C., *Bloodstain Patterns on Human Skin, Journal of the Canadian Society of Forensic Science,* Vol. 12, No. 3, pp. 134–141, Sept., 1979.

Pex, J.O. and Vaughn, C.H., *Observations of High Velocity Blood Spatter on Adjacent Objects, Journal of Forensic Sciences,* Vol. 32, No. 6, pp. 1587–1594, Nov., 1987.

Piotrowski, E., *Uber Entstehung, Form, Richtung und Ausbreitung der Blutspuren nach Heibwunden des Kopfes,* K.K. Universitat, Wein, 1895.

Pizzola, P.A., Roth, S., and DeForest, P.R., *Blood Droplet Dynamics-I, Journal of Forensic Sciences,* Vol. 31, No. 1, pp. 36–49, Jan., 1986.

Pizzola, P.A., Roth, S., and DeForest, P.R., *Blood Droplet Dynamics-II, Journal of Forensic Sciences,* Vol. 31, No. 1, pp. 50–64, Jan., 1986.

Stephens, B.G. and Allen, T.B., *Back Spatter of Blood from Gunshot Wounds - Observations and Experimental Simulation, Journal of Forensic Sciences,* Vol. 28, No. 2, pp. 437–439, April, 1983.

Sutton, T.P., *Bloodstain Pattern Analysis in Violent Crimes.,* Department of Pathology, Division of Forensic Pathology, University of Tennessee, Memphis, 1993.

White, R.B., *Bloodstain Patterns of Fabrics—The Effect of Drop Volume, Dropping Height and Impact Angle, Journal of the Canadian Society of Forensic Science,* Vol. 19, No. 1, pp. 3–36, 1986.

Medical and Medicolegal Aspects of Bloodshed at Crime Scenes

5

WILLIAM G. ECKERT, M.D.

Many factors affect the amount or volume of bleeding that will occur after an injury. Among the important considerations are the age, muscularity and general health of the individual as well as the anatomic location and condition of the major vessels in the injured area of the body.

Age and Muscularity

A muscular individual may be able to absorb impact from a blunt instrument resulting in no more than a hematoma of the soft tissues. Muscle mass may interfere with the penetration of a knife or other sharp object. Projectiles may be slowed in their penetration into muscle mass depending upon their caliber and velocity. In these instances the amount of internal and external bleeding may be minimized. In contrast, those individuals with less muscle mass including children and the elderly may sustain more severe injury and increased bleeding in a given situation. The elderly victim may also have a thin bone structure which provides limited support to prevent serious injury.

General Health

The presence of natural diseases such as cirrhosis of the liver, hemophilia, malignancies and vitamin deficiencies may delay coagulation of blood and permit severe internal and external hemorrhaging in cases where only minor trauma is involved. The continued use of medications such as aspirin as well as prescribed anticoagulants for the treatment of heart and circulatory diseases also encourage excessive bleeding of individuals due to the extended clotting time of the blood. The rapidity of death of a victim also affects the quantity of internal and external bleeding such as with acute myocardial infarction or ruptured aneurysm. In these instances there may be a relatively short period of bleeding.

Figure 5.1 Patterned abrasion on back of a victim consistent with having been produced by an impact with a 2 × 4 wooden board. A stab wound is located to the right of the patterned abrasion.

Types of Wounds Associated with Blunt Force Injuries

An abrasion is the forcible removal of the outer layers of skin due to friction created by contact with a rough surface. Bleeding is usually minimal and confined to areas of capillary damage in the dermal layer of the skin. A patterned abrasion may be associated with the object that produced it (Figure 5.1). A bruise or contusion is characterized by hemorrhage of blood into skin tissue or organ due to rupture of blood vessels without an accompanying tear or defect of the surface of the skin or outer layer of the organ. Patterned contusions may also be associated with the object that produced them (Figure 5.2). A laceration is a tear of the skin or underlying tissues or organs due to either a shearing or crushing force due to blunt trauma. Skin lacerations are often irregular with abraded contused margins and occur most commonly over bony areas such as the head (Figure 5.3). Threads of nerve, elastic, and connective tissue fibers and blood vessels referred to as tissue bridges are usually present connecting the opposite sides of the laceration (Figure 5.4).

A fracture is essentially a laceration of a bone. Blunt force injuries that produce bruising and lacerations often produce fractures of underlying bony structures which can further damage underlying tissue and increase the internal and external hemorrhaging at the wound site.

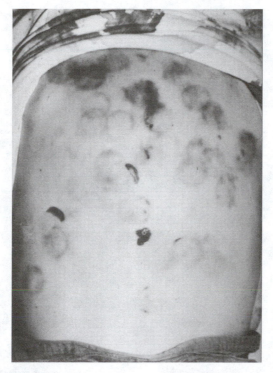

Figure 5.2 Multiple circular-shaped contusions on the back of a victim consistent with having been produced by impacts with the rounded surface of a hammer which fractured the spine and ribs. The victim died as the result of blunt force trauma to the head.

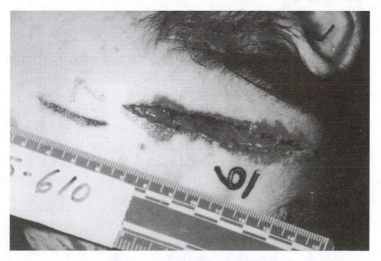

Figure 5.3 Linear lacerations on right side of head of victim exhibiting tissue bridging produced by impact with a blunt object.

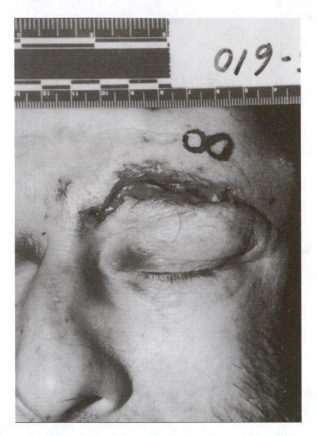

Figure 5.4 Linear laceration, above left eye of victim, exhibiting tissue bridging produced by impact with a blunt object.

Types of Wounds Associated with Sharp Force Injuries

An incised wound is produced by sharp-edged weapons such as knives, razors, and shards of glass. Characteristically, the length of the wound is greater than its depth. Bleeding can be rapid and severe especially in the case of incised arteries. A stab wound is produced by a pointed instrument and characteristically the depth of the wound exceeds the length (Figure 5.5). The typical weapon is a knife but other weapons such as scissors, ice picks and screw drivers are not uncommon. In knife attacks it is common to see a combination of incised and stab wounds inflicted upon a victim. Defense wounds may be present on the arms and hands of a victim as well as offensive wounds sustained by the attacker received when the fingers and palm come in contact with the blade (Figures 5.6 and 5.7).

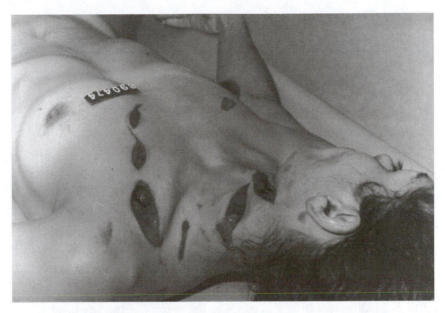

Figure 5.5 Incised and stab wounds in chest and right elbow area of victim.

Figure 5.6 Defensive incised wound on right palm of victim.

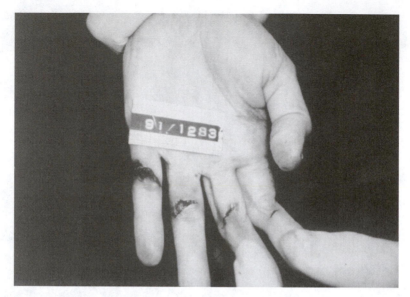

Figure 5.7 Offensive incised wounds of the fingers of the left hand produced by the assailant's fingers sliding over the blade of the knife during the attack.

Types of Wounds Associated with Gunshot

A penetrating gunshot wound is characterized by an entrance site but no exit wound. Correspondingly, a perforating gunshot wound is characterized by both an entrance and an exit wound. Exit wounds may be larger than entrance wounds due to projectile deformation and bony fragment production as the projectile passes through the body. This often results in the production of a greater amount of forward spatter than back spatter as well a greater amount of bleeding. Gunshot entrance wounds are further classified based upon their appearance at increasing ranges of discharge. Tight or hard contact gunshot wounds in areas of a thin layer of skin and tissue overlying bone often produce stellate lacerations radiating from the central defect. These stellate-shaped entrance wounds may be larger than the accompanying exit wound (Figure 5.8 A and B). The muzzle blast of a weapon fired in contact with a body may cause blowback of blood, tissue and fabric several inches down the barrel. The skull may fracture extensively with evisceration of the brain tissue. Massive destruction of the head often occurs when the muzzle of the firearm is within the mouth at time of discharge (Figure 5.9). A loose or near contact gunshot wound of entrance usually does not produce splitting of the wound edges.

Depending upon the caliber of the weapon, the blow back and back spatter is considerably lessened in quantity and may be absent in cases of intermediate and distant range gunshot wounds of entrance.

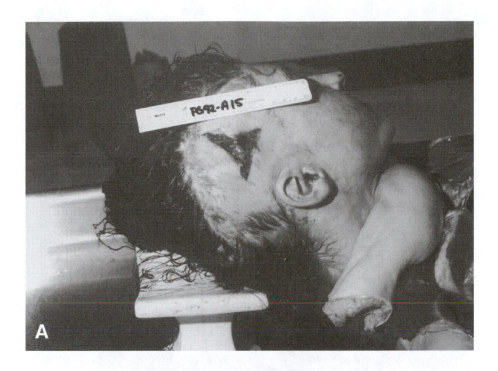

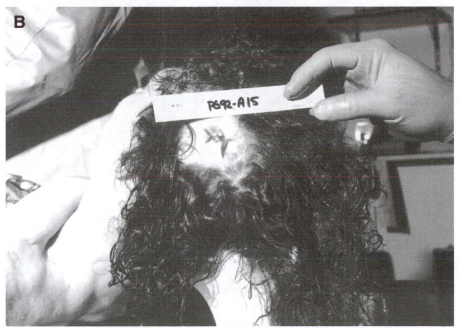

Figure 5.8 (A) Stellate-shaped contact gunshot wound of the right side of the head; (B) irregularly-shaped exit wound on left side of head of same victim.

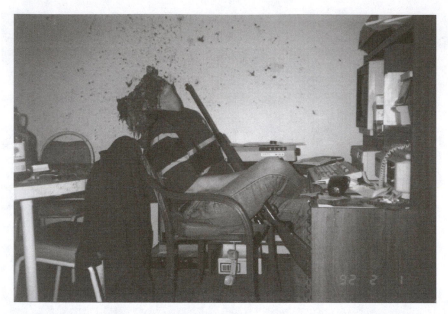

Figure 5.9 Self-inflicted gunshot wound with massive destruction of head and brain evisceration resulting from barrel of rifle in mouth at time of discharge as victim sat at computer.

Wound Location and Major Vessel Disruption

The relationship between the location, characteristics and severity of a wound and the body structure, organs and major vessels involved is critical in the assessment of internal and external bleeding of a victim. Amputation or destruction of the head, abdominal cavity or extremities will by their very nature produce massive blood loss while a lethal puncture or stab wound may produce minimal bleeding (Figure 5.10). The number of injuries and the increased number of anatomic areas involved increase the number of bleeding sites. Thus multiple gunshot wounds, lacerations, or stabbing and incised wounds to any area of the body often produce massive bleeding.

The susceptibility of the organ or vessel in the body to injury is an important consideration. The brain is in a protected cavity surrounded by the skull and unless direct blunt force or penetrating trauma occurs, it is perhaps the best protected organ in the body. The head offers variable amounts of bleeding depending upon the area, extent and type of injury sustained by a victim. Scalp lacerations may produce severe bleeding especially when the temporal arteries are involved. Intoxicated individuals frequently fall and suffer head injuries of this type that, when unattended may result in a fatal consequence. In a case in New Orleans, an intoxicated person was arrested and placed in a jail cell overnight. At some point during the night, the inmate fell and struck his head on the bed frame in his cell. He developed severe shock and died with his head hanging over the edge of the bed while bleeding. It was estimated that he lost approximately 1500 ml of blood which had accumulated on the floor of his cell. It is common to encounter skull fractures, evisceration of the brain and massive bleeding in numerous cases of fatal gunshot and blunt trauma. However, there are many documented cases of survival after sustaining severe head injuries. A victim survived an attack with a roofing ax where the skull was able to resist deep penetration. In another case, an individual sustained a severe shotgun wound of the face and survived the ordeal despite being without medical attention for 48 hours. The victim lost a large quantity of blood in his residence during this period of time. He was finally found by a friend who discovered him in a semi-comatose state on his bed. There was evidence that the victim had removed his bloody clothing, taken a shower, shaved and used the toilet during this period of time. The blast from the shotgun traveled upwards and severely damaged the right side of his face including the orbit of the eye (Figure 5.11). Some pellets remained in the brain but the victim has recovered and is living a normal life.

Figure 5.10 Massive destruction of the head and blood loss due to self-inflicted shotgun wound.

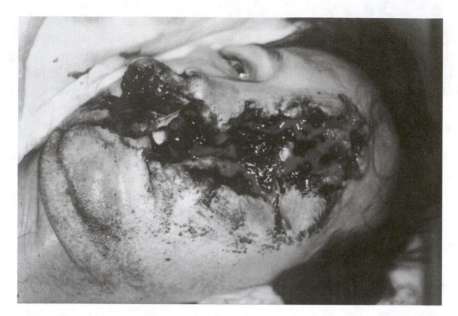

Figure 5.11 Non-fatal shotgun wound to the left side of the face of victim.

Penetrating gunshot wounds of the head may produce minimal bleeding from the entrance site. This may indicate a relatively rapid death or minimal intracranial pressure associated with the injury. Blunt force trauma that produces basal skull fractures may only show evidence of bleeding from the nose or the ear in the absence of external lacerations.

The nose and mouth are prominent structures that are frequently injured due to their location and may produce considerable bleeding due to their vascularity. Significant bleeding is usually associated with fractures to the nose and sinuses, as well as certain medical conditions such as nasal polyps, blood disorders, or hypertension. Oral hemorrhages result from fractures of the jaw, lacerations of the mouth and tongue, as well as esophageal varicies or hemoptysis. The mouth and nose are also associated with active bleeding to the respiratory tract including the lungs and trachea as the result of trauma, infections, tumors, or chemical inhalation. Death due to asphyxiation may also cause bleeding from the nose and mouth. A couple were found deceased and bound in a bomb shelter in the basement of their home (Figure 5.12). Death was attributed to ligature strangulation. The husband had bled considerably from the nose and mouth with no directly associated trauma to those areas. The bleeding was considered due to the effect of prescribed anticoagulants taken by the husband for a heart condition in conjunction with ruptured capillaries in the airway passages (Figure 5.13).

Figure 5.12 Victims found bound and strangled in basement bomb shelter of their home.

Figure 5.13 Dripping and transfer of blood on floor from nose and mouth of male victim.

Injuries to the neck produced by penetration of a projectile or by slashing or stabbing with a sharp instrument may produce severe bleeding due to the severance of the jugular vein or the carotid arteries. These major vessels of the neck are located near the surface and have a fixed structure beneath them and are perhaps the most vulnerable vessels in the body. The resulting hemorrhage is massive and disabling. Bleeding from the carotid arteries is rapid as it exits under pressure. The resulting bloodstain patterns are distinctive in their appearance. Death may ensue quickly due to acute blood loss and reduced oxygen supply to the brain. A young woman survived a brutal attack in which she sustained in excess of 35 stab wounds. Many of these stab wounds were inflicted to the head but did not penetrate the skull. A large kitchen knife was left embedded into her neck which was later removed in the emergency room (Figure 5.14 A and B). Despite extensive blood loss, the victim survived the attack and made a complete recovery.

The organs of the chest including the heart, lungs, and aorta are located within the rib cage and are thus protected from all but severe injury to the chest. The amount of bleeding may be minimal to none when the injuries are not severe. Chest wounds of a blunt nature will cause hemothorax formation but often no external bleeding unless there is hemoptysis from an injured lung or crushed chest. Penetrating injuries to the chest related to gunshot or stab wounds often produce more internal bleeding than external bleeding unless there is a perforation of the heart or aorta or a large, gaping wound of the chest wall. In these situations there may be an unimpaired flow of blood from the external wound site. The blood volume that may accumulate in the pericardial cavity after heart penetration may reach a volume of 100 to 200 ml. The effect of this blood accumulation in the pericardial sac acts as a hydraulic impediment to the movement of the heart. If there is injury to the coronary artery, there may be further reason for cardiac standstill and death. The amount of bleeding into the chest cavities after lung injury or aortic transection may be in a range of 1000 to 1500 ml. On one occasion where a robbery victim was stabbed in the anterior chest wall, he collapsed and regained consciousness only to be stabbed again in the back. At autopsy the knife outline produced by the stabbing in the back was clearly visible through the massive blood clot in the chest cavity produced by the initial injury.

In the abdominal cavity there is protection of the organs in the upper area where the lower rib cage is still a very significant protective factor. In the pelvic area the bones of the pelvis serve to protect the lower abdominal cavity organs including the bladder, rectosigmoid region, and large vessels below the abdominal aorta bifurcation. Injuries to the abdomen from blunt or penetrating trauma may show bleeding that may occur over a period of

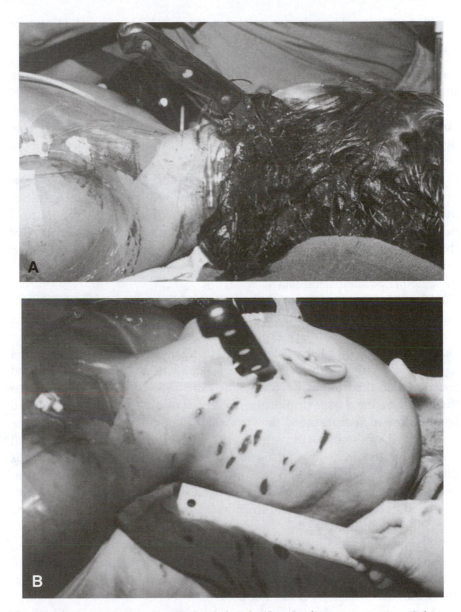

Figure 5.14 (A) Knife embedded in left side of neck of surviving victim; (B) view of multiple stab wounds of the head of same victim.

time greater than that seen in chest injuries. A large entrance wound produced by shotgun discharge in the abdominal cavity will produce great damage to the abdominal wall as well as to the internal organs in that region. The liver is a frequent target for injury because of its size and location and may bleed over an extended period of time unless there are numerous sites of tear or rupture. The spleen is an extremely vascular organ and its rupture is associated with rapid bleeding, shock, and ultimate death in the absence of medical intervention. Trauma to the kidneys may produce very serious bleeding depending upon the extent of the injury. Aortic injury or rupture produced severe bleeding in the chest and abdominal cavity that may rapidly produce shock and ultimate death unless rapid surgical intervention is available. Bleeding from mesenteric artery tears or injuries may be relatively slow depending upon the site of the injury. In a recent case involving a tear of the superior mesenteric artery of a child, a total of 750 ml of blood was observed in the abdominal cavity. The death occurred hours after injury, which was more of a squeezing injury than a blow. Damage to mesenteric vessels may impede circulation to portions of the intestine and result in delayed intestinal necrosis and perforation in surviving victims. The separation or fracture of the pelvis may produce a slowly forming retroperitoneal hematoma which may produce shock a day or more after injury. This is common in victims of vehicular accidents and falls.

Bleeding from urethral, anal, or vaginal orifices may be associated with natural disease including tumor formation, and polyps that may cause spontaneous as well as voluntary expulsion of blood. Significant bleeding may also occur during the menstrual period. During the investigation of a suicidal hanging of a female who utilized a bed sheet, a large accumulation of blood was noted on the front of her blue jeans which had continued to drip onto the floor creating a large drip pattern and pool of blood. This was produced by a profuse menstrual blood flow from the victim.

There may also be an unnatural cause for bleeding from anal or vaginal orifices due to mechanical intrusion by foreign bodies or objects such as dildos, broom handles, etc. These intrusions may be associated with an assault upon the victim or may be acts of self abuse by the persons themselves. In the absence of an accurate history, these injuries may not be able to be identified as self-inflicted.

The femoral arteries and veins are also located in a vulnerable position, but they do not have a fixed body behind them so that their injury potential is much less than that of the neck vessels. However, the vessels of the elbows and wrists are located in vulnerable areas.

Large amounts of bleeding by a victim due to major injury can be designated as quantities in excess of 200 ml or 6 ounces, and small amounts as less than that quantity. Large amounts of bleeding are associated with such events as decapitation, crushing of the head by blunt force, explosive destruction of the body, amputation of an extremity, shotgun injuries to various areas of the body and slashing or stabbing with numerous varieties of sharp instruments. Denudement of large areas of skin and tissue such as may occur with motor vehicles and other types of machinery may produce massive bleeding. Minimal bleeding may occur in a variety of situations. A short post-injury survival time may reduce bleeding of a victim. The bleeding from a lacerated face, nose, or mouth may be small in volume. In those areas of the body that lack large blood vessels, injury may not produce excessive bleeding. Bleeding from the nose or ear associated with skull fracture may be minimal. There may be some bleeding associated with multiple abrasions from blows or as a result of friction from contact with a surface onto which a victim has been thrown.

The amount of blood flow will vary in different anatomic regions of the body and is an important consideration not only for medicolegal purposes but also for the emergency medical team and emergency room physicians who may treat the victim in a trauma unit.

Significance of Blood Loss Evidence

The combined examination of bloodstains on the victim, assailant, weapon, and scene should be a routine procedure in all cases. For the forensic pathologist there are additional parameters and factors that should be considered in conjunction with blood at the scene which involve the amount or volume of blood that has been shed. There is also a need to relate the quantity of blood with the nature of the bleeding and the anatomic site of bleeding. This may be especially helpful in those cases where the victim has been injured or killed at the scene and removed to another location.

Examination of the blood at the scene may also be used as a source of information as to the survivability of the victim after injury. The careful examination of the blood accumulation may reveal additional tissue such as hair, skin, and brain tissue whose presence would help establish not only the injury site on the victim but also the capabilities of the victim after injury and an approximation of post-injury survival time. The appearance of the blood may also provide information regarding the origin of blood from the body. Lung injuries often result in frothy blood in the mouth associated with respirations of the victim. There may be evidence of the coughing up or vomiting of blood that would be significant. A cut to the sides of the neck may result in the severance of the carotid artery and produce a rapid spurting type of bleeding and rapid disability of the victim with death occurring very shortly after the injury at the location where the attack took place. This would also apply to accidental or suicidal injuries to areas of the body where arteries are accessible.

Abdominal or chest wounds very often have little or no extrusion of blood since blood may accumulate within the body cavities. The clothing may become soaked and impede further extrusion of blood from the body.

Clothing which is tight against the skin of a victim may impede the outward flow of blood from the body. A prone or supine body may have blood leakage owing to gravity depending upon the position of the body. A chest wound on a victim who is on his back may show little evidence of external bleeding but when the body is turned over considerable blood may leak from the chest cavity. If the circulation is impaired by the rapid drop of blood pressure prior to death, external blood loss may be minimal. Cold temperatures may limit the extent of bleeding in a victim because of the body's reaction to preserve internal heat by peripheral vessel contraction.

The determination of the period of time that the blood has been present on a surface may be an issue as well. This may relate to the clotting time of blood as well as the drying time of quantities of blood on a particular surface and may have to be determined by experimental work as discussed in Chapter 4. The character of the blood at the scene must be described as to the degree of drying and clotting. The blood clots will change after a period of time with visible separation of the serum from the clot. It may be possible to relate the appearance of the blood clot and drying of blood to its approximate time of deposition. Although it is variable, one might expect a considerable amount of dried blood at a scene 24 hours after injury. The environment and type of surface upon which the blood is deposited are important considerations with experiments of this type.

Attempts to evaluate cases in which blood loss evidence is a crucial factor have to be based on the fact that the known volume of blood present in a normal person is in the range of 5000 to 6000 ml or 5 to 6 liters (Figure 5.15). When the vascular system of a victim is disrupted so that the blood is able to leak or leave the vessels, the stability of the body will change. Blood may leave the circulatory system externally or accumulate within the cranial, thoracic, pericardial, or peritoneal cavities. When 20 to 25% of the blood volume is lost from the circulation (1000 to 1500 ml), the first symptoms of shock are imminent. This is significant when one also considers this change in conjunction with injuries to a specific organ such as the heart, lungs, or brain whose dysfunction will produce additional changes to impair the victim. The rate of bleeding is also a factor that will vary according to the portion of the vascular system that is injured.

The degree of intoxication involving alcohol and/or drug use may have an indirect effect on the amount of bloodshed. After injury, the activities of intoxicated victims may be related to their reduced sense of inhibition and unusual behavior, and increased physical activity may increase bleeding because of the increased action of the heart. Persons may exhibit aggressive behavior which may include attacks on others producing additional injuries, jumping from heights, or attempting to break away from law enforcement officers there to assist them.

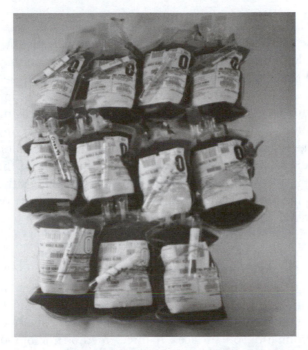

Figure 5.15 The average quantity of blood in the human body represented as units of blood is approximately 5000 to 6000 ml or 5 to 6 liters.

The volume of blood loss becomes important for several reasons including the evaluation of the degree of activity of a victim after he or she has received a lethal injury. Estimations of external blood volume should be made at the scene as well as internally during the postmortem examination by measuring the volume of free blood present in the various body cavities. The rapidity of death after the wound has been sustained is an important factor to evaluate plus the possibility that the assailant's clothing received victim's blood during the struggle or attack.

The various situations where blood evidence becomes important do not always involve criminal cases as in the case of the accidental leakage of blood from a surgical patient when intravenous tubing became disconnected and significant blood loss occurred. The questions were how to measure the blood loss in a quantitative manner and to evaluate the significance of the blood loss in relation to the death of the patient. Unexpected internal bleeding may bring up questions as to cause and what measures of medical treatment would have been effective under the proper conditions. The question of activity after a lethal injury is frequently asked during testimony in trials. The degree of external and internal bleeding must be carefully evaluated in these cases.

Estimation of Blood Volume at the Scene

In those cases where there is a scene with substantial quantities of blood present and the absence of a victim, important information may be derived from careful study of the character of the bloodstains and the quantity of blood that was shed. The location of the victim at the time of injury and the site and nature of injury may often be determined as well as movement of the body after injury to include evidence of dragging or carrying the victim from the scene (Figure 5.16 A and B). An estimation of the volume of blood in a particular location may assist with the determination of the site representing a primary or secondary scene. In the absence of a body the estimation of blood volume present may give an indication of the severity of injury and expected survival time. Various methods have been utilized to estimate the volume of blood present in bloodstains. Herbert MacDonell developed experiments utilizing volumes of blood in 50 ml increments applied to a surface similar to that containing the unknown volume of blood. The resultant areas of the known and unknown bloodstains are measured by the diameter or grid method and compared to estimate the volume of blood in a bloodstain (Figure 5.17). Dr. Henry Lee also developed methods for blood volume determination on surfaces. A direct method for bloodstains on a non-absorbent surface involved a constant derived by determining the relative weight of 1.0 ml of liquid blood compared to the weight of 1.0 m of dry blood. The weight lost during drying was 0.78 grams. The constant for weight loss was 0.78 divided by.24 which equals 4.2. The original bloodstain was scraped or lifted from its surface and weighed. A formula was developed utilizing the constant for the weight loss of a dry bloodstain.

A direct method for blood volume estimation on absorbent surfaces such as carpet involved weighing the bloodstained surface and subtracting the weight of an unstained area of that surface similar in size. The difference in weight was utilized to estimate the volume of blood shed on that surface.

Dr. Lee developed an indirect method for blood volume estimation on large areas which involved the weighing of a measured unit of bloodstained carpet or other surface and comparing this finding to the weight of a measured unit of unstained surface. He further developed an indirect photograph weighing method by determining the relative unit weights of stained and unstained areas of the photograph. He then applied blood to a unit area of unstained material similar to that depicted in the photograph to calculate the volume of the original bloodstain.

Conclusion

The medicolegal considerations of bloodshed and blood loss due to various types of injuries by the forensic pathologist can be an important

Figure 5.16 **(A)** Location of victim of sexual assault/homicide at time of initial injury and bloodshed. **(B)** View of drag pattern in blood leading to final position of victim. Note interruption in drag pattern with pooling of blood in location where victim was positioned for a period of time prior to final position.

Figure 5.17 Measurement of the area of a bloodstain produced by a known quantity of blood on a carpet by a grid method to be compared with bloodstains found at scene on similar carpet.

source of information for the crime scene investigator and bloodstain analyst. It is especially significant when the questions relating to the postinjury survival time, the postmortem interval, the location of severe or lethal injuries in a specific location and helps to address the issue of likelihood of death of an individual when the body has be disposed of in another location. These applications of bloodstain interpretation have significance in both criminal and civil litigations.

References

DiMaio, V.J.M., *Gunshot Wounds*, CRC Press LLC., Boca Raton, FL, 1993.

DiMaio, D.J., DiMaio, V.J.M., *Forensic Pathology*, Elsevier Science Publishing Co., New York, NY, 1989.

Lee, Henry C., Estimation of Original Volume of Bloodstains, *Identification News*, July, 1986.

Lee, Henry C., Pagliaro, E.M., Gaensslen, R.E., *Bloodstain Volume Estimation*, IABPA *Newsletter*, October 1986.

Lee, Henry C., Pagliaro, E.M., Gaensslen, R.E., *Determination of the Volume of a Single Bloodstain*, AAFS Annual Meeting Abstract B-12, 1986.

MacDonell, H.L., *Bloodstain Patterns*, Laboratory of Forensic Sciences, Corning, NY, 1997.

Tedeschi, C.G., Eckert, William G., Tedeschi, L.G., *Forensic Medicine, A Study in Trauma and Environmental Hazards*, W.B. Saunders Co., Philadelphia, PA, 1977.

The Documentation, Collection, and Evaluation of Bloodstain Evidence

6

STUART H. JAMES

General Considerations

Physical evidence is defined as any and all materials or items that may be identified as being associated with a crime scene, which, by scientific evaluation, ultimately establishes the element of the crime and provides a link among the crime scene, the victim, and the assailant. The proper recognition, documentation, collection, preservation and examination of physical evidence are crucial to the successful reconstruction of a crime scene and litigation in a criminal proceeding. Physical evidence may be present at the crime scene whether it be indoors or outside, on a vehicle, on the victim, on the assailant, and/or his environment. There is frequently transfer of blood and trace evidence between victim and assailant.

It is important to recognize that the study and interpretation of bloodstains at a crime scene should be integrated within the systematic approach to the examination of all types of physical evidence and crime scene reconstruction (Table 6.1). The initial bloodstain evaluation at a crime scene should be able to provide the investigator with the general nature of the activities that took place and relative movements of victim and assailant. A complete analysis of bloodstains at a scene where there exist numerous complex stain patterns may require hours or days of work involving measurements, projections of angles of impact, sketches, diagrams and extensive photography. Conversely, a crime scene may provide relatively little information with respect to bloodstains that is not already apparent to the investigator. In any event, the bloodstain evaluation should be coordinated with the overall documentation, collection, preservation, and examination of the other types of physical evidence that may be present at the crime scene. The major time-consuming details of bloodstain interpretation can usually be accomplished after the crime scene has been processed for other types of physical evidence. In most cases the search and collection of trace evidence such as hairs, fibers, and fingerprints can be given priority over evaluation

Table 6.1   Outline for Interpretation of Bloodstain Evidence

Scene

Secure scene and exclude unauthorized persons.
Avoid alteration of bloodstains.
Photograph victim and associated bloodstains prior to moving victim.
Photograph weapon if present and secure it.
Note environmental conditions.
Conduct preliminary evaluation of overall bloodstains and patterns.
Move body cautiously.
Collect trace evidence.
Complete search and recognition of bloodstains and patterns.
Photograph bloodstains including close-up view with measuring device.
Take bloodstain measurements including locations, widths, lengths, angles of impact convergences, and origins.
Make preliminary sketches and diagrams.
Perform preliminary blood testing if desired.
Collect, tag and identify bloodstained items.
Perform string reconstruction if desired.

Assailant

Examine assailant and his environment.
Photograph and document clothing and
  other physical evidence.
Obtain appropriate blood samples.

Autopsy of Victim

Photograph body, clothed and unclothed
  including injuries.
Secure clothing, physical evidence and
  blood samples.
Obtain autopsy report, x-rays, and medical
  data.

Laboratory Reports

Blood identification and individualization.
Trace evidence, ballistics, and other
  physical evidence.

Bloodstain Reconstruction

Final diagrams and bloodstain
  experiments.
Bloodstain interpretation of scene, clothing,
  and other items.
Correlation with autopsy and laboratory
  reports.

Final Conclusions and Report

of the bloodstain patterns. In those instances where trace evidence coexists with bloodstain evidence, consultation and communication between investigators and laboratory personnel at the scene will minimize unnecessary contamination, alteration, or destruction of physical evidence. Initial documentation and photography of bloodstain evidence are essential.

In actual practice, the crime scene environment can be indoors within a room or rooms of a house or other structure, outdoors, or can involve an automobile or other type of transportation vehicle. Not infrequently all these environments may be involved in the commission of the same crime and all may be sources of physical evidence, especially in cases where a victim has been killed in one location and transported to another. The subsequent actions of the assailant may produce additional sources of physical evidence involving disposition of a weapon or other incriminating materials. The assailant's clothing is a valuable source of bloodstain evidence as well as trace evidence, especially when it is acquired within a reasonable time and has not been subjected to extensive washing.

The indoor crime scene is for the most part protected from the elements and easily preserved for extended periods of time. Usually, there should be no need to hasten the processing of the scene. Occasionally, complications arise with the examination of a victim and crime scene in public places such as restaurants, stores, and airports because there is pressure to clean up the scene as quickly as possible. In all situations, unauthorized persons should be denied access to the scene. Those entering the scene should be cautious in order to minimize the unnecessary tracking of wet blood thereby altering significant bloodstain patterns and produce artifacts.

The crime scene, including bloodstain evidence, should be documented with high-quality color photographs including a close-up view with a scale of reference prior to moving the body or otherwise altering the scene. The use of a video camera is very useful to document the undisturbed scene as well. The bloodstains on the body and clothing should be photographed from above and from all sides. Close-up photographs of small bloodstains on the body should be taken with a measuring device in view. Turning the body for further examination should be done cautiously to minimize alteration of adjacent bloodstains and to avoid the creation of additional bloodstain patterns on the floor or clothing of the victim. Consistency of blood clots and degree of drying of the blood on the body and surrounding area should be documented with the ambient temperature. After the body has been removed, any remaining wet pools of blood should not be disturbed in order to avoid the production of artifacts.

In most circumstances there is no pressing need to remove a deceased victim from the scene. The body should remain undisturbed until the necessary observations and evaluations have been completed by the investigators. In those cases where medical attention is given to a surviving victim, the scene may be subject to unavoidable alteration. Often it is necessary for a victim to be moved to a more suitable position or location for the administration of medical treatment and emergency procedures. Alteration of bloodstains and creation of new bloodstains and other artifacts may be produced as a result. It is important to recognize these alterations at the crime scene. Activities at the scene during medical intervention should be documented by the investigator. In those cases where the activities of the emergency medical team (EMT) personnel and removal of the victim to the hospital precede the arrival of the investigator, it is important to consult with the medical personnel regarding the original position of the body and the undisturbed condition of the scene upon their arrival. Many EMTs make observations and take notes regarding the environment of the victim as well as movement and treatment rendered at the scene. They should be able to produce records of interventions made for a victim that may have produced bloodstains or altered those already present.

When a victim has been transported to a hospital it is important to retrieve physical evidence, including victim's clothing, projectiles and so forth, from the emergency room before they are grossly altered or lost. The sheets or blankets used on the victim during transport in an ambulance should be collected for these items may contain valuable trace evidence that became dislodged from the victim.

Small bloodstains, spatters, and thin smears of blood will dry rapidly at the scene and will usually remain intact on a surface. There are, however, instances where flaking and ultimate alteration of bloodstains will occur after relatively short periods of time. This phenomenon may occur when there is excessive air movement as created by a fan and when the target surface is wet owing to various heating devices including heated waterbeds. Certain surfaces such as waxed floors may not hold bloodstains very well. In these circumstances slight disturbances can cause bloodstains to become dislodged.

Preliminary testing of blood may be made on dried stains after they have been properly documented and photographed. This may be accomplished with the use of Leucomalachite green, phenolphthalein or an equivalent reagent. This technique is especially helpful when the stains are suspect in nature. In many household crime scenes, reddish brown stains may be easily mistaken for blood and elimination of these stains permits concentration on the actual bloodstains present.

A diligent search for inconspicuous bloodstains at a crime scene should be made using a good light source such as photo floodlights. Many surfaces may be dirty and discolored or the patterns or texture of the surface may blend in with the bloodstains that are present. There also may be areas of the crime scene where there has been an attempt to wipe up the blood or otherwise clean the surface. Blood may still be present especially in cracks in floors and walls. Luminol spray is often used to locate inconspicuous bloodstains. It cannot be overemphasized that the location of all bloodstains and patterns at a scene should be adequately photographed including a close up view with a measuring device. Documentation of bloodstains must be accurate with respect to their size, shape, and distance from a common locus for incorporation into graphs and diagrams.

Directionality, points of convergence, angles of impact, and origins should be determined on all surfaces for graphic representation or reconstruction with the use of strings at the scene. It is important to study bloodstain patterns to determine the object or objects that may have produced them. There are instances where the sequence of activities may be determined. For example, the presence of medium-velocity blood spatter impacted over a bloodstain transfer shoe- or handprint may indicate the presence of a certain individual prior to or during the physical activity producing the spatter and not at a subsequent time.

It is important to keep in mind the possible activities of an assailant at the scene not only during the assault but also after the incident has taken place. Assailants may produce bloodstain patterns with the victim's blood or in some instances with their own blood if they have sustained an injury during the altercation with the victim. A bloody knife, for example, may be wiped on a surface leaving a visible pattern. Various items may be used to wipe blood from the assailant's hands including towels, tissues, furniture, rugs, and drapes. Partial blood transfer hand- or fingerprints may be deposited on door edges, knobs, handles and light switches. Bathrooms should be thoroughly examined for bloodstain evidence. Assailants may deposit or transfer blood on sinks, toilets, shower stalls, or tubs during their attempt to clean up prior to leaving the scene. Sink traps and tub traps should be examined and water samples taken to be tested for the presence of blood. A thorough search should be conducted for discarded weapons and bloodstained clothing. An assailant may leave bloodstained cigarette butts or other personal articles such as glasses at the scene. As previously discussed, the clothing of the assailant may provide valuable bloodstain evidence. Evaluation of the transfer of bloodstains and patterns of victim's blood on the assailant's clothing will in many cases indicate the type of physical activity necessary to produce them. Correct interpretation of bloodstains on assailant's clothing can help to establish the probability of his presence at the scene and involvement with the assault on the victim. Often the reason offered by the assailant for his bloodstained clothing can be refuted.

The same principles of recognition, documentation, collection, preservation, and examination of physical evidence that are utilized for crime scenes indoors apply to crime scenes outdoors. Exterior scenes are not as likely to be altered or cleaned by the assailant but the nature of the terrain and environment including weather conditions may significantly alter the appearance of such physical evidence as bloodstains and cause difficulty in their recognition. Bloodstains and patterns may be absorbed into soil or otherwise altered by wind, rain, snow, or ice. It is important to consider the existing weather conditions and their effect on existing bloodstains and their interpretation. Outside target surfaces are more likely to consist of rougher textures than those inside. The interpretation of bloodstains on rock, concrete, and grassy areas may be more difficult with respect to directionality and angle of impact. Bloodstains that have been subjected to moisture may undergo alterations in appearance and appear diffuse and diluted. Blood flow patterns will spread on wet surfaces like ice and appear to be of greater volume as the blood is diluted. In freezing temperatures bloodstains and spatters have been observed to retain their characteristics fairly well and remain quite suitable for interpretation.

Photography and documentation of outdoor crime scenes should be accomplished as soon as possible and practical for the obvious reason that unexpected weather changes may alter the scene considerably and obliterate physical evidence. Bloodstained items should be processed and removed before these changes occur. It may be necessary to videotape and/or photograph the scene at night with the use of strong light sources. The use of a ladder or truck with a boom is useful for overall photographs of the outdoor scene. The weather may not hinder additional photography the following day but if weather change becomes a detrimental factor the night photography is crucial.

It may be necessary to collect soil samples for the demonstration of bloodstain locations. Bushes, leaves, and various outdoor debris should be examined closely for evidence of bloodstains. In certain cases the absence of significant bloodstain evidence may be associated with the dumping of a victim subsequent to the fatal injury's having occurred elsewhere. If sufficient time has elapsed for blood on the body to dry, the existing flow patterns may not be consistent with the present position of the victim.

Prompt examination of road surfaces for evidence of bloodstain patterns during the investigation of pedestrian-vehicular accidents may reveal impact sites and directionality of blood spatter that can assist in the repositioning of the victim and reconstruction of the accident. In addition to examination of road surfaces for bloodstain patterns in pedestrian-vehicular accidents, the vehicle exterior often provides substantial bloodstain evidence in the area of impacting surfaces and undercarriage of the vehicle. The undercarriage of the vehicle should be examined while the vehicles is on a hydraulic lift in a garage.

The examination of vehicle for bloodstain evidence may provide valuable physical evidence in various types of investigations. The interior of vehicles should be examined in a systematic manner and be divided into sections including the trunk. Each area should be photographed and examined separately. The trunk or interior of a vehicle may reveal bloodstain evidence relating to transportation of a victim, bloody clothing, or objects. The assailant may have transferred his own or victim's blood onto door and window handles, steering column, gear shift or dashboard controls, seats, or floor pedals.

In cases of motor vehicle accidents involving injury to driver and/or occupants, the evaluation of bloodstain evidence may help to resolve the issue as to the actual driver of the vehicle and the seat location of passengers. This may be accomplished by characterization of bloodstain patterns and impact sites relative to specific types of injuries in addition to blood grouping and testing of genetic markers.

Methods for Conducting Crime Scene Searches

In order that bloodstains and other physical evidence are not overlooked it may be necessary to employ an extensive, systematic plan, especially in cases in which the scene encompasses a large area. The scene should be surveyed initially and a search plan formulated that will be suitable for the individual case. Any proximal and obvious physical evidence should be photographed, documented, and collected prior to the initiation of an extensive search in order to avoid alteration or destruction of physical evidence by numerous searchers in an area.

The initial survey and evaluation of the scene may suggest the nature of items sought and the method of search most desirable for the particular case. The use of search patterns may be useful. There are several types of search patterns commonly used depending upon the scene environment and the preference of the investigators (Figure 6.1). Zone or quadrant search patterns are usually more applicable to indoor scenes and vehicles. Strip, grid, spiral, and wheel search patterns are more commonly utilized for large areas and outdoor scenes. The particular method used is not as critical as the manner in which the search is conducted.

1. **Zone.** The area is divided into quadrants that may be further subdivided to allow examination of small sections of an area in a systematic manner.
2. **Strip.** The area is visualized as a rectangle and is searched along paths parallel to one side with each succeeding path parallel and adjacent to the preceding one until the entire area has been traversed.

3. **Grid.** The area is visualized as a rectangle subdivided into squares. The squares or grids are examined systematically in two directions perpendicular to each other.

4. **Spiral.** The area is searched in a counter-clockwise manner forming a spiral beginning at the center of the area and spiraling outward until the entire scene has been examined.

5. **Wheel.** The area is considered to be roughly circular. The search begins at the center of the circle and progresses outward along a radius of the circle as in following the spoke of a wheel. A return can be made along the same radius back to the center of the circle. Successive radial paths are searched in a similar manner until the entire 360 degrees of the circle have been examined.

Crime Scene Diagrams

Good photography is essential for the proper documentation of the crime scene but photographs may not always depict relative distances between objects and other details that are best demonstrated with sketches or diagrams. A diagram is the graphic illustration of the crime scene and items within the scene that are pertinent to the investigation. The primary purpose is good orientation to the scene. A diagram will contain only essential items whereas photographs may be overcrowded with detail. It should show overall view, geographic location, size, and position of objects at the crime scene. A good diagram of a crime scene should complement the photographs and

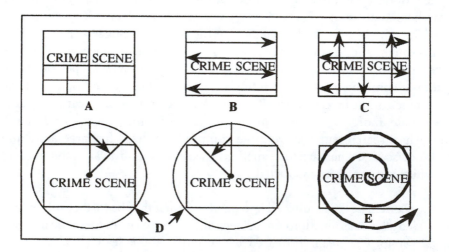

Figure 6.1 Crime scene search methods. **(A)** Quadrant zone method; **(B)** strip method; **(C)** grid method; **(D)** wheel method; **(E)** spiral method.

together provide the investigator, and eventually a jury, a clear picture of the scene. Some good general rules for crime scene diagrams are as follows:

1. Get a general, visual idea of the layout before collecting data and measurements. Use photographs for reference if available.
2. The person reading the tape measure should record the measurements.
3. Measure from finished wall to finished wall and record dimensions of the room.
4. Note that "all measurements are approximate".
5. Note direction in which doors swing.
6. Note position of doors, windows, and light fixtures.
7. Include only essential items of furniture, fixtures and so forth to avoid clutter in sketch.
8. Measurements of the location of movable objects should be noted in reference to at least two fixed objects so they may be relocated to their original position at a later time.
9. Note position of magnetic north.
10. Note the position from which photographs are taken.
11. Sketch outline of area first and then record objects.
12. If there is more than one body at the scene, number them.

There are two types of diagrams. The first is considered to be rough and is usually completed at the scene. The second is the finished or final diagram which is to be used in court. The rough sketch or diagram should be retained with the notes of the crime scene. The two-dimensional diagram system utilizing length and width is the most widely used (Figure 6.2). The three-dimensional system shows four walls, ceiling and floor and is useful for construction of a scale model of the scene (Figure 6.3). Whether a two- or a three-dimensional diagram system is utilized, it should contain essential information and not be cluttered with too much detail making it difficult to interpret. A variety of computer programs are available for the production of these types of diagrams (Figure 6.4 A and B). Multiple diagrams and overlays of a crime scene can be constructed from the basic sketch. Diagrams of bloodstain locations and convergences should show the location of the victim and only relevant nearby objects in order to demonstrate effective graphical representation.

There are three basic types of plotting methods:

1. **Rectangular.** The objects are located by right-angle measurements from fixed baselines such as walls (Figure 6.5).
2. **Triangulation.** Measurements are taken from two or more points to locate objects (Figure 6.6).

3. **Transecting baseline.** Baseline is established through center of area
and objects are located from baseline. **Z** is the baseline which is equi-
distant along **X** and **Y** and parallel to **ab**. Point **A** is located by measuring along **Z** to **a** and **b** and then at right angles perpendicular to **A**
(Figure 6.7).

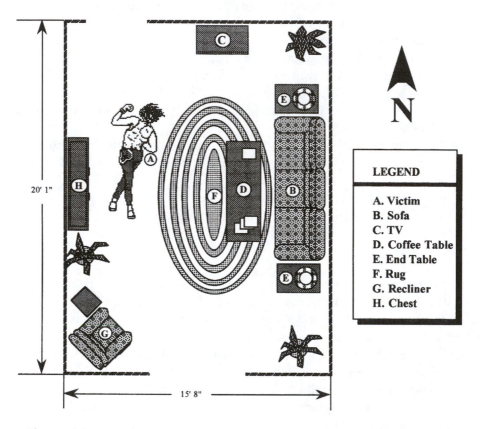

Figure 6.2 Two-dimensional crime scene diagram generated by computer.

The scale of scene sketches and diagrams depends upon the size of the
area to be measured. Small rooms can be scaled to the order of 1/2 inch
equals 1 foot. Larger rooms may be scaled to the order of 1/4 inch equals 1
foot. Outside locations may be scaled to the order of 1/8 inch equals 1 foot
or 1/2 inch equals 10 feet.

The basic materials needed for sketching at crime scenes are as follows:

- Tape measures (100 feet and 10–20 feet)
- Assorted rulers and triangles
- Graph paper and sketching paper

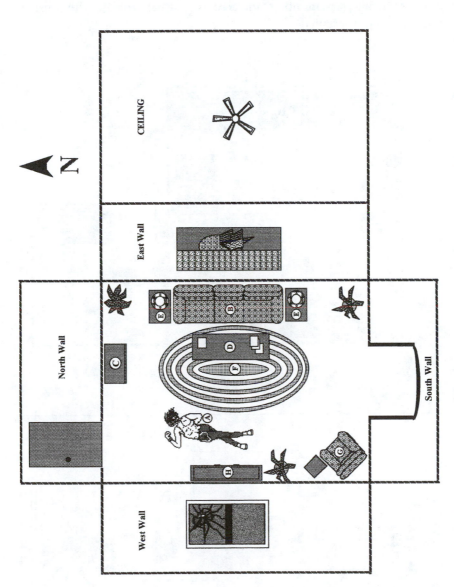

Figure 6.3   Three-dimensional crime scene diagram generated by computer.

- Appropriate pencils, pens, and eraser
- Templates (building interiors, body, etc.)
- Compass

Press on or touch letters, numbers, and arrows (excellent for use with finished diagrams and photographs).

A

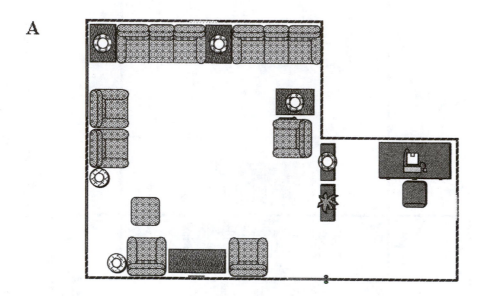

B

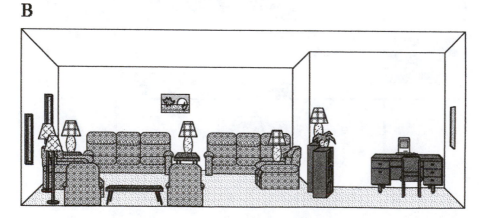

Figure 6.4 Two- and three-dimensional generated by computer: crime scene diagrams **(A)** two-dimensional; **(B)** three-dimensional.

Figure 6.5 The rectangular method of plotting.

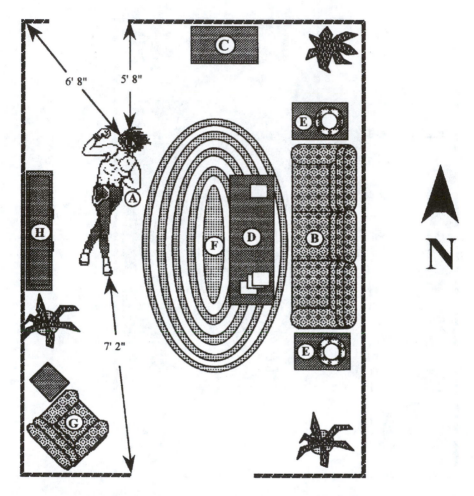

Figure 6.6 The triangulation method of plotting.

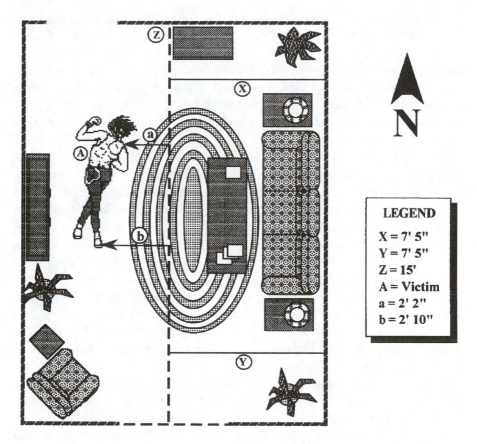

Figure 6.7 The transecting baseline method of plotting.

Collection and Preservation of Bloodstain Evidence

The identification of blood and forensic serological studies for species determination, grouping, genetic marker and DNA individualization are utilized in conjunction with bloodstain interpretation and are often mutually beneficial to the reconstruction of a crime scene. Both disciplines are important sources of physical evidence. In some cases the bloodstain interpretation may provide more valuable information, whereas in others the serological studies may be more revealing and informative. The value of each should be considered when the investigator is preparing to remove bloodstained objects and individual stains from the crime scene for submission to the laboratory. It is of ultimate importance to photograph and document adequately the location, size, and shape of bloodstains prior to their collection and removal from the crime scene.

The extent of ABO grouping, testing of genetic markers and DNA analysis in bloodstains that is possible in a given case depends on many factors including the age of the blood, the quantity of the blood available, the environmental conditions to which the blood has been exposed, and the degree of contamination that has occurred. Generally, with a limited sample available and with older samples, fewer systems can be tested. Exposure of the blood to extreme heat is detrimental. Also, it should be recognized that laboratories differ in their abilities and techniques to individualize dried bloodstains. Hospital and clinical laboratories are better equipped to individualize fresh blood in blood banks for transfusion and in cases involving paternal disputes. Many forensic laboratories have developed sophisticated techniques for the individualization of dried bloodstains. Occasionally, the surface upon which the blood has been deposited may provide a source of contamination and limit the extent of blood individualization, for example, on soiled clothing, floors, and vehicle exteriors where large deposits of crushed insects have accumulated. In all cases it is mandatory to collect, for comparative purposes, a negative control sample from an unstained area on the same surface from which the bloodstain is to be collected.

Putrefied blood presents many problems for the serologist because of the contaminating effect of bacteria, fungi, and the enzymatic breakdown of blood components and often produces misleading or inconclusive testing results. Blood may decompose if not packaged properly. For this reason, bloodstained articles should not be packaged wet or sealed in airtight plastic bags which may accumulate moisture. Individual packaging of completely dry bloodstained articles in clean paper bags is most desirable. Crusts and scrapings of bloodstains may be packaged in clean, folded paper or clean plastic containers. It is important during the collection process not to handle bloodstains or control areas with hands or fingers which may contaminate the samples with the blood group substances of the collector if that person is a secretor. All items should be properly labeled and identified for chain of custody purposes.

The following general guidelines are recommended to help ensure optimal results in the proper collection and preservation of bloodstain evidence. Investigators should consult with the specific forensic laboratory in order to follow particular protocols and to resolve the issues that may arise.

1. If there is a sufficient quantity of wet, pooled blood at a scene, approximately 5 to 10 ml should be collected with a pipette or medicine dropper and placed into a glass tube containing preservative and anticoagulant. Appropriate tubes containing sodium fluoride and potassium oxalate to preserve blood samples are available commercially or

may be provided by the laboratory. Always check with the laboratory personnel for their preference of blood preservative for specific procedures. The wet blood samples should be refrigerated prior to submission to the laboratory.

2. A moist bloodstain on a nonabsorbent surface such as glass or metal may be collected by adding a small amount of sterile physiological (0.9%) saline to the stain and mixing it thoroughly with an applicator stick and retrieving it with a pipette or medicine dropper. A control sample should be collected in a similar fashion. Both should be refrigerated.

3. Water or other liquids to be tested for blood should be placed into clean jars or other leak-proof containers and refrigerated.

4. When feasible, the entire bloodstained article or object should be collected as evidence after the bloodstains have thoroughly dried and their locations have been photographed and properly documented.

5. Do not fold wet clothing or bedding and do not package it in a wet condition. When bloodstained sheets, blankets, or pillow cases are removed from a bed or other location, it is important to document top, bottom, left side, right side, and which surface is up or otherwise folded as it was at the scene. Clothing and bedding items should be suspended in a clean area for drying purposes over clean paper to collect any trace evidence that may become dislodged during the drying process. Do not use a hair dryer or heating element to hasten drying. The papers under the dried items should be folded and submitted with the individual articles. The items should be folded and packaged individually in order not to further disturb the bloodstains.

6. Rugs or carpets may be lifted and removed in their entirety in many cases. If this is not feasible, the bloodstained portions and control areas should be cut and removed after photography and proper documentation and then packaged in clean paper.

7. If it is not feasible or practical to submit the entire bloodstained surface or object, the bloodstains may be scraped with a clean scalpel or razor blade onto clean paper. To avoid cross-contamination, individual disposable blades should be used. Be sure to scrape control surfaces as well. The papers may then be folded, taped and properly identified or transferred to clean plastic containers for submission to the laboratory.

8. If collection of a bloodstain by scraping is not desirable, as with a thin smear on a surface or a bloodstain absorbed into a rough surface such as concrete, it may be best removed by wetting the stain with physiological (0.9%) saline and collecting it with a pipette or medicine

dropper and placing into a clean, glass tube and refrigerating. Control samples should be collected in a similar fashion.

9. An alternative method for the removal and collection of dried bloodstains from smooth surfaces is to moisten a sterile cotton swab or swatch with a physiological (0.9%) saline and rub the stain from the surface. A control sample should be collected in a similar fashion and the samples refrigerated or frozen.

10. Collection of blood samples from the victim at the time of postmortem examination is within the protocol of the medical examiner or forensic pathologist. Consultation with the pathologist will help ensure that sufficient blood is obtained for all procedures necessary, including the toxicological and serological studies. The blood should be collected in separate tubes for each purpose with the appropriate preservatives and anticoagulants.

11. Authority for collection of blood samples from suspects or defendants is obtained through appropriate legal procedures. The forensic laboratory that will test the samples should be consulted to ensure that proper samples are collected by a physician, registered nurse, or licensed medical technologist with the proper rules of chain of custody observed in each case.

Examination of Bloodstained Clothing

The careful examination of bloodstained clothing and footwear often provides valuable information for accurate reconstruction of a violent crime. Bloodstain patterns on the clothing of a victim and assailant may represent the activity, position, and movement of each during and subsequent to an attack or struggle after blood has been shed. Examination of bloodstained garments may be difficult and stain patterns may be complex and sometimes partially obscured on blood-soaked material but a diligent examination is often quite rewarding. Blood found on the clothing of a victim is usually that of the victim, but do not assume this always to be so. Difficult to explain features of bloodstain patterns and inconsistent directionalities of individual bloodstains on the victim's clothing may represent blood of the assailant rather than that of the victim. Bloodstain interpretation of patterns on a suspect's clothing will help confirm or refute explanations offered by the suspect concerning the reason for his bloodstained clothing. For optimal results certain procedures and precautions should be observed:

1. The bloodstained clothing of a victim should be carefully removed after initial photography and preserved to avoid contamination and the production of artifacts.
2. Clothing that is haphazardly cut from a victim causes many problems of bloodstain reconstruction. If clothing must be cut from the victim, it should be done in an orderly fashion avoiding bloodstain patterns if possible. Perforations, tears, and other defects in the fabric should not be altered during the removal process.
3. Wet garments should not be folded together or packaged in a damp condition. Blood transfers may occur as well as possible bacterial contamination of the bloodstains which may hinder blood grouping procedures. It is best to hang and air-dry bloodstained clothing over clean paper in a secure location prior to packaging in paper bags.
4. Trace evidence collection and other special tests and procedures such as examinations for gunshot powder patterns and residue testing should be conducted before extensive bloodstain pattern examination is undertaken.
5. Bloodstain interpretation and serological studies on clothing should be coordinated and appropriate sites chosen for serological and DNA testing. If certain bloodstains must be removed they should be carefully photographed and their exact location documented. One experienced in bloodstain interpretation can suggest grouping and individualization of bloodstains in specific areas that will assist the reconstruction. Remember that the source of all blood on victim's clothing may not be that of the victim.
6. If the clothing of the victim was cut prior to removal at autopsy it can be extremely helpful to restore it by sewing or taping to conform to its original configuration before bloodstain pattern study is begun.
7. The use of a mannequin is helpful in orienting the location of bloodstains as they were while the victim or assailant wore the garments (Figure 6.8).
8. The investigator should study the original scene photographs of the victim at the time the clothing examination is being conducted. This will alert him to the possibility of artifacts being produced during removal and subsequent handling of the garments prior to examination.
9. Clothing should be adequately described in conjunction with the observed bloodstain patterns. Significant bloodstains should be measured and sketched showing their directionalities, relative sizes, shapes, and appearances. Be cautious with the interpretation of physical appearance and directionality of bloodstains on fabrics. Close-up photographs should be taken with a measuring device in place.

10. A good light source is essential especially when small spatters are being examined on dark clothing and denim materials.
11. For photographic and demonstrative purposes the location of small blood spatters may be better visualized by encirclement with white binder reinforcements (Figure 6.9).
12. Mirror images of bloodstains may be created when wet, bloody clothing is folded.
13. Alternate clean or void areas on bloodstained clothing may indicate folds in the clothing during bloodshed. Void areas on clothing may also indicate the presence of an intermediate object (Figures 6.10 and 6.11).
14. Search carefully for bloody weapon transfer patterns especially in association with stabbing and blunt force injuries.
15. If blood has soaked through clothing be sure to determine upon which side of the fabric the blood initially made contact (Figures 6.12 and 6.13).
16. Always check the pockets of assailant's garments for blood transferred from the assailant's hands.
17. An assailant frequently steps in blood at a scene. Be sure to check the soles of assailant's footwear for bloodstain evidence.
18. When prone victims are beaten with a blunt object or kicked, medium-velocity blood spatters are usually found in the region of the assailant's lower trouser legs, shoes and shirt sleeves. Be sure to examine the underside of the cuff areas as well as the shoes and socks of suspects in these situations (Figure 6.14).
19. The rear trouser leg and rear of the shirt of an assailant may receive cast-off bloodstain patterns from a bloody weapon when it is swung over the shoulder while an assailant is on his knees administering the blows to a prone victim.
20. A careful search for bloodstain evidence should be conducted on the suspect's clothing in those cases where sufficient time has elapsed for the clothing to have been washed. There is always the possibility that some detectable blood may have survived the cleaning procedure. The effect of water on bloodstained clothing including washed areas may show hemolysis and dilution of bloodstains. Evidence of diffusion of blood to areas previously not bloodstained may be recognizable.
21. Bloodstained clothing and footwear of the assailant may be the source of blood transfer fabric patterns and impressions on walls, doors, floors, and other objects at the scene (Figure 6.15). When duplicating patterns of this type for purposes of comparison always use the same material upon which the original pattern was produced.

22. The use of a stereomicroscope is very useful for the visualization of small bloodstains on dark fabrics and thick-knitted materials.

23. Leucomalachite green reagent, phenolphthalein or other presumptive tests for blood may help distinguish blood from spots of foreign substances (paint, tar, etc.). This type of presumptive testing may prove useful during bloodstain examination of clothing, especially in the case of small spatters and areas not previously tested by a serologist that are important for the final interpretation. For purposes of further confirmatory tests for blood and DNA analysis care should be taken not to use all the sample for presumptive tests.

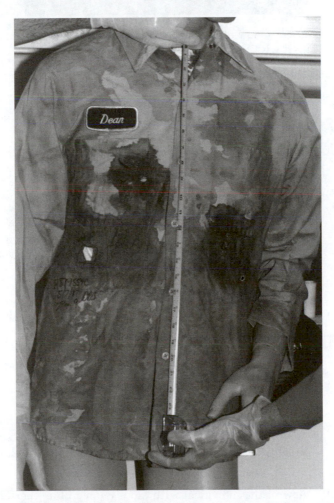

Figure 6.8 Placing the bloodstained shirt on a mannequin assists with the location and evaluation of the bloodstains.

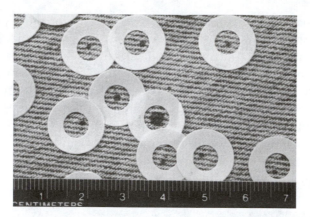

Figure 6.9 Close-up view of medium-velocity impact blood spatters on denim material, enhanced with the use of white reinforcements..

Figure 6.10 View of the individual with bloodstained blue jeans and a clean shirt. He claimed to have carried the victim following an attack by another. Note the V-shaped void area on the upper front of the blue jeans, not consistent with the type of shirt he is wearing.

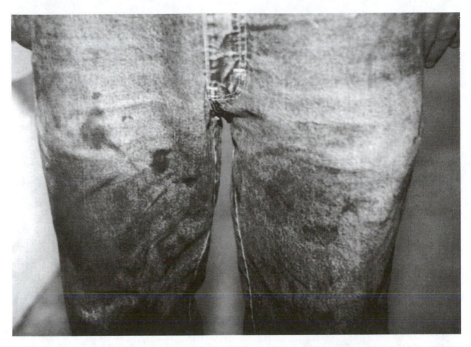

Figure 6.11 Close-up view of void area on the upper front of blue jeans.

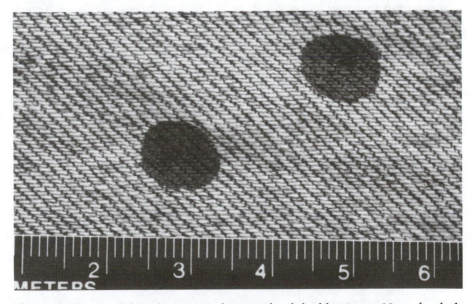

Figure 6.12 Small bloodstains on the outside of the blue jeans. Note the dark color and the small crusts of blood on the surface of the jeans.

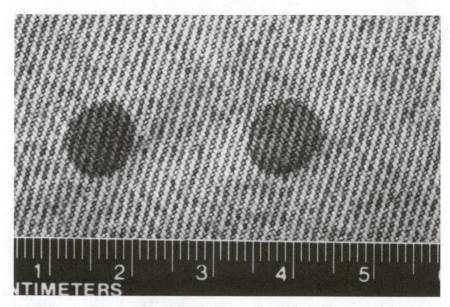

Figure 6.13 The same small bloodstains, on the inside of the blue jeans, that have soaked through the material to the opposite side. Note the lighter appearance of the stains.

Figure 6.14 Small blood spatters, contact transfer stains, and flow patterns of blood on left she of assailant.

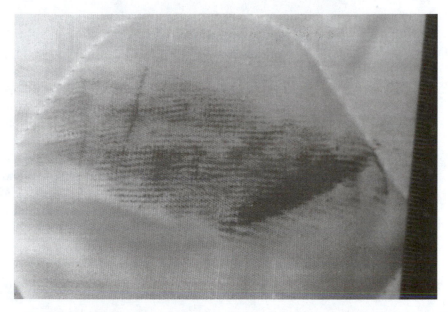

Figure 6.15 Blood transfer pattern on the bedspread created by contact with the bloodstained trousers of the assailant.

References

Adelson, L., *The Pathology of Homicide*, Ch. 2. Charles C Thomas Co., Springfield, IL. 1974.

Califana, A. and Lekov, J., *Criminalistics for the Law Enforcement Officer*, Chapters 2, 7. McGraw-Hill Co., New York, NY. 1978.

Cunliffe, F. and Piazza, P., *Criminalistics and Scientific Investigation*, Prentice-Hall, Inc., Englewood Cliffs, NJ. 1980.

Curran, W., McGarry, L., and Petty, C., *Modern Legal Medicine, Psychiatry, and Forensic Science*, Chs. 3,5,6. F.A. Davis Co., Philadelphia, PA. 1980.

Deforest, P., Gaensslen, R., and Lee, H., *Forensic Science - An Introduction to Criminalistics*, Appendix Two. McGraw-Hill Co., New York, NY. 1983.

Department of the Treasury, *Forensic Handbook*, United States Government Printing Office, Washington, DC. 1975.

Eckert, W., Editor., *Introduction to Forensic Sciences*, 2nd Edition, CRC Press, LLC, Boca Raton, FL. 1997.

Eckert, W., *Investigation of Deaths and Injuries*, Medicolegal and Forensic Investigation Series. Ch. 1. The International Reference Organization in Forensic Medicine, Wichita, KS. 1987.

Fatteh, A., *Handbook of Forensic Pathology*, J.B. Lippincott, Philadelphia, PA. 1973, Ch. 1.

Federal Bureau of Investigation, *Handbook of Forensic Science*, United States Government Printing Office, Washington, DC. 1974.

Fisher, A.J., *Techniques of Crime Scene Investigation*, 5th Edition, CRC Press, LLC, Boca Raton, FL. 1993.

Fisher, R. and Petty, C., Eds. *Forensic Pathology—A Handbook for Pathologists*, National Institute of Law Enforcement and Criminal Justice. Law Enforcement Assistance Administration, United States Department of Justice, Washington, D.C. 1977, Ch. 5.

Fox, R. and Cunningham, C., *Crime Scene Search and Physical Evidence Handbook*, United States Department of Justice, National Institute of Law Enforcement and Criminal Justice, Washington, D.C. 1973.

Geberth, V.J., *Practical Homicide Investigation*, 3rd Edition, CRC Press LLC, Boca Raton, FL. 1996.

Geberth, V.J., *Practical Homicide Investigation—Checklist and Field Guide*, CRC Press LLC, Boca Raton, FL, 1997.

Harris, R., *Outline of Death Investigation*. Charles C Thomas Co., Springfield, IL. 1973, Ch. 10.

Hughes, D., *Homicide Investigation Techniques*, Charles C Thomas Co., Springfield, IL. 1974, Ch. 2.

Jones, L., *Scientific Investigation and Physical Evidence*, Charles C Thomas Co., Springfield, IL. 1959, Ch.1, 10–11.

Kirk, P., *Crime Investigation*, 2nd Edition, John Wiley & Sons, New York, NY. 1974, Ch. 3.

MacDonell, H.L., *Crime Scene Procedures*, Forensic Sciences, Vol. 2, Cyril Wecht, Ed., pp. 35-5–35-23. Matthew Bender, New York, NY. 1983.

Merkeley, D., *The Investigation of Death*, Charles C. Thomas Co., Springfield, IL. 1957, Ch. 10–11.

O'Brien, K. and Sullivan, R., *Criminalistics—Theory and Practice*, 2nd Ed., Holbrook Press Inc., Boston, MA. 1972, Ch. 3.

O'Hara, C., *Fundamentals of Criminal Investigation*, 2nd Edition, Charles C Thomas Co., Springfield, IL. 1970.

O'Hara, C. and Osterburg, J., *An Introduction to Criminalistics—The Application of the Physical Sciences to the Detection of Crime*, Indiana University Press, Bloomington, IN. 1974, Ch. 3–4.

Osterburg, J., *The Crime Laboratory—Case Studies of Scientific Criminal Investigation*, Indiana University Press, Bloomington, IN. 1968.

Polson, C., *The Essentials of Forensic Medicine*, 2nd Ed., Charles C Thomas Co., Springfield, IL. 1967.

Redsicker, D.R., *The Practical Methodology of Forensic Photography*, CRC Press LLC., Boca Raton, FL. 1991.

Saferstein, R., *Criminalistics—An Introduction to Forensic Science*, 2nd Ed. Ch. 2–3. Prentice-Hall Inc., 1981.

Snyder, L., *Homicide Investigation*, 3rd Ed., Springfield, IL. Charles C Thomas Co., Englewood Cliffs, NJ. 1977, Ch. 1–2, 4.

Spitz, W. and Fisher, R., *Medicolegal Investigation of Death*, 2nd Ed., Charles C Thomas Co., Springfield, IL. 1980, Ch. 15, 25.

Svensson, A. and Wendell, O., *Techniques of Crime Scene Investigation*, 2nd Ed., Elsevier Science Publishing Co., New York, NY. 1965.

Swanson, C., Chamelin, N., and Territo, L., *Criminal Investigation*, Goodyear Publishing Co., Santa Monica, CA. 1977.

Turner, R., *Forensic Science and Laboratory Techniques*, Charles C Thomas Co., Springfield, IL. 1949, Ch. 2–3.

Weston, P. and Wells, K., *Criminal Investigation*, 3rd Ed., Prentice-Hall, Inc., Englewood Cliffs, NJ. 1980.

The Detection of Blood Using Luminol

7

DALE L. LAUX, M.S.

"Fausak had never experienced anything like it. He felt as if he were in a sci-fi movie. Initially, there was the same pale green light. It got greener and brighter. It began to glow. And through its luminosity he could see the trail of blood. The trail was solid, but with streaks in it, as though someone had taken a big wet mop and wrung it out and dragged it along the floor. The length of the bloody trail measured some 55 feet.

"The shimmering glow hung in the air, above Fausak's knees. It had become so bright that he could see the faces of the forensic men and the chemists."*

Introduction

The fascinating chemical luminol which produces a bright luminescence when in the presence of the most minute amounts of blood is without a doubt a clear asset to the investigators repertoire. Chemiluminescence occurs when a molecule capable of fluorescing is raised to an excited level during a chemical reaction. Upon its return to the ground state, energy in the form of light is emitted. Only a few molecules are known to emit appreciable amounts of light, and of those, luminol is one of the most outstanding. Much of the early work with luminol occurred in Germany, and consequently, many of the articles require translation. The following text, however, is an attempt to unravel the history of luminol and its use in the detection of blood.

Discovery

A very good historical treatise of luminol's discovery and mechanism of action appears in Gaensslen's *Sourcebook* (1983). Most reports cite A. J. Schmitz as the first to synthesize luminol in 1902; however, a paper by Gill

---

* Maas, Peter. 1990. *In A Child's Name: The Legacy of a Mother's Murder*, New York, New York: Simon and Schuster, p. 112.

153

states luminol's discovery to be around 1853. What is certain is that in the early 1900s a chemical having chemiluminescent properties was available and being studied. A better understanding of the chemical's nature came about in 1928 with Albrecht's investigations. This study demonstrated that hypochlorites, plant peroxidases and blood greatly enhanced the luminescence of the compound with hydrogen peroxide. Albrecht also speculated on a mechanism for the reaction.

In 1934, Huntress and co-workers published an article describing a method of synthesis for the compound and coined the term luminol. Gleu and Pfannstiel (1936) prepared luminol and found that the alkaline solution, with the addition of hydrogen peroxide or sodium peroxide, produced an intense luminescence with hematin. This was independently confirmed by Tamamushi and Akiyama (1938).

Luminol caught the attention of the forensic science world after the extensive studies by Specht (1937). Upon the suggestion of Gleu and Pfannstiel, Specht studied fresh and old bloodstains as well as milk, coffee, sperm, saliva, urine, feces, and other body fluids. He tested numerous materials such as wallpaper, fabrics, leather, oils, varnish, wood, grass, leaves, and soil. Interestingly, he tested metals (copper, steel, brass, lead, and zinc) and obtained negative results. In the presence of hypochlorite, a weak luminescence was produced. The test was said not to interfere with subsequent crystal or spectral tests, nor with serological tests for species or blood groups. Specht demonstrated the ability to photograph the positive luminol reaction and obtained quality photographs of blood on various substrates including an outdoor setting. Two preparations of luminol were used and were applied as an aerosol with a glass sprayer. Specht found that dried stains produced a more intense chemiluminescence than fresh blood which produced only a "weak glow". According to Specht, the older the bloodstain, the more intense the reaction, with blood traces a year old or more yielding luminescence. Specht commented on the ability to cover large areas of a crime scene or large pieces of evidence quickly with luminol and recommended that luminol be used for medicolegal examinations, believing that it was quite specific for blood.

A very nice paper by Proescher and Moody (1939) confirmed many of Specht's findings and made three important observations:

- While the test is presumptive, large areas of suspected material can be examined rapidly.
- Dried and decomposed blood gave a stronger and more lasting reaction than fresh blood (three-year old stains gave a brilliant luminescence).
- If the luminescence disappears, it may be reproduced by the application of a fresh luminol-hydrogen peroxide solution; dried bloodstains may thus be made luminescent many times over.

These authors were also among the first to describe parameters for obtaining photographs of the luminescence produced.

McGrath (1942) found the luminol reaction to be rather specific for blood, testing a wide variety of substrates including serum, bile, sputum, pus, seminal stains and feces obtaining no reaction. However, he recommended that the test should not be used as a specific test for blood. He recommended that after its application, which should be kept to a minimum, the stain be photographed and allowed to dry. The stain is then available for all the usual serological analyses. McGrath was unable to detect any differences between stained and unstained samples. Nevertheless, he used a sprayed area with no luminescence as a control for typing purposes.

Luminol's preparation has changed over the years. Specht (1937) used a mixture of luminol, calcium carbonate and hydrogen peroxide or luminol with sodium peroxide. Proescher and Moody (1939) used sodium carbonate with hydrogen peroxide or sodium peroxide. McGrath (1942) used the methods of both Specht and Proescher and Moody and noted a trace of inherent luminescence of the solution on preparation which could be removed with the addition of indazolon-4-carboxylic acid.

Essentially, the preparation requires luminol, the addition of a base (to make the solution alkaline) and an oxidant. Grodsky et al. (1951) described the preparation of a solution composed of 0.07 g sodium perborate in 10 ml water, to which is added 0.01 g luminol and 0.5 g sodium carbonate.

Weber (1966) published a preparation of luminol consisting of the following stock solutions:

- 8 g sodium hydroxide in 500 ml water
- 10 ml 30% hydrogen peroxide in 490 ml water
- 0.354 g luminol in 62.5 ml of 0.4 N sodium hydroxide diluted to 500 ml with water

The test reagent is prepared by mixing 10 ml of each of the above stock solutions with 70 ml of water. This preparation was stated to be an improvement over earlier ones in that it reacted well with fresh bloodstains and was more sensitive to dilute blood samples.

The Luminol Reaction

Some proteins possess a non-peptide portion called a prosthetic group. The prosthetic group is intimately involved in the biological function of the protein. Such is the case for hemoglobin. The prosthetic group for hemoglobin is heme and it is involved in the transport of O_2 and CO_2 in the body.

Heme contains iron bound to the pyrrole system known as porphin. In the normal function of hemoglobin in the body, the iron atom does not undergo change in valence as oxygen is bound and lost; it is in the Fe(II) state. Upon aging and subsequent oxidation, the iron atom changes from heme to hemin or hematin; with this transformation comes a change in the color of the stain from red to brown. It is this conversion that is crucial to the subsequent oxidation/reduction reactions that are ultimately used to test for the detection of blood.

The reactions of luminol, or 3-aminophthalhydrazide, with blood producing what is termed chemiluminescence are complex. Many authors have made attempts to describe the reaction. Early studies by Albrecht (1928) indicated that luminol (Figure 7.1) was oxidized to form intermediate compounds (Figure 7.2-II) which were hydrolyzed in the basic solution to yield a dianion, phthalic acid (Figure 7.2-III), and N_2H_2. The dianion would further react with N_2H_2 and form nitrogen, light and luminol (Figure 7.3-IV). Since Albrecht could only isolate unchanged luminol from the reaction mixture after chemiluminescence had ceased, he thought that luminol itself was the light emitting species.

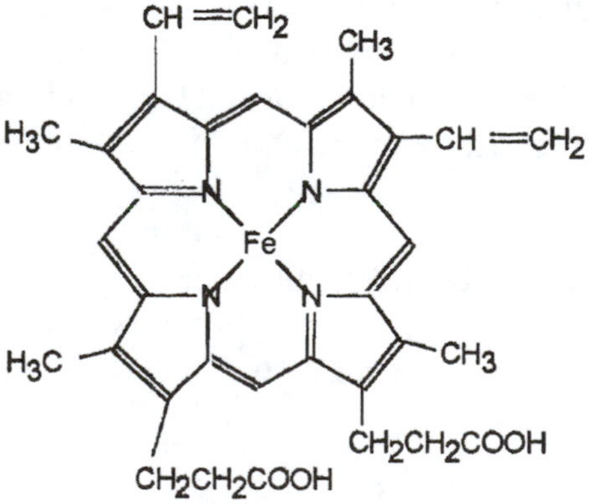

Figure 7.1 Heme.

Proescher and Moody (1939) correctly predicted the structure of luminol in acid (Figure 7.3A) and the tautomeric structures (Figure 7.3B and 7.3C) in alkaline solutions.

Form (a) gave a strong blue luminescence. It was believed that the chemiluminescence was produced by oxidation in an alkaline solution of either form (b) or (c). The authors speculated that the reaction proceeded as in the Albrecht mechanism.

The Albrecht reaction was seriously challenged in the early 1960s. Erdey et al. (1962) speculated that depending on the pH, hydrogen peroxide exists

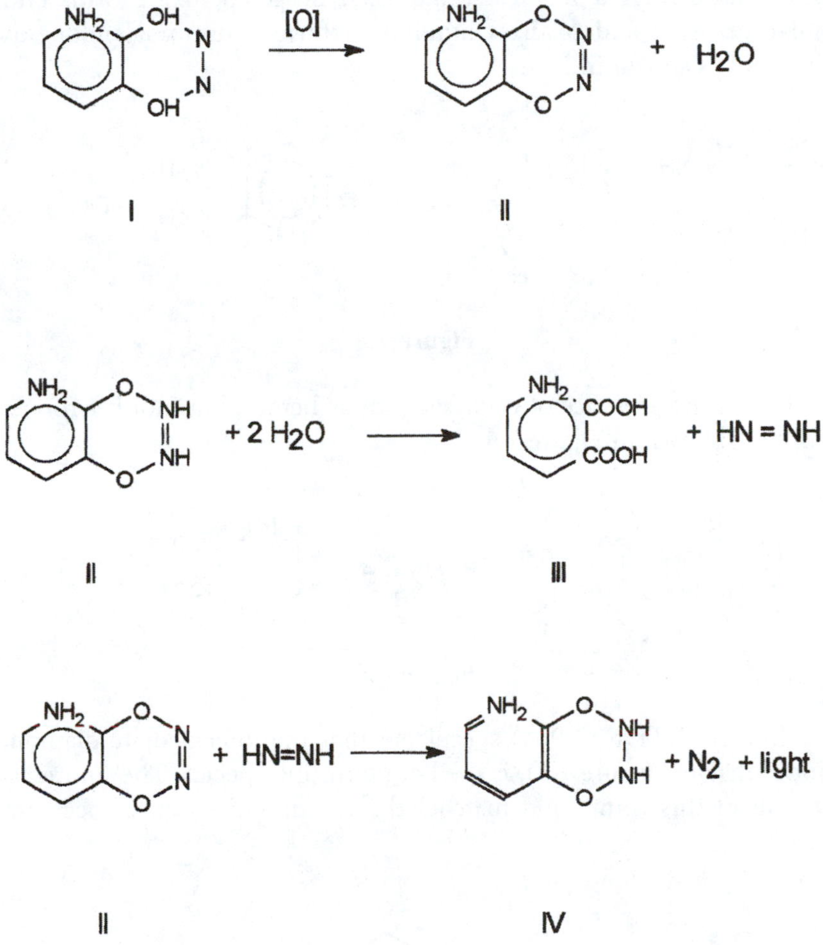

Figure 7.2 The Albrecht Mechanism (from Gaensslen 1983).

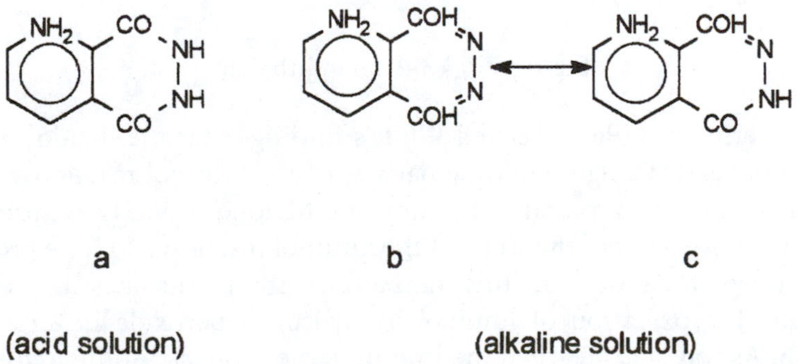

Figure 7.3 Luminol structures in solution (from Proescher and Moody 1939).

in different forms. At a pH greater than 12, hydrogen peroxide forms a trans-annular peroxide and oxidizes luminol to form a luminol endoperoxide compound as shown in Figure 7.4.

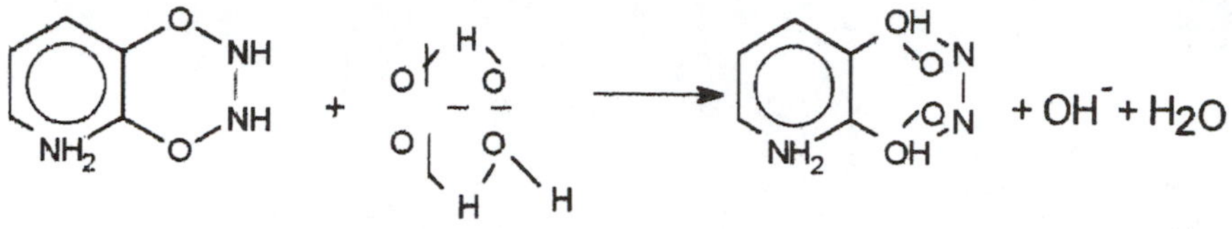

Figure 7.4

Then in the presence of catalysts such as hemin, luminol is irreversibly oxidized as shown in Figure 7.5.

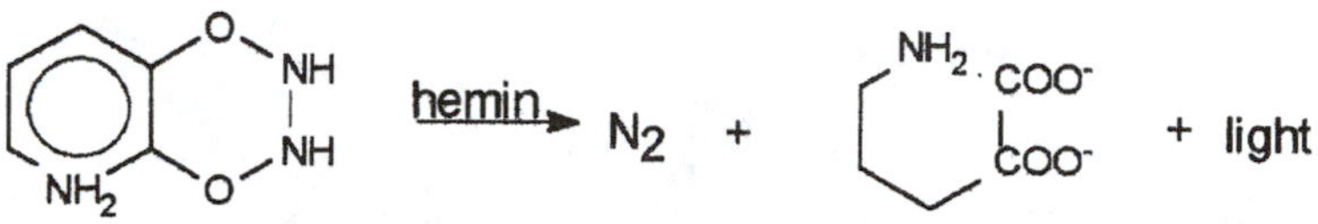

Figure 7.5

White et al. (1961, 1964) speculated that the intermediate dianion, 3-aminophthalate (Figure 7.6), is the light emitting species. The fluorescence spectrum of this compound matches the chemiluminescence spectrum of luminol.

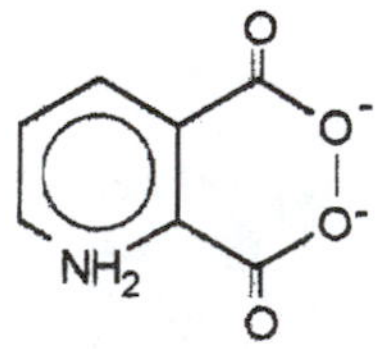

Figure 7.6   3-Aminophthalate.

Gundermann (1965) restated White's findings that the dianion is both the product and the light emitting particle of the luminol reaction.

Finally, and most recently, Thornton and Maloney (1985) have presented an excellent overview of the study of the luminol reaction and have proposed a reaction of their own. In this mechanism, the hemin acts as a catalyst triggering the oxidation of luminol by hydrogen peroxide in an alkaline solution. As was stated earlier, the iron in heme can exist in different states.

The normal valence for iron in hemoglobin is in the Fe(II) ferrous state. Upon aging of the bloodstain, hemoglobin is converted to methemoglobin and the iron is oxidized to the Fe(III) ferric state. Upon the addition of hydrogen peroxide, the iron is oxdized to a transition state Fe(IV). At the time of the oxidation of luminol, the Fe(IV) is reduced to Fe(III), thus allowing the iron in heme to participate in another reaction. This phenomenon may explain the finding that stains can be dried and sprayed with luminol repeatedly, often times resulting in brighter luminescence on latter applications as a result of the further conversion of heme to hemin in the stain. The exact mechanism of luminol's reaction with blood may not be completely understood but the final outcome can be dramatic and provide the investigator with important information. It is for this reason, after all, that luminol is being used. It is luminol's preparation, application and interpretation that will now be considered.

Preparation of Luminol

A number of preparations for luminol exist. Two of the most commonly used preparations are detailed in Tables 7.1 and 7.2. The preparation described by Grodsky et al. (1951) has an advantage in that the components can be placed in a luminol "kit" in the trunk of a car or crime scene vehicle and remain there indefinitely. The dry ingredients can be placed in discarded plastic 35-mm film containers which conveniently hold the amounts of sodium perborate and sodium carbonate required to make 500 ml of solution. The 0.5 g of luminol required can be stored in a 1.5 ml microfuge tube. It is important to dissolve the sodium perborate first in 500 ml of distilled water *before* adding the luminol and sodium carbonate. Sodium perborate does not dissolve completely if all the reagents are mixed at once. The preparation of the solution should be performed in a 500 ml volume (or greater) plastic container. *Never* use water from the crime scene to prepare the reagent as "hard" water or well water often contains chemicals which may cause a severe background luminescence.

Table 7.1   Preparation of Luminol According to Grodsky, Wright, and Kirk (1951)

1. Weigh out 3.5 g sodium perborate and add to 500 ml distilled water.
2. Stir until dissolved.
3. Add 0.5 g luminol and 25 g sodium carbonate.
4. Stir until dissolved.
5. Let stand 5 minutes.
6. Decant solution into plastic spray bottle.
7. Use immediately. The reagent does not keep well once prepared.

Note: The chemicals may be stored dry and in separate plastic film containers until needed.

Table 7.2 Preparation of Luminol According to Weber (1966)

Stock Solutions:
  8 g sodium hydroxide in 500 ml distilled water (0.4 N)
  10 ml 30% hydrogen peroxide in 490 ml distilled water (0.176 M)
  0.354 g luminol in 62.5 ml 0.4 N sodium hydroxide to final volume of 500 ml (0.004 M)

Store Stock Solutions in a Refrigerator

Test Solution:
  10 ml solution (A) + 10 ml solution (B) + 10 ml solution (C) + 70 ml distilled water

Final Volume = 100 ml working solution

After thoroughly shaking the mixture, the solution should be allowed to stand for several minutes allowing any undissolved ingredients to settle. The solution is then decanted into a plastic spray bottle. If mixing is performed in the spray bottle, the end of the nozzle will most likely clog.

This author prefers to use the luminol preparation described by Weber (1966). This preparation has two advantages over the preparation of Grodsky et al. First, it is reported to be more sensitive than other luminol preparations due to the lower concentrations of reagents which tend to be inhibitory. Second, the lower concentrations of reagents make it safer to use.

There are some disadvantages however. First, the preparation of this luminol solution is more difficult and probably could not be accomplished by an investigator in the field from scratch. Second, it has been observed that the luminescence produced by this preparation does not last as long as others and may require repeated sprayings during photography.

Nevertheless, this author prefers to use the Weber formulation. Stock solutions are kept refrigerated. Preparation of the working solution is easy and can be accomplished in the field very quickly from previously prepared stock solutions.

A word of caution here: although luminol is not a known carcinogen, the mutagenic effects are not known at this time. According to Material Safety Data Sheets available at the time of this writing, luminol is very dangerous in case of eye contact (irritant) and may irritate eyes causing redness, watering and itching. Sodium perborate is harmful if inhaled or swallowed, can cause eye and skin irritation and is irritating to mucous membranes and the respiratory tract. Sodium carbonate is toxic and a severe eye, skin and mucous membrane irritant. Dusts or vapors may cause mucous membrane irritation with coughing, shortness of breath and gastrointestinal changes. Sodium hydroxide is corrosive and an irritant and may irritate the eyes and skin upon contact. Hydrogen peroxide can cause irritation of the eyes and is a severe irritant for lungs and the respiratory tract.

Since the luminol preparation is applied as an aerosol, protective equipment is recommended. Dust and mist respirators, splash-proof safety goggles, gloves, and protective clothing are suggested (Color Plate 1*). Contact lens wearers may notice that they are more sensitive to the luminol mist than others and should be certain to wear eye protection without air vents. It is recommended that contacts *not* be worn during the luminol application.

The luminol application should not be conducted in the presence of an audience. Limit the number of people in the room for their own safety.

Interpretation of Luminescence

Luminol is a presumptive test and has been found to react with plant peroxidases (fresh potato juice), metals (Figure 7.7) and some cleaners (esp. hypochlorites). This author has found it to react with soil, fresh bleach solution and cigarette smoke inside cars. It does not react with semen, saliva or urine.

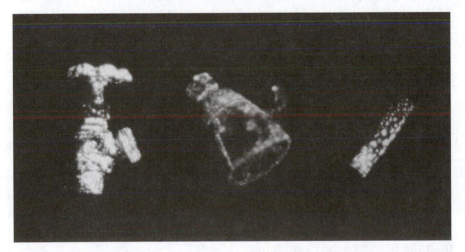

Figure 7.7 Luminescence given off by metal objects. From left: water valve, shower head, copper pipe.

Upon reaction with metals, there will often be a "twinkling" or "rippling" of the luminescence instead of an even, long-lasting glow as with blood. It is possible to obtain an even, long-lasting, moderate glow from an old porcelain sink or bathtub that has been exposed to cleaners.

Luminol's reaction with a true bloodstain produces an intense, long-lasting, even glow frequently in patterns such as spatters, smears, wipes, drag marks, or even footwear impressions (Color Plate 2). Caution should be

* Color Plates follow page 162.

exercised when an entire object luminesces such as a sink, carpet, automobile seat, etc., as this is most likely due to background luminescence. In the case of carpeting, a sofa or chair should be moved and the area sprayed to check for luminescence. If luminescence appears, it is probably due to a cleaner or something in the substrate.

Use of Additional Presumptive Tests

After any positive reaction with luminol, the stained area should be circled with a grease pencil or other suitable marker. The stained area should be checked again with another reagent for blood such as tetramethybenzidine (TMB), phenolphthalein, or o-tolidine. A clean, dry cotton-tipped swab should be wiped lightly over the area of luminescence. The reagents can be applied directly to this swab and the swab can be examined for its reaction. The luminol preparations do not induce a false positive reaction with either TMB, o-tolidine or phenolphthalein (Laux, 1991).

Interpretation of Patterns

Blood can be deposited upon an object in many ways. Blood can be transferred by contact, splashed, projected, and cast-off by many different means upon a vast array of surfaces. Compound this with the ways and means of cleaning up the bloodstains and the investigator can be faced with difficulties in locating stains.

Luminol is a valuable tool for the investigator since it not only discloses the presence of blood but its distribution. Often times, in "cleaning up", blood is distributed over a larger area making the detection with luminol easier. The fact that blood is present and was cleaned up is often more important than the typing of the bloodstains.

Experience is the best educator in locating and interpreting bloodstains with luminol and it is recommended that the new investigator witness several demonstrations of luminol at crime scenes before interpreting any themselves. No mock crime scenes can duplicate all the variables in the real world.

Finally, the investigator should be aware of and recognize the following samples of blood distribution possible at crime scenes which have been cleaned up:

- High-velocity spatters associated with gunshots
- Cast-offs from weapons, tools, etc.
- Pooled blood that has soaked into carpet padding, cracks in wood floors, between tiles, etc.

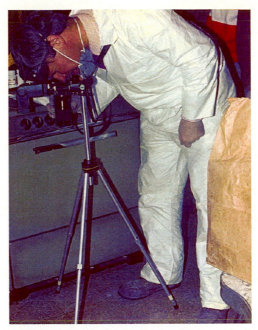

Plate 1. Protective clothing, including eye goggles, dust and mist respirators, and gloves, should be worn during luminol application.

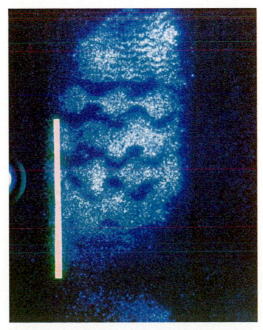

Plate 2. Footwear impression in blood as developed with luminol. Note the luminescent tape in the photograph as a reference.

Plate 3. Luminol photograph utilizing a bounce flash during the luminol exposure. Note the blood spattering and the left handprint on the wall and the smearing on the carpet.

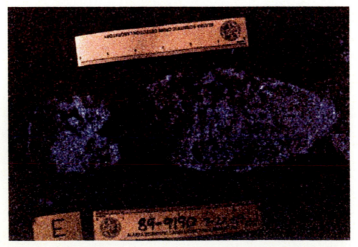

Plate 4. Close-up luminol photograph of the shoe impression found in Case 2. Note the "V" notch cut out of the heel.

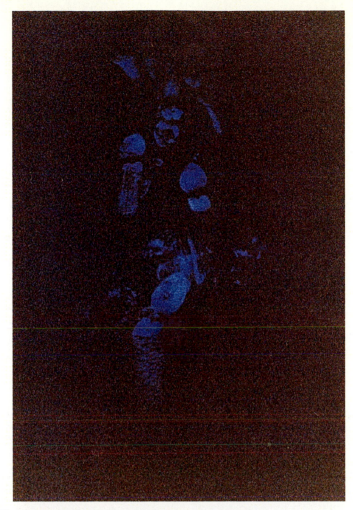

Plate 5. Overall view of the trail of shoe impressions in Case 2.

JPD Case #89-9190
DPS Lab #89-1514
Item #185 Right Shoe Sole

9-21-89 jw

89-1514 #185 Right 9-13-89
ALASKA SCIENTIFIC CRIME DETECTION LABORATORY

Plate 6. Photograph of the right shoe from the male suspect in Case 2. Note the "V" notch in the heel which corresponds to the shoe impressions discovered at the scene. (Plate 4)

Plate 7. Trail of luminescent latent footwear impressions developed with luminol at the the crime scene from Case 3.

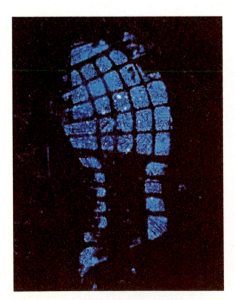

Plate 8. Close-up photograph of latent footwear impression from Case 3 without fill-in flash.

Plate 9. Close-up photograph of latent footwear impression from Case 3 with fill-in flash.

- Wipe/smear marks associated with cleaning
- Footwear impressions
- Drag marks along walls, floor, etc.
- Partial or entire handprints on walls, furniture, etc.
- Outlines of weapons, cleaning tools, etc.

One should look for clear-cut demarcations of luminescence. An excellent example of the different types of blood distribution one may encounter is in Lytle and Hedgecock (1978).

Effect of Substrates

The luminol test, like most analyses, can be quite easy at times, and difficult at times. One of the most important considerations facing the investigator when using the reagent is the nature of the substrate possessing the stain. Absorbent materials such as fabric, carpeting, etc., are fairly easy to analyze and stains on materials such as these can be resprayed and photographed successfully.

Non-absorbent substrates such as glass, vinyl, porcelain, tile, and linoleum are more difficult to examine. Stains on materials such as these will quickly "run" when sprayed (Figure 7.8). The investigator should use a minimum amount of reagent (use fine-mist spray bottle) and be ready to photograph the stain quickly. Reapplication of the reagent on these types of surfaces is usually not successful.

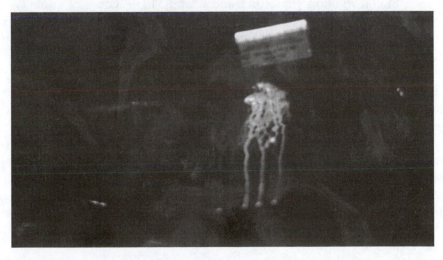

Figure 7.8 Luminol reagent "running" down the side of a vinyl car seat during application.

When one is asked to analyze a large room with linoleum, ceramic tile, etc., luminol can be applied and large areas can be covered quickly. However, should luminescence appear, spraying should be immediately halted. If photographs are desired, a camera should be set-up with a tripod over areas *not yet sprayed*. These areas can be photographed with a flash, the room darkened, luminol applied, and photographs of the luminescence obtained. Gradually, the entire area can be covered and photographed. As stated earlier, re-application of the reagent on these types of surfaces is usually not successful and the investigator often gets only one chance to obtain photographs.

Collection of Samples

After bloodstains are located, it is customary to collect the stains and take them to the crime laboratory. Obviously, if the object with the bloodstain can be moved, the entire object should be taken to the crime laboratory. This allows for the analyst to sample and collect stains to their own specifications.

If the bloodstained object cannot be moved, e.g., walls, floors, ceilings, etc., the stains can be collected on cotton threads or swabs. A very diffuse stain, on a wall for example, may be best collected on the end of a dry cotton tipped swab by rubbing the swab tip over the entire stain. Allow the swab to dry and place it inside a *paper* evidence envelope. Label the envelope accordingly. Controls should be collected by swabbing an area of the substrate that has been sprayed but does *not* exhibit luminescence.

Various sources list luminol's sensitivity ranging from 1 in a million to 1 in a billion dilution (Proescher and Moody 1939; Grodsky et al. 1951; Weber 1966; Kirk, Lytle, and Hedgecock 1978). However, these results were often obtained photographically with long exposures. A more practical dilution one may expect to see in the field is 1 in 1000.*

Tests conducted by this author on bloodstains ranging from fresh to several years old revealed that the luminol preparations exhibited strong luminescence on all samples equally well except the very fresh samples which exhibited little or no luminescence. Stains over 17-years old stored at room temperature produced luminescence. It is recommended that luminol *not* be used on very fresh stains (e.g., the day of the bloodshed) but rather wait a few days to allow for ample degradation of the heme. Pretreatment of the stains with hydrochloric acid (Ballou 1995) is not recommended as it may have deleterious effects on any subsequent typing attempts and appears to decrease sensitivity and increase the level of background luminescence (Lytle and Hedgecock 1978).

---

* This is the concensus derived from student's observations in classes conducted by the author.

Effects of Luminol on the Subsequent Analysis of Bloodstains

Generally, when luminol is used, it is because a visual search with the naked eye has not revealed any bloodstains. Keeping this in mind, if bloodstains are discovered with luminol, chances are that there is not a great deal of blood present. Further tests on bloodstains that have been sprayed with luminol have been performed with varying degrees of success.

A brief mention of luminol's effect on the typing of bloodstains appeared in Lytle and Hedgecock (1978). They mentioned that luminol does not prevent subsequent identification tests or ABO grouping but does interfere with erythrocyte acid phosphatase and phosphoglucomutase typing.*

Most studies with luminol have shown that the reagent does not interfere with subsequent confirmatory tests (Specht 1937; Proescher and Moody 1939; McGrath 1942). Duncan et al. (1986) studied the effects of superglue, ninhydrin, black powder and luminol on the subsequent analysis of bloodstains and found that luminol did not interfere with catalytic examinations, crystal tests for hemoglobin, species tests or ABO blood grouping by absorption elution. They reported that enzyme typing was affected with a weakening or destruction of the entire band pattern.

Grispino (1990) tested Specht's original luminol preparation and a modified formulation on many subsequent blood tests. He found, as before, that the reagents did not affect presumptive tests, hemochromogen crystal formation, or species testing by the precipitin method. He found that luminol treatment did diminish the ability to detect blood group antigens by absorption elution. Luminol also routinely denatured most blood enzymes he studied after a short exposure.

Laux (1991) studied the effects of two preparations of luminol, those of Grodsky et al. and Weber et al., on the subsequent analysis of bloodstains. The results were consistent with those observed by others. Luminol had no effect on further presumptive chemical tests, the Takayama confirmatory test, species identification by rocket electrophoresis, and ABO typing by absorption elution. Depending on the amount of blood detected by luminol and the manner in which it is collected, one may be able to determine the species origin and the ABO grouping of a sprayed bloodstain with the limiting factor being sample size.

Laux found that protein markers were affected by both preparations of luminol with a general decrease in band intensity. Phenotyping of bloodstains with the enzymes ESD, PGM, PGM subtyping, GLO, ADA, and AK was possible. The most deleterious effects of luminol were on the Group IV system with distortion of hemoglobin migration and decrease of PEPA and CA II bands to the point that they could not be typed.

---

* These were the only enzymes studied at the time.

Hochmeister et al. (1991) tested the effects of presumptive reagents on DNA typing of bloodstains and semen stains. Their results indicated that the amount of DNA yielded and its quality as typed by RFLP was the same from luminol treated bloodstains as uncontaminated controls.

Cresap et al. (1995) studied the effects of luminol and Coomassie Blue on DNA typing by PCR. Based on their study, luminol had no effect on the ability to obtain PCR results and "field investigators should feel free to use both luminol and Coomassie Blue as appropriate when searching a crime scene for bloodstains".

Keep in mind that luminol is generally used as an investigative tool in cases where bloodstains are not readily observed and is often used as a last resort. In such cases, there is probably not a sufficient amount of blood for more than a confirmatory test and perhaps species identification. Should luminol be used and lead one to pooled blood, spraying of these stains should be avoided. However, should large bloodstains become inadvertently sprayed with luminol, they should be allowed to dry completely and retained as research has shown that it may be possible to generate some useful serological information from them.

Photography

Shortly after the discovery of luminol and its recommended use in the detection of blood at crime scenes, it was apparent that photography of the distribution of blood was important. One of the first to obtain photographs of bloodstains with luminol was Specht (1937). Proescher and Moody (1939) briefly described photographing the luminol reaction.

Zweidinger et al. (1973) described the photographic parameters required to obtain both 35-mm photographs and Polaroid photographs using Polaroid Type 410 Trace Recording film (ASA 10,000). They noted that drawbacks existed in using Polaroid film to record luminescence including the fact that there is no permanent negative and no adjustments can be made in the length of exposure.

Lytle and Hedgecock (1978) photographed bloodstains they prepared on a variety of surfaces and cleaned up with soap and water. They obtained best results with Kodak Tri-X film developed in HC 110 developer. They used Nikon and Pentax 35-mm single-lens reflex cameras using 35- and 50-mm f/1.4 lenses. A 30-sec exposure often sufficed in capturing the luminescence. Longer exposures often resulted in overexposure of the luminol and in the swamping of the luminescence by ambient light under field conditions.

Thornton and Murdock (1977) made brief mention of making double exposures by placing a piece of cloth over the flash unit and exposing the negative again after recording the luminescence. Gimeno and Rini (1989) and Gimeno (1989) expanded on this technique describing detailed procedures for obtaining "fill-flash time exposures" which resulted in both the luminescence and the object being clearly visible in the resulting photograph. The photographs are dramatic when successful but practice is recommended before this method is tried in the field.

Niebauer et al. (1990) describes a more conventional way of obtaining luminol photographs, a method they refer to as a "film overlay negative system". In this method, the crime scene is recorded using ambient light (or flash) on one negative. The luminescence is recorded in total darkness on the next negative.

Critical to this technique is the use of a tripod and a luminescent ruler or target of known dimensions. This ensures that the two photographs are of the same area and can be directly compared.

Recently, rather good photographs have been obtained by many investigators by simply "bouncing" a flash off a nearby wall during the luminol exposure. This method adds a sufficient amount of light to visualize the object without washing out the luminescence (Color Plate 3).

Trial-and-error with your own equipment is simply the best way to succeed. The following procedures are to assist you in the set-up and actual photography of the bloodstain. They should be taken as starting points and used for guidance only.

1. Setup
   - A 35-mm camera with "bulb" setting is recommended. A fast 50-mm fixed lens is suggested. The f-stop should be at the lowest setting (i.e., the aperture is fully open) for luminol photographs. A shutter release cable should be attached to the camera.
   - A tripod is necessary for luminol photography. Fluorescent tape placed on the ends of the legs and near the top of the tripod helps to locate it in the dark. A flash unit should be attached to the camera for flash photos and be shut off or disconnected for the luminol photography.
   - Kodak T-Max 400 or Tri-Max Pan 400 black and white print films or color 400 ASA print films are acceptable.
2. Flash/Dark Sequence
   - A photograph of the object with a flash should be taken prior to the luminol photographs. The camera and flash should be prepared for a flash photograph. The camera lens should be parallel with the object being photographed. A fluorescent ruler or tape of known length must be in *both* the flash and luminol photographs.

- After the flash photograph is taken, the flash should be shut off or disconnected. The f-stop should be at the lowest setting. The camera should be set for "B" or bulb. The room is darkened, and the reagent is applied. Using the shutter release cable, the luminol photograph is obtained. The stain can be re-sprayed during the luminol photograph to enhance the reaction.

3. Exposure
   - Research by the author has shown that a 30 to 45 second exposure with one of the recommended films captured the luminescent image very well.*

Report Writing

The fact that the blood was found (verified by a confirmatory test) and the distribution of that blood should be stated in a precise and clear manner. Unusual features of the stains such as spatters, smears, pooling, footwear impressions, direction of travel, etc., should naturally appear in the report. The exact way in which the facts are put to written word is obviously up to the individual. The following examples of reports are to be used for guidance only.

- Application of luminol to the section of carpet submitted to the laboratory revealed the presence of luminescence in several areas. Chemical tests on extracts made from these areas were positive, however, species tests for human blood were negative.
- The examination of the interior of the vehicle with luminol revealed a luminescent pattern on the inside passenger window. Analysis of the pattern revealed it to be consistent with a high velocity spatter. Chemical and immunological analysis of the stain revealed the presence of type "A" human blood.
- Examination of the floor in the kitchen with luminol revealed the presence of stains extending from the stove to the doorway. These stains exhibited characteristics of a right tennis shoe with a suction-type pattern and lead from the stove towards the doorway. Chemical and immunological analysis of the stains revealed the presence of human blood.

---

* Luminescence of varying degrees was produced using a series of filters placed over pieces of luminescent tape. Photographs were taken with exposures from 1 sec to 120 sec. It was found that more of the fainter images were captured on film as the exposure times were increased up to 30 to 45 sec. Increasing the exposure time beyond this point did not increase the intensity of the luminescence obtained on film.

Testimony

The key here to remember is that luminol is a *presumptive* test for blood—nothing more. It is useful in that it not only indicates where blood is located but also patterns of blood distribution. Further analysis of the stain must be made before the stains can be called bloodstains.

Luminol has been accepted in court as a recognized tool in the detection of bloodstains. With knowledge and experience, it should be recognized by the investigator that luminol has an important role in the detection of bloodstains.

Case Studies

Case 1

Two female friends made arrangements for an evening out and one of the women went home to change. This was the last time the victim was seen. The next day, the daughter of the victim reported her mother's disappearance to the police.

The victim was married and authorities questioned her husband regarding his wife's disappearance. They were known to have had a stormy marital relationship. The husband stated that he had seen his wife leave their trailer home with a person in a red pick-up truck and that was the last time that he had seen her.

Examination of the inside of the victim's trailer commenced approximately one week after her disappearance (see Figures 7.9 to 7.12). The inside of the trailer was in disarray with clothes piled about and dirty dishes in the sink and on the table. No bloodstains were found during routine examination in daylight. When luminol was applied to the darkened living room, several areas of luminescence developed including marks on the surface of the couch cushions (Figure 7.10) and on the couch with the cushions removed (Figure 7.12). Enough blood was found on the couch to type the ABO group and several protein markers. Blood from the parents of the victim was typed and it was determined that the blood found on the couch could have originated from a child of the couple and was found in only 5% of the general population. The husband could not have been the source of the blood.

The husband was found guilty of murder. The body of the victim was never found. The finding of blood at the home was important in establishing that a crime had occurred. The fact that luminol demonstrated that the bloodstains had been cleaned up was important in linking the husband to the crime.

Figure 7.9   Photograph of the couch taken from the crime scene in Case 1.

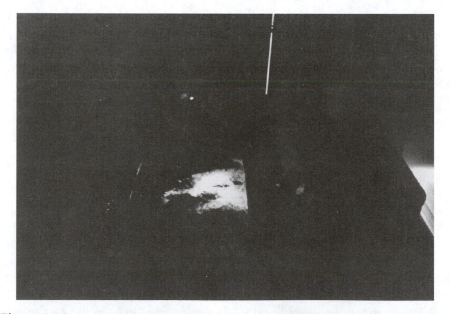

Figure 7.10   Luminol photograph of the souch in Figure 7.9 showing the distribution of blood over the surface of the cushions. Note the smeared blood on the center cushion and the partial handprint on the right cushion. The circle at the top of the couch is a penny that was used as a reference. This is not recommended; a luminescent ruler or tape should be used as a reference instead.

Figure 7.11 Photograph of the couch from the crime scene in Case 1 with the cushions removed.

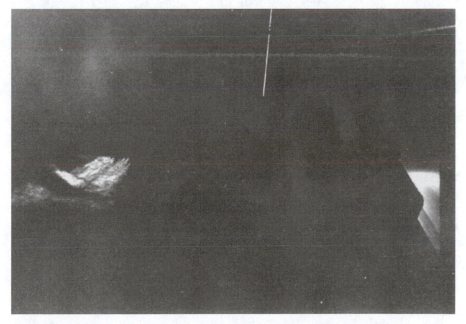

Figure 7.12 Luminol photograph of the couch in Figure 7.11 with the cushions removed. Note the attempts at cleaning and the smeared blood.

Case 2

(Contributed by James R. Wolfe, Alaska State Crime Lab.)

Alaska State Crime Lab personnel responded to a homicide in which the victim had died from numerous stab wounds. Examination of the victim's residence revealed evidence of a prolonged struggle in which a large amount of blood had been spattered throughout the living room. No visible bloody shoe impressions were located during the course of a detailed scene search. After completion of physical evidence collection, luminol was applied to the carpeted floors. Vivid, luminol-reactive shoe impressions were found leading from the bloodstained living room, down a hallway, and back to where a missing VCR had been located.

Close-up photographs of the individual shoe impressions were taken (Color Plate 4) along with overall views of the trail of shoe impressions (Color Plate 5). These shoe impressions were relatively unique in that they appeared to have been made by a cowboy boot with a deep "V" notch on the heel.

The scene search also located the empty box from which the missing VCR had come, with the respective serial number. This information was crucial in developing a suspect. Two days later, an Alaska State Trooper responded to a residential disturbance call at which the missing VCR was located in the suspect's bedroom. A female and male suspect were arrested. During booking, the male suspect tried to hide his cowboy boots which were found to have a hand-cut "V" on the heel (Color Plate 6). It was later discovered the male suspect had recently been released from a Colorado State penitentiary where notches had been cut.

Laboratory comparison of the luminol impressions at the scene to the suspect's boots confirmed the scene impressions were made by a boot of the same sole design with the same type of notch cut in the heel. Since the unknown impressions were all located on carpet, insufficient detail was present for a positive identification. However, graphic displays of the impressions and the boots at trial provided powerful circumstantial evidence not only linking the suspect to the scene, but also displaying his movements after the stabbing. The male suspect was convicted of first degree murder.

Case 3

(Contributed by Chris W. Beheim, Alaska Dept. of Public Safety
Scientific Crime Detection Lab.)

Alaska State Crime Laboratory personnel responded to the scene of a brutal double homicide in Nome, Alaska. The victims, a mother and her daughter, were found murdered in the bedroom of their residence. Both had been stabbed numerous times. A knife handle with a broken off blade was found on the floor next to the bodies. Autopsy results revealed that two different knives had been used during the assault.

The floor of the residence was processed with luminol and a trail of latent footwear impressions was developed (Color Plate 7). These impressions led from the bedroom into an area of the kitchen where knives were stored. The impressions then led back into the bedroom. Impressions on the kitchen floor showed the best detail and close up photographs were taken (Color Plates 8 and 9).

A suspect was later apprehended and his shoes were submitted to the laboratory for comparison to the luminol photographs. Test impressions made from the suspect's shoes matched the luminol impressions with respect to size and outsole tread design. One of the luminol photographs exhibited sufficient detail as to show accidental characteristics from a small cut located on the edge of the suspect's right shoe.

The footwear impressions visualized by luminol proved to be the crucial piece of evidence in this case as the suspect later admitted to being in the residence but adamantly denied ever entering the kitchen. He later pled guilty to the crimes.

References

Albrecht, H.O. 1928. Uber die Chemiluminescenz des Aminophthalaurehydrazids. *Z. Phys. Chem. (Leipzig)*, 136:321–330.

Ballou, S.M. 1995. Moves of Murder. *Journal of Forensic Sciences*, 40(4): 675–680.

Cresap, T.R., et.al. 1995. The Effects of Luminol and Coomassie Blue on DNA Typing by PCR. Presented at the 47th annual American Academy of Forensic Sciences Meeting, Seattle, WA.

Duncan, G.T., Seiden, H., Vallee, L., and Ferraro, D. 1986. Effects of Superglue, Other Fingerprint Developing Agents, and Luminol on Bloodstain Analysis. *Journal Assoc. Anal. Chem.*, 69(4):677–680.

Erdey, L., Pickering, W.F., and Wilson, C.L. 1962. Mixed Chemiluminescent Indicators. *Talanta*, 9:371–375.

Gaensslen, R.E. 1983. *Sourcebook in Forensic Serology, Immunology, and Biochemistry*, Superintendent of Documents, U.S. Government Printing Office, Washington, DC.

Gill, S.K. 1983. New Developments in Chemiluminescence Research. *Aldrichimica Acta*, 16:59–61.

Gimeno, F.E. 1989. Fill Flash Color Photography to Photograph Luminol Bloodstain Patterns. *Journal Forensic Identification*, 39:305–306.

Gimeno, F.E. and Rini, G.A. 1989. Fill Flash Photo Luminescence to Photograph Luminol Blood Stain Patterns. *Journal Forensic Identification*, 39:149–156.

Gleu, K. and Pfannstiel, K. 1936. Uber 3-Aminophthalsaure-hydrazid. *J. Prakt. Chem.*, 146:137–150.

Grispino, R.R.J. 1990. The Effect of Luminol on the Serological Analysis of Dried Human Bloodstains. *Crime Laboratory Digest*, 17(1):13–23.

Grodsky, M., Wright, K., and Kirk, P.L. 1951. Simplified Preliminary Blood Testing. An Improved Technique and Comparative Study of Methods. *J. Crim. Law Criminol. Police Science*, 42:95–104.

Gundermann, K.D. 1965. Chemiluminescence in Organic Compounds. *Angewandte Chemie* (International Edition), 4:566–573.

Hochmeister, M.N., Budowle, B., and Baechtel, F.S. 1991. Effects of Presumptive Test Reagents on the Ability to Obtain Restriction Fragment Length Polymorphism (RFLP) Patterns from Human Blood and Semen Stains. *Journal of Forensic Sciences*, 36(3): 656–661.

Huntress, E.H., Stanley, L.N., and Parker, A.S. 1934. The Preparation of 3-Aminophthalhydrazide For Use in The Demonstration of Chemilumines-cence. *J. Amer. Chem. Soc.*, 56:241–242.

Laux, D.L. 1991. Effects of Luminol on the Subsequent Analysis of Bloodstains. *Journal of Forensic Sciences*, 36(5):1512–1520.

Lytle, L.T. and Hedgecock, D.G. 1978. Chemiluminescence in the Visualization of Forensic Bloodstains. *Journal of Forensic Sciences*, 23:550–555.

McGrath, J. 1942. The Chemical Luminescence Test For Blood. *British Medical Journal*, 2:156–157.

Niebauer, J.C., Booth, J.B., and Brewer, B.L. 1990. Recording Luminol Lumines-cence in its Context Using a Film Overlay Method. *J. Forensic Ident.*, 40(5):271–278.

Proescher, F. and Moody, A.M. 1939. Detection of Blood By Means of Chemilumi-nescence. *J. Lab. and Clin. Med.*, 24:1183–1189.

Specht, W. 1937. The Chemiluminescence of Hemin: An Aid For Finding and Rec-ognizing Blood Stains Important For Forensic Purposes. *Angewante Chemie*, 50:155–157.

Tamamushi, B. and Akiyama, H. 1938. Mechanism of the Chemiluminescence of 3-aminophthalhydrazide. *Zeitschrift Fuer Physikalische Chemie*, 38: 400–406.

Thornton, J.I. and Maloney, R.S. 1985. The Chemistry of the Luminol Reac-tion—Where to From Here? *Calif. Assoc. Crim. Newsletter*, Sept:9–16.

Thornton, J.I. and Murdock, J.E. 1977. Photography of Luminol Reaction in Crime Scenes. *Criminol.*, 10(37):15–19.

Weber, K. 1966. Die Anwendung der Chemiluminescenz des Luminols in der ger-ichtlichen Medizin und Toxicologie. I. Der Nachweis von Blutspuren. *Z. Gesamte Gerichtl. Med.*, 57:410–423.

White, E.H. 1961. The Chemiluminescence of Luminol. In: *Light and Life*, ed. W.D. McElroy and B. Glass. Johns Hopkins Press, Baltimore, MD, pp. 183–195.

White, E.H. and Bursey, M. M. 1964. Chemiluminescence of Luminol and Related Hydrazides: The Light Emission Step. *J. Amer. Chem Soc.*, 86: 941–942.

Zweidinger, R.A., Lytle, L.T., and Pitt, C.G. 1973. Photography of Bloodstains Visualized By Luminol. *Journal of Forensic Sciences*, 18:296–302.

Case Studies in Bloodstain Pattern Interpretation

8

STUART H. JAMES

The following presentations of cases have been selected for their value and contribution to the application and understanding of bloodstain pattern interpretation as a tool for the reconstruction of events that occurred during and subsequent to bloodshed at death scenes in cases of gunshot, blunt force, and cutting/stabbing injuries. These cases were investigated for law enforcement agencies, prosecutors, or defense attorneys in various areas of the country and abroad, with court testimony provided in many instances. The interpretation of the bloodstains, and reconstruction of events, are based on a combination of scene examination and/or review of scene photographs and other documentation including autopsy reports and photographs and crime laboratory reports provided by the law enforcement agency involved.

It is the position of the authors that the interpretation of bloodstains from photographs, without the benefit of scene examination, should be conservative. Photographs do not always depict the entire scene nor all of the bloodstains that may be present. They may be of varying quality in terms of exposure and distortion and unfortunately do not always contain a scale of reference or measuring device. It is also imperative to correlate observed bloodstains with autopsy findings and all physical evidence especially the serological studies of the collected blood samples. This chapter describes 18 cases including 12 which have occurred since the first edition of *The Interpretation of Bloodstain Evidence at Crime Scenes* by Eckert and James in 1989, and 6 which have been retained from the prior text because of their interpretative value.

Gunshot: Case 1

A young man and his live-in girlfriend, who had a documented history of domestic disputes, were seen arguing and drinking heavily in a neighborhood bar. They left together at closing time.

Figure 8.1   View of the victim in a sitting position with upper body and head leaned forward.

Early the following morning, the boyfriend called police to report that his girlfriend had apparently shot herself during the night while they slept together in the same bed. He denied any involvement in the shooting and further related to police that he slept through the night and did not hear a gunshot.

Police arrived at the scene and found the victim in the bedroom of the apartment. She was observed to be in a sitting position on the left side of the bed with her feet on the floor and her upper body and head leaned forward between her legs. Her arms and hands were draped in front of her close to the floor. A small caliber revolver was present on the floor between her left hand and left foot. (Figure 8.1) A gunshot entrance wound was present above her right eye with a heavy concentration of soot within the periphery of the wound (Figure 8.2). There was no exit wound. Blood originating from the wound had dripped downward onto the left foot and floor and created numerous satellite spatters of blood on the palmar surface of the right hand (Figure 8.3). The great toe area of the right foot had showed similar satellite spatters of blood. A large pool of partially clotted blood had accumulated on the floor in the area beneath the weapon. The left hand showed moderately heavy bloodstaining on the left thumb and forefinger as well as numerous satellite spatters on the inner lateral and ventral aspects of the hand (Figure 8.4). To the left of the left hand on the floor was a Semicide® wrapper which also showed numerous satellite spatters of blood. The satellite spatters on the left hand and wrapper had resulted from blood dripping into

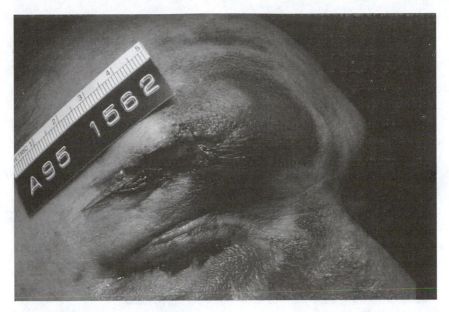

Figure 8.2 Gunshot wound of entrance above the right eye of the victim with an abundance of soot present.

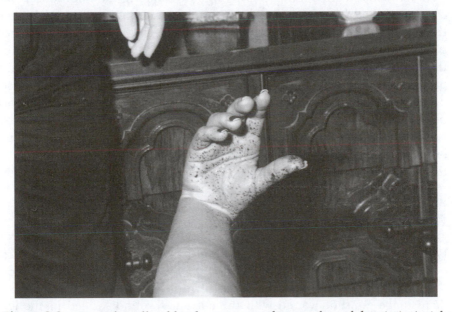

Figure 8.3 View of satellite blood spatter on palmar surface of the victim's right hand.

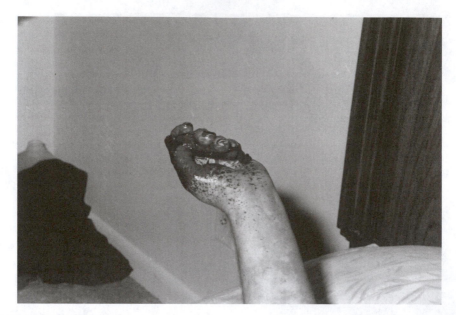

Figure 8.4 View of the left forearm and hand of victim showing bloodstained thumb and fingers with satellite blood spatter on base of the thumb and wrist.

blood. However, the observed positions of the left hand and the wrapper were not consistent with blood dripping into blood in that location. It was concluded that the left hand and the wrapper were moved to the left after the deposition of the satellite spatter occurred. This conclusion is further supported by the presence of a void area on the left edge of the toe area of the left foot which is consistent with the original position of the left hand partially over the left foot (Figure 8.5) They were in that position when blood dripped onto them and created the satellite spatter. No satellite spatter was observed on the weapon. Based upon these facts, it was concluded that the left hand was moved away from the left foot subsequent to blood dripping onto the hands creating the satellite and the weapon was later placed between them in an effort to stage a suicide.

Gunshot Injuries: Case 2

Police were called to the scene of a fatal shooting of a black male which occurred in the residence of his girlfriend in a suburban area of a city on the west coast (Figure 8.6). Death was attributed to a penetrating intermediate range gunshot wound with the entrance wound located in the left posterior parietal scalp. A distorted copper jacketed large caliber projectile was retrieved from the superior right temporal lobe of the brain. The path

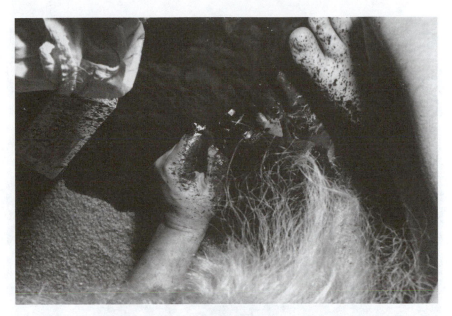

Figure 8.5 View taken from above head of victim showing the satellite blood spatter on the right toe area, blood on left toe with visible void on top surface of left foot. The firearm is located between the left hand and left foot.

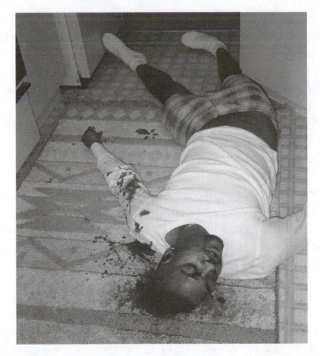

Figure 8.6 Victim on the floor of the kitchen to the right of the oven.

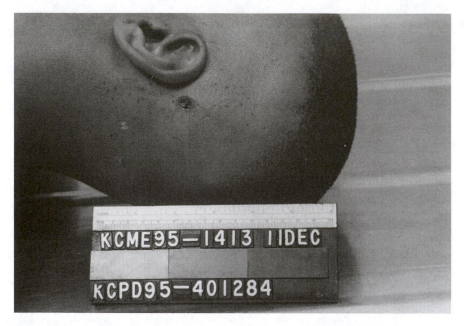

Figure 8.7 Location of the entrance wound behind the left ear, with considerable stippling around wound site.

of the projectile was determined to be left to right, back to front with a slightly upward inclination. An oval area of stippling measuring approximately 4 × 3 3/4 inches surrounded the entrance wound (Figure 8.7).

Further investigation into the circumstances of this death revealed that the victim was a cocaine dealer who was engaged in an argument with one of his buyers regarding payment for a recent transaction. It was alleged that the victim verbally threatened the family of the drug user whereupon the user produced a weapon and fired a single shot into the head of the drug dealer. Based upon the location of blood spatters on surfaces close to the floor it was suspected that the shooting was execution style with the victim on his knees rather than standing as the suspect related in his statement to the police. The suspect was arrested and charged with first-degree murder.

The scene of this homicide was the kitchen of the residence. The victim was lying on his back in front of an oven. According to the victim's girlfriend, the oven door was often partially ajar with the oven on to provide additional heating for the kitchen.

The oven door was completely open and parallel to the floor (Figure 8.8). Blood transfer stains were present on the left arm and hand of the victim. Small circular to oval-shaped blood spatters with a downward directionality were present on the lower portion of the oven and the right side adjacent kitchen cabinet door to a height of approximately 13 inches above the floor

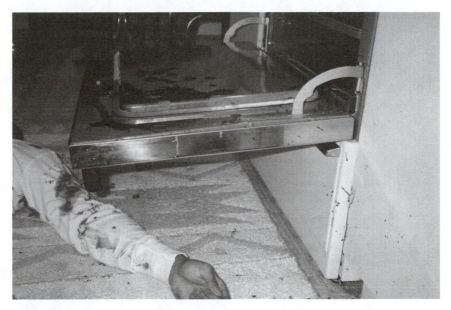

Figure 8.8 View of the open oven door in relation to the left arm and hand of the victim.

(Figures 8.9 A and B). A smaller but similar bloodstain pattern was observed to the left of the open oven door on the lower left side adjacent kitchen cabinet (Figure 8.10).

The inside horizontal surface of the open oven door shows a pooling of blood which is somewhat altered by an object contacting the bloody surface. Additionally there is an extensive drip pattern of blood with surrounding satellite blood spatter on the inside of the oven door. Many of the large, circular bloodstains contain spine-like projections indicating a directionality to the left of the open oven door. An elongated angular bloodstain with a downward directionality located on the right side of the open oven door nearest the oven indicated that the oven door was only partially ajar at the time that stain was deposited. That stain also showed some horizontal motion from right to left as one would face the oven (Figure 8.11 A and B). Drips of blood from a source above have been deposited on the left side of the open oven door close to the oven (Figure 8.12).

It was concluded that the blood spatters on the lower kitchen cabinetry to the left and right of the open oven door were not high-velocity impact spatters created by gunshot. The victim initially bled from his head wound when the source of blood was above the oven door permitting blood to drip onto that surface for a period of time. The initial bloodshed occurred when the oven door was just partially ajar and the remainder of the blood was deposited with the oven door in the observed horizontal position. As the victim was falling

Figure 8.9 (A, B) Small blood spatters, showing downward directionality, on the lower portion of the oven and the right side of the adjacent kitchen cabinet.

from right to left relative to the oven to his final position it is likely that his arm or hand contacted the oven door and caused the previously deposited blood to spatter. This type of activity as well as the creation of satellite blood spatter from blood dripping into blood likely produced the small spatters of blood that were present on the lower cabinetry on both sides of the oven. The

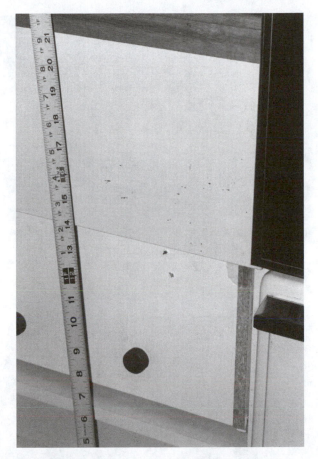

Figure 8.10 Small blood spatters to the left of the oven door on adjacent kitchen cabinet.

final position of the victim was not considered to be a likely position to assume from a kneeling position after receiving the fatal shot. However, due to the absence of high-velocity impact blood spatter, the exact position of the victim at the time the shot was fired could not be determined. The defendant pled guilty to second-degree murder just prior to trial. This case demonstrates again that small spatters of blood in the size range of medium- to high-velocity impact blood spatters can be created by events other than gunshot.

Gunshot Injuries: Case 3

Police responded to a 911 call from a grandmother who upon returning to her residence which she shared with her daughter and grandson found them dead in a bunk bed in the child's room (Figure 8.13). The boy was in the

Figure 8.11 **(A, B)** Drip pattern of blood on the inside of the open oven door with angular bloodstain on lower right inside edge of oven door.

upper bunk with the blanket and sheet pulled up to his shoulders in a normal, prone sleeping position. The right side of his head rested on his right wrist and his left hand was beneath his nose and mouth. A contact gunshot wound was present in the center of his forehead (Figure 8.14). The projectile exited the rear of the head and re-entered his right arm (Figure 8.15).

Figure 8.12 Drops of blood deposited on left inside edge of oven door.

Figure 8.13 Young boy on upper bunk and mother on lower bunk in bedroom, each with a gunshot wound of the head.

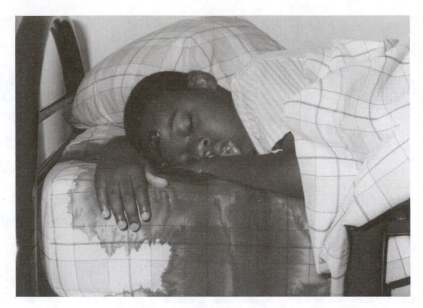

Figure 8.14   View of young boy in sleeping position with entrance wound in center of forehead.

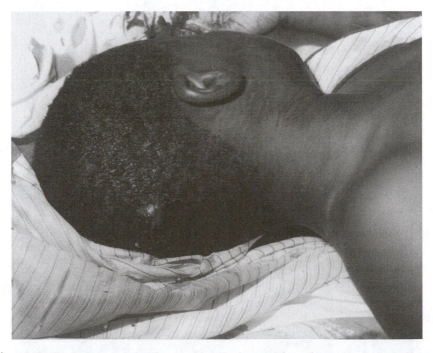

Figure 8.15   Exit wound at back of head of young boy through which bullet re-entered his right arm.

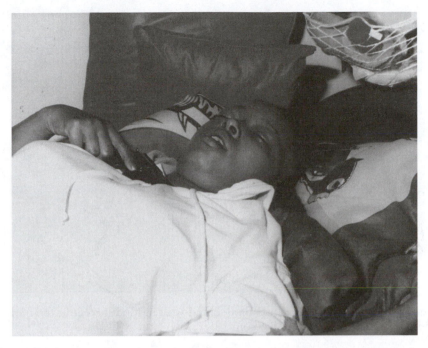

Figure 8.16   View of mother in lower bunk with the weapon beneath right hand.

The mother of the young boy was located in the lower bunk on her back in the opposite direction of her son. She sustained a single contact wound of the right side of her head within the hairline with a revolver on her upper front chest with her right hand resting over the right side of the weapon. High-velocity back spatter was absent from her right hand and none was observed on the revolver or the immediate area of her head (Figure 8.16).

On the wall and a doll on the bed at the feet of the mother there was a bloodstain pattern which proved to be the blood of her son who was in the upper bunk (Figure 8.17). This appeared initially to investigators to be high-velocity impact spatter which suggested to them that the son was shot in the lower bunk and placed in the upper bunk afterwards. However, there was no bloodstain evidence to indicate that the child had been moved after bloodshed, but shot in the position in which he was initially found. The physical evidence and postmortem examinations of the victims were consistent with a homicide/suicide but the explanation of this bloodstain pattern remained unresolved.

Further review of this case showed substantial bleeding had occurred on the upper bunk which accumulated around and beneath the child (Figure 8.18). It was evident that blood had flowed over the head of the upper bunk forward of the boy's head and dripped downward. The railing of the lower

Figure 8.17 Bloodstain pattern on doll and wall beyondthe feet of the mother, which proved to be blood of her son.

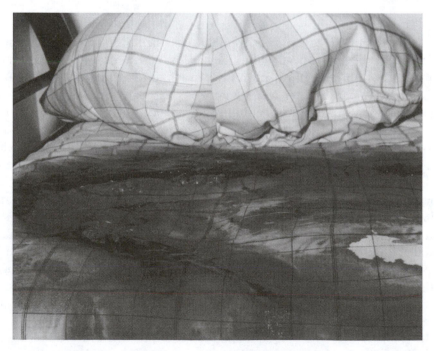

Figure 8.18 Blood accumulation on upper bunk, below head and shoulders of the young boy.

Figure 8.19 Bloodstain pattern on wall opposite lower bunk railing on which blood had dripped producing satellite blood spatter.

bunk forward of the feet of the mother was the target for this dripping blood. The blood droplets struck this railing at a rapid rate and created a large quantity of satellite spatter which impacted the adjacent wall. Opposite to and above the rail, many of the blood spatters were circular to oval in shape within a size range of medium- to high-velocity blood spatter (Figure 8.19). Below this area the pattern extended downward on the wall in an elongated streaking fashion. There were numerous overlapping bloodstains where droplets had struck previously deposited bloodstains (Figure 8.20). This bloodstain pattern was not high-velocity impact blood spatter as previously thought by investigators but rather a low-velocity event that created many small bloodstains in that particular size range. It was important to visualize the entire bloodstained area which in this case readily explained the mechanism that created a very unusual pattern that was initially misinterpreted. This led investigators to suspect that the case was a double homicide. The case was finally ruled a homicide/suicide. A background investigation of the mother revealed that she had recently been diagnosed with incurable cancer and was despondent over the future of herself and her son. Apparently she did not want to burden the grandmother with raising the child. The strange twist of this case was that the postmortem examination of the mother did not reveal any evidence of existing malignancy.

Figure 8.20 Lower portion of the same satellite bloodstain pattern showing more elongated bloodstains.

Gunshot Injuries: Case 4

The victim, in this case a 35-year-old white female, resided with her boyfriend in a small, single-level home where several incidents of domestic violence fueled by excessive alcohol consumption and use of marijuana had been reported in the past. The couple argued and fought frequently as described by their friends and neighbors in an otherwise quiet neighborhood. On the night of the fatal incident, the boyfriend placed a call to 911 to report that his girlfriend had been shot. Police and paramedics responded immediately to the scene. The victim was located on the living room floor near the kitchen being held by the boyfriend in a partially upright position as he was attempting mouth to mouth resuscitation. The victim was given emergency treatment at the scene and transported to a local hospital where she was pronounced dead.

Postmortem examination of the victim revealed a single shotgun wound of entrance in the sternal area of the chest with a wound trajectory of front to back and slightly right to left horizontally (Figures 8.21 and 8.22). The victim was clad in a turquoise-colored sweatshirt and blue jeans. A defect in the front chest area of the sweatshirt corresponded to the entrance wound.

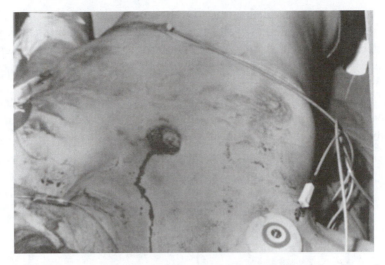

Figure 8.21   Shotgun wound of entrance in the sternal area of the chest of victim.

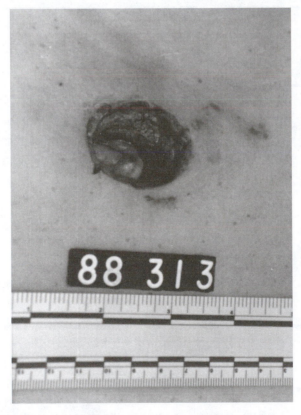

Figure 8.22   Close-up view of the shotgun wound of entrance determined to have been inflicted from greater than two feet and less than five feet in distance.

X-ray examination revealed numerous shotgun pellets in the right pleural cavity identified as #6 shot. Powder-pattern tests performed on the sweatshirt using the Central Arms, 12-gauge, double-barreled shotgun and Winchester, 12-gauge #6 shot shell revealed the muzzle to target distance to be greater than two feet and less than five feet.

The scene of this shooting was measured and photographed in detail by the investigating agency (Figure 8.23). The physical layout of the premises is described as follows: the front entrance on the south side of the house opened

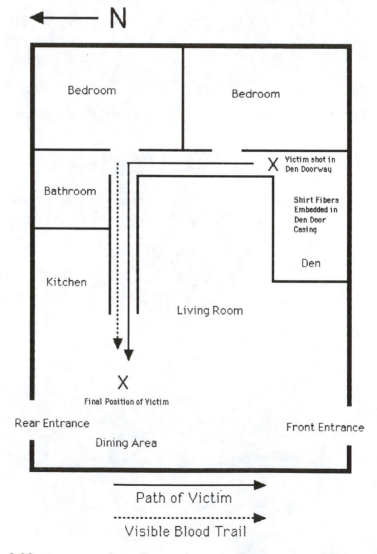

Figure 8.23 Diagram of residence where shooting occured showing path of victim and visible blood trail. Not drawn to scale.

into a living room with the rear entrance and kitchen on the north side of the residence. The victim was located in the living room near the entranceway to the kitchen. Extending to the east from her location on the living room floor was a hallway which led to the master bedroom and bathroom at the northeast end of the house. At this point, the hallway turned at a right angle to the south and terminated at the entrance to the den. A second bedroom was located adjacent to the den in the southeast corner of the house.

Photographs of the scene showed the shotgun and two knives on the hallway floor between the den and the bathroom (Figure 8.24). The bloodstain patterns photographed in this case are confined to the L-shaped hallway and the floor of the living room. The final position of the victim was established to be the floor of the living room. It was also concluded that this was the only area in which she was on the floor subsequent to receiving the fatal shotgun wound. The central issue in this case was the determination of the location of the victim at the time the shot was fired relative to the position of the boyfriend who admitted firing the fatal shot, stating it was self defense. He described to the police that his girlfriend threatened him with a knife in each hand. As she advanced towards him in this manner, he retreated to his den in the southeast

Figure 8.24 The shotgun and the knife on the hallway floor.

corner of the house and grabbed his shotgun from a rack on the wall. When she advanced into the doorway of the den he fired in self defense since he was trapped in the den. As she stumbled backwards into the hallway he grabbed her before she fell and dragged her down the hallway to the living room floor where he attempted mouth to mouth resuscitation before calling 911.

The interpretation of the bloodstains in the hallway by the investigators indicated to them that the shooting occurred in the hallway near the master bedroom and the bathroom with the boyfriend located down the hallway nearer to the living room. This would have permitted the boyfriend a means of retreat and escape from the premises.

The theory of sequence of events by the investigators was enhanced by the lack of blood in the hallway between the den and the master bedroom and their interpretation of high-velocity bloodstains on the hallway floor between the master bedroom and the bathroom. In this area as well as on the bathroom door were small circular to oval bloodstains measuring 0.5 to 2.0 ml in diameter which are typically produced as the result of exhaled blood droplets (Figure 8.25). There was also a blood transfer pattern on the tiled hallway floor in this area consistent with having been produced by a left hand wet with blood with evidence of fingers wiping through the blood while it was still wet on the floor (Figure 8.26 A and B).On the hallway floor on the north side leading to the living room is a series of blood drip patterns and projected bloodstains which lead to the final position of the victim on the living room floor (Figure 8.27 A and B).

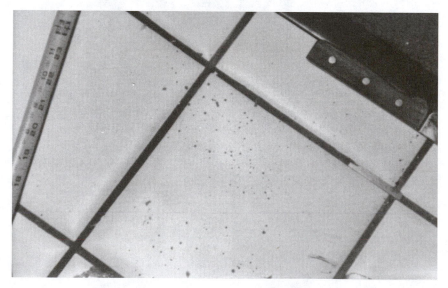

Figure 8.25 Exhaled bloodstain pattern on hallway floor near the knife and shotgun.

Figure 8.26 (**A**) Blood transfer pattern consistent with that produced by a blood-ied left hand. (**B**) Close-up view of blood transfer pattern consistent with left hand with an exhaled bloodstain pattern to the left of the transfer pattern.

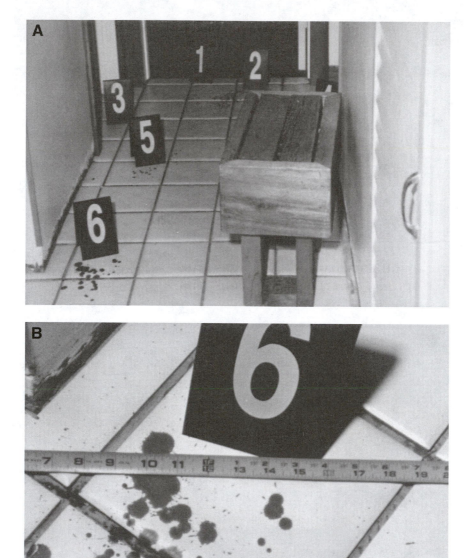

Figure 8.27 (A) Series of drip patterns of blood on the hallway floor leading to the living room of the residence. (B) Close-up view of drip pattern of blood on the hallway floor.

Subsequent to the police investigation, the boyfriend was arrested and charged with second-degree murder. Although maintaining his version of self-defense, he eventually pled guilty to a lesser charge of manslaughter. Prior to sentencing, the crime scene, the police photographs, and physical evidence were re-examined at his request by a private forensic scientist. The bloodstains at the scene were relatively intact since the bloodstained areas were protected by a plastic covering and were not appreciably altered. The living room, hallway as well as entrances to the bathroom, bedrooms and the den were tested with luminol and phenolphthalein to locate any latent bloodstained areas. A possible trace of blood was located on the carpet in the den just inside the doorway. Examination of the hallway floor near the entrance to the den revealed some tiny clumps of turquoise fibers. Similar tiny clumps of turquoise fibers were discovered on the carpet within the den within a radius of approximately 2 feet in from the doorway (Figure 8.28).

Figure 8.28 View of hallway looking from the doorway of the den towards the bedrooms and the bathroom.

Examination of the casing of the doorway of the den revealed the east side casing to be free of blood or fibers. Examination of the west side casing in an area between 4' 9" and 5' 6" above the floor revealed numerous clumps of turquoise fibers adhering to the enamel paint. Some of these fibers were embedded into the paint (Figures 8.29 and 8.30). Sterile saline swabs taken

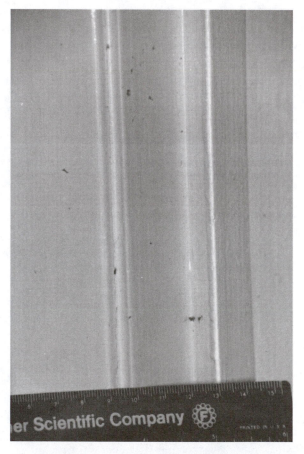

Figure 8.29 Clumps of turquoise fibers embedded into the paint of the west side of the den door casing.

on this area on the door casing produced a positive reaction with phenolphthalein. A clean control area was negative for blood. Samples of the turquoise fibers were collected from the den carpet near the door, the hallway floor near den doorway and the casing of the den door. These fibers were examined microscopically and compared to fibers from the turquoise sweatshirt worn by the victim and were found to be indistinguishable and were consistent with having a common source.

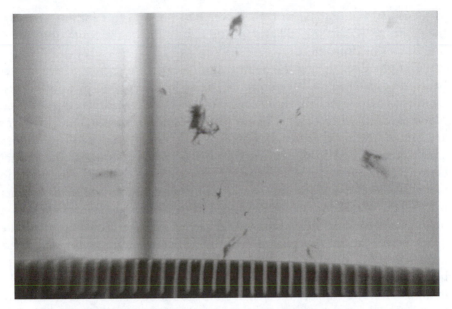

Figure 8.30   Close-up view of ihe embedded turquoise fibers.

Based upon these findings, it was concluded that the victim was most likely standing in the doorway of the den facing inward and very close to the west side den door casing. The shotgun pellets passed through her turquoise sweatshirt and into the right side of her chest. Clumps of turquoise fibers from the entrance wound site of her sweatshirt were projected with explosive force into the enamel surface of the west den door casing. Turquoise fibers were also deposited on the den carpet and the hallway floor near the entrance-way to the den.

The relative lack of bloodstains at the entrance to the den may be explained by the nature of the wound, the clothing worn by the victim and the muzzle to target distance from which the shot was fired. This type of trauma produces an open pneumothorax or sucking chest wound which produces negative intrapleural pressure during inspiration and expansion of the chest reducing external bleeding. There was no doubt extensive internal bleeding. External bleeding may also be minimized by the placing of a hand over the wound site as a victim would reflexively do, compressing the wound like a pressure dressing. Clothing will also absorb considerable blood from a wound before the blood is deposited on nearby surfaces.

High-velocity impact blood spatter was not observed in this case. The production of back spatter from a single entrance wound is dependent upon several factors. Back spatter may not be seen associated with wounds of the chest or abdomen. The muzzle to target distance is usually contact to close range for significant back spatter to occur. In this case, the muzzle to target distance was determined to be between 2 to under 5 ft. Clothing covering the entrance wound site will also greatly reduce the quantity of back spatter due to its shielding effect.

The blood spatter on the hallway floor near the entrance to the master bedroom as well as the bathroom door initially interpreted by police investigators as high velocity is more consistent with spatter produced by exhaled blood droplets when there is injury to the respiratory tract. These patterns are sometimes misinterpreted as high velocity due to the size of the stains. The victim moved from the entranceway of the den towards the master bedroom and bathroom while exhaling small droplets of blood. Her left hand wet with blood from previous contact with her chest wound made contact with the hallway floor near the entrance to the master bedroom. The blood flow from the victim created drip patterns and some projected blood on the north side of the hallway leading to the living room. Examination of her blue jeans showed a blood flow pattern present on her left side consistent with her proceeding backwards and possibly being assisted down the hall to the living room. The transfer bloodstains on the mouth, chest, and trousers of the boyfriend are consistent with touching the victim while she was bleeding as well as the administration of mouth to mouth resuscitation (Figure 8.31).

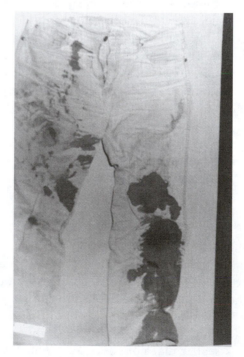

Figure 8.31 The trousers of the boyfriend showing bloodstained areas following of mouth to mouth resuscitation and contact with the victim subsequent to the shooting.

The case was presented to a grand jury which decided that the boyfriend had acted in self defense in the den and dismissed the case. Under the former plea bargain, the boyfriend was facing up to seven years in state prison. Six months after gaining his freedom, the boyfriend was killed in a one-car vehicular accident that was alcohol-related. A strange twist of fate, to say the least.

Gunshot Injuries: Case 5

After a short courtship and tumultuous marriage, a wealthy surgeon chose to file for divorce. The property settlement and alimony were in dispute, due to the wife's request for additional cash. When the husband failed to respond to pages by his associates over a weekend period, his secretary notified the local authorities. Police were dispatched to the residence where they were met by the wife. She stated she had not seen or heard from her estranged husband for the past three days. Police then asked for permission to search the home. During this period of time the wife ventured into the basement den. Police in the house heard her exclaim "He's down here, and he's not breathing!"

The husband was discovered on a couch in the basement, dead from a gunshot wound to the head (Figure 8.32). Postmortem examination revealed the victim to be a 55-year old white male weighing approximately 261 pounds and measuring approximately 6 ft 5 in. in height. Rigor mortis had largely

Figure 8.32 View of the victim positioned on couch in the basement den.

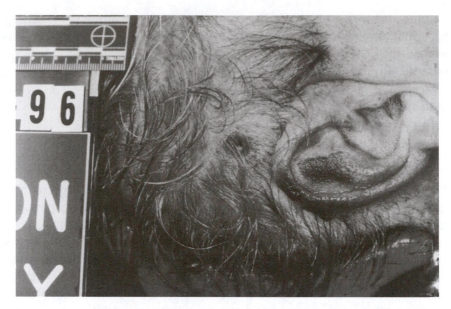

Figure 8.33 Gunshot wound of entrance on the right side of the head above the ear showing soot deposition and burning of the ear skin.

dissipated and livor mortis was fixed primarily on the left side of the victim. A gunshot wound of entrance was present on the right side of the head located 3/4 of an inch above the superior attachment of the right ear, measuring 3/16 of an inch in diameter. Stippling was noted on the skin up to one inch from the entrance wound. There was a zone of soot deposition and burning of the skin on the pinna of the ear (Figure 8.33). A .38-caliber projectile was recovered slightly left of the medial canthus of the left eye, 1 1/2 inches left of the midline and 1 inch above the nasion. The path of the projectile was from the right to the left, and back to front. A separate wound track extended anteriorly toward the lateral aspect of the right eye terminating in a small laceration above and behind the right eye. A projectile fragment is recovered from this area.

At the scene, the victim was observed to be fully clad in shirt, trousers, and socks with his shoes on the carpet nearby. He was resting on his left side, his head on a pillow on the arm of the couch with his legs resting on the floor at the midsection of the couch in front of a coffee table. His arms were extended outward from his upper body, with his right arm resting over the left and his hands draped over the edge of the couch (Figure 8.34). Evidence of a second gunshot is present on the couch cushion near his arms. This is characterized by a perforation in the cushion surrounded by an area of soot (Figure 8.35). A .38 revolver rested on the carpet below his hand at the right side of his body. The livor mortis displayed a prominent pattern in the left hand but was not present in the right hand (Figure 8.36). This pattern did

Figure 8.34 Close view of victim on couch showing position of arms draped over edge. Note area of soot on cushion to the right of the left hand of victim.

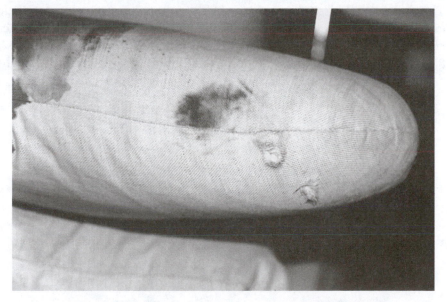

Figure 8.35 Closer view of area of soot deposition with perforations in cushion.

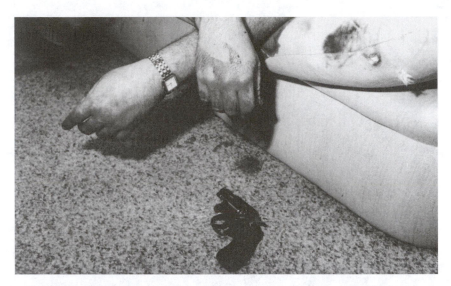

Figure 8.36 Dependent livor mortis on the left hand of victim.

not coincide with the position in which the victim was found and indicated movement of the hand subsequent to the fixing of the livor mortis.

The bloodstain patterns observed in this case also demonstrated that the position of the victim was altered after the injury and bloodshed had occurred. The victim was alive long enough to exhale blood and produce a characteristic expirated bloodstain pattern on the palmar surface of his right hand, inner right arm, shirt, and trousers as well as on the couch cushion (Figures 8.37, 8.38, 8.39, 8.40). The exhaled bloodstains on the palmar surface of the right

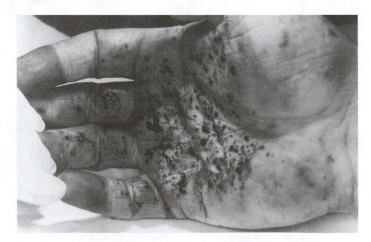

Figure 8.37 Expirated bloodstain pattern on the palmar surface of the victim's right hand.

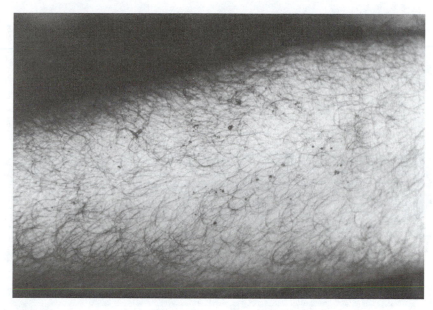

Figure 8.38   Expirated bloodstain pattern on the inside of vthe ictim's right arm.

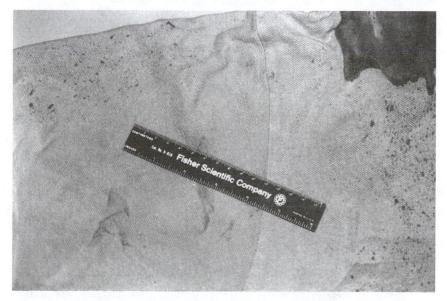

Figure 8.39   Expirated bloodstain pattern on the right side of the victim's shirt.

Figure 8.40   Expirated bloodstain pattern on the couch cushion near victim's head.

hand must have been produced when the hand was close to the facial area of
the victim as he was exhaling blood. Some blood had spattered back onto the
face of the victim. In addition, a transfer pattern of blood on the dorsal side
of the right hand indicated contact with an area wet with blood prior to its
final position. Upon removal of the victim, a small spatter of blood was
observed beneath the victim, which could not have reached that location from
the present position of the body. Also observed on the cushion beneath the
head of the victim was a greenish discoloration of the dried bloodstain indicating a considerable length of time since its deposition. On the front edge
of the couch there were several projected, partially clotted bloodstains which
were produced at least three to fifteen minutes after bloodshed. There are also
some unclotted bloodstains on the edge of the cushion which appear to have
been wiped by something with a right to left motion before they dried (Figures
8.41 and 8.42). These bloodstains could not have been produced by any
activity of the victim himself but rather by another person or activity. Some
of these stains were not visible until after the pressure of the victim was
released from the cushions, again indicating movement of the victim prior
to his final position. There was no high-velocity spatter present on the surface
of the couch or other nearby surfaces to assist with the determination of the
position of the victim at the time he received his fatal gunshot wound. However, a small blood flow pattern from the right forehead wound created by a
portion of the projectile was consistent with the present observed position of
the victim's head on the pillow (Figure 8.43).

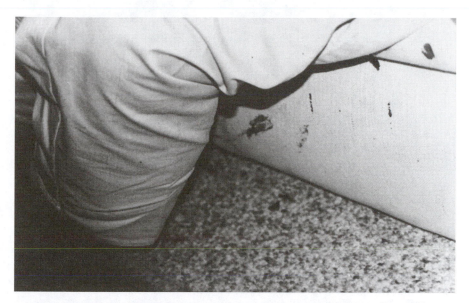

Figure 8.41 Partially clotted and unclotted projected bloodstains on front edge of couch behind victim's left leg.

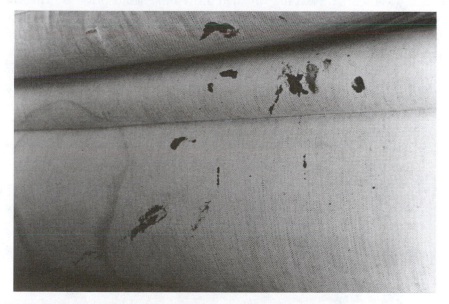

Figure 8.42 Closer view of partially clotted and unclotted projected bloodstains on front edge of couch behind victim's left leg.

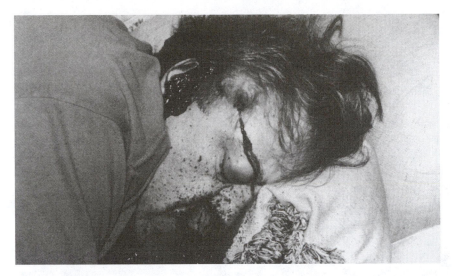

Figure 8.43   Blood flow pattern on the right side of the victim's head.

The second gunshot was of considerable interest in this case since it is known that individuals intent on suicide occasionally test-fire a weapon prior to the fatal discharge. In addition, based upon the movement of the victim's hands and the presence of gunshot residue on his hands as contended by the state, it was theorized that the wife had moved his hands prior to firing the second shot. This movement would have been necessitated in order to produce definitive gunshot residue on his hands consistent with suicide. Close examination of the soot covered area on the cushion with a hand-held microscope revealed that the soot covered a portion of the exhaled bloodstain pattern (Figure 8.44). This would indicate that the bloodshed preceded the

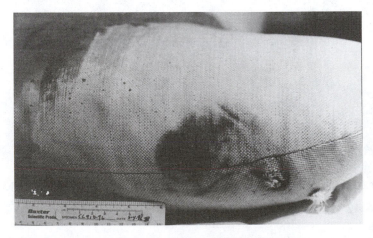

Figure 8.44   Soot covering portion of exhaled bloodstain pattern on cushion.

second gunshot. This observation was confirmed by an experiment conducted by forensic scientist William Best of North Carolina. Best spattered blood on a similar fabric and then discharged a similar weapon at close range. He then fired the weapon at close range into the fabric followed by the spattering of blood. The sequence in each instance was easily distinguished.

Bloodstain evidence testimony at trial was crucial in this case to show that movement of the victim had occurred after the time of death and that bloodstains could not have been produced by activity of the victim. The jury did not hear the evidence of the sequence of the soot and exhaled bloodstain patterns seen on the cushion since this observation was made by a defense expert who agreed with the prosecution's bloodstain expert and was not called upon to testify. The wife was convicted of first degree murder and sentenced to life in prison.

Gunshot Injuries: Case 6

At approximately 4:20 AM, a telephone call was received at a county communications center from a man who stated that his 16-year old son had just shot his mother, two brothers, and himself. Police and medical personnel responded to the scene at 4:50 AM. Four victims were found in the trailer residence and three were pronounced dead at the scene (Figure 8.45). The fourth, the16-year-old son, expired several hours later at a local hospital. The husband, who had made the initial call, was not injured but was admitted to the hospital for observation. Upon questioning, the husband stated that he was asleep in his bed with his wife when he was awakened by the sound of a gunshot. He crawled out of the bed so as not to disturb his wife and ran down the hallway where he observed his 16-year old son coming towards him. The son was clad only in underwear.

Figure 8.45 Trailer residence where the four victims were found dead at the scene.

The husband further stated that he passed by his eldest son, and proceeded to the front of the trailer. At this time, he heard two additional shots, coming from the direction of his bedroom. As he walked back to the master room, he observed the teenager approaching from the back room, with a pair of socks and a gun in his hand. At this point, the husband realized that his wife and infant had been shot. As he dialed 911, he heard a fourth shot. He remained in the bedroom until the police arrived.

The wife was found in the bed of the master bedroom, at the south end of the trailer. She had sustained a gunshot wound of entrance on the left side of her nose (Figure 8.46). A heavy blood flow pattern originating at the wound site had flowed downward by gravity across her left cheek, over the fingers of her left hand, and onto the edge of the pillow beneath her head. This bloodstained area was noted to be dry by medical personnel at the scene. The directionality of the blood flow pattern was consistent with her observed reclined position in the bed (Figure 8.47). The lateral aspect of her left hand which was exposed to the site of the entrance wound, contained small circular to oval bloodstains, likely resulting from high-velocity back spatter from the entrance wound. Stains of this type provided additional criteria to prove that the victim was shot while in bed in her observed position. Her skin was noted to be gray and cold to the touch. The postmortem examination revealed the gunshot to be of close range with massive brain injury. A .22-caliber projectile was recovered from the brain.

Figure 8.46 View of wife, on the bed of the master bedroom, with gunshot wound of entrance on left side of nose.

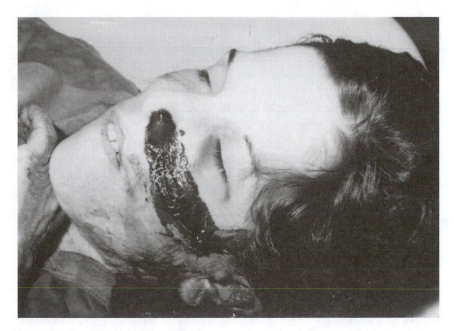

Figure 8.47 Closer view of gunshot wound of entrance on left side of nose of victim with flow pattern of blood from nose across the cheek.

The second victim, a male infant was found in a crib of the master bedroom, near the bed of the mother (Figure 8.48). He had sustained a gunshot wound of entrance in the proximity of his right ear. A heavy blood flow pattern originating from the site of the gunshot wound of entrance had flowed downward by gravity, across the lower portion of the right jaw and right neck, onto the sheet and mattress beneath the body (Figure 8.49). This was consistent with bloodshed occurring at a time in which the infant would have been in the observed reclining position. Blood-tinged serum stains were present at the rear of each arm of the pajama, as well as across the top of the shoulders. These had resulted from expressed serum from the clotted pool of blood beneath the victim diffusing upward due to capillary action, through the fabric of the pajama. Paramedics noted that his skin was cold and that blood in the area of the wound was dry. A police investigator noted that the blood soaked pajamas the infant wore were also dry notably in the area of the upper right arm (Figure 8.50). A postmortem examination revealed massive brain injury from a .22-caliber projectile which was recovered from the brain.

The third victim, a 14-year old white male was also found in his bed, in a room to the north of the master bedroom. He had sustained a gunshot wound of entrance above his left eye. Blood had flowed downward by gravity

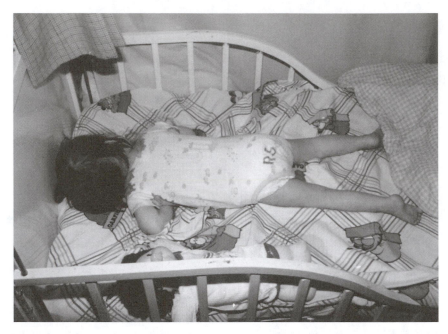

Figure 8.48   View of the second victim, a male infant, in a crib in the master bedroom who sustained gunshot wound of entrance near right ear.

Figure 8.49   Flow pattern of blood, originating from site of entrance wound, flowing downward across right jaw and neck.

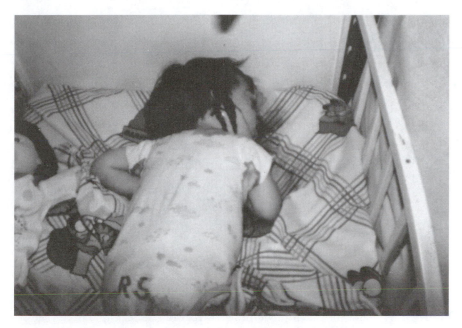

Figure 8.50 Areas of dry diffused blood near upper right shoulder of infant victim.

from the wound site across the left temple to the hairline where it saturated the hair and ear area, forming a large pool of blood beneath the head on the pillow (Figure 8.51). The directionality of this bloodstain pattern was also consistent with bloodshed occurring from a gunshot wound being inflicted at the time the victim was in the observed reclined position in bed. There was smearing of the blood on the left cheek, as well as at the edges of the blood flow pattern immediately above the left ear lobe, indicating alteration or partial removal of blood prior to the complete drying of the blood stain. Medical personnel noted foam in the mouth area. His skin was cold to the touch. Blood around the wound appeared dry. Postmortem examination revealed a close-range gunshot wound which entered above the left supra-orbital ridge with a projectile recovered from the brain.

The 16-year old male, who died later at the hospital, was found on a couch in the living room with a gunshot wound entrance in the upper lip (Figure 8.52). Examination of the couch on which the victim was located revealed a heavily blood-soaked pillow, partially covering additional blood-stains. It was apparent that the pillow had been moved (Figure 8.53). It's previous position would have been adjacent to the right arm of the sofa and occupying the void area on the couch cushion. A blood drip pattern was also noted on a nearby table. A .22-caliber Beretta semi-automatic hand-gun was found at his right side near his hip beneath his right hand. The postmortem examination revealed massive brain injury due to a .22-caliber

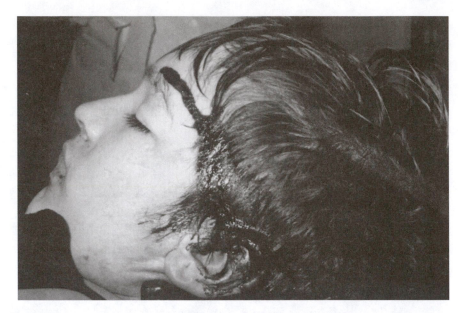

Figure 8.51 View of the third victim, a 14-year-old male, found in his bed with an entrance wound above the left eye.

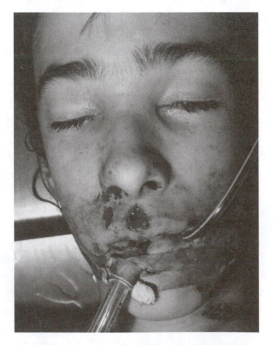

Figure 8.52 The fourth victim, a 16-year-old male, with gunshot wound of entrance in upper lip.

Figure 8.53   Blood-soaked pillow on couch on which the 16-year-old victim was found.

projectile which was recovered. The range of fire was indeterminate. Examination of the socks purportedly held by the eldest son revealed three gunshot penetrations to be present through the two socks in coincident areas. The socks were found to be positive for gunshot residue in the area of these holes. Transfer bloodstains were noted on the socks (Figure 8.54). Typing of the bloodstains revealed them to contain AB and O antigens which was consistent with a mixture of blood of the mother and her three

Figure 8.54   Socks exhibiting gunshot penetrations, gunshot residue, and blood transfer stains.

sons. It was concluded that the socks were likely used in an attempt to muffle the shots or shield the shooter from receiving bloodstains. This accounts for the lack of sooting or powder particles around the wounds of entry of the victims.

The bloodstain evidence in this case revealed that the mother, a 14-year old son, and the infant son were most likely shot while asleep. The 16-year old son received a gunshot wound on the couch in a reclined position.

The most important feature of this case was the postmortem interval relative to the statements given by the husband at the time he made his call and thereafter at the hospital and the observations made by medical personnel and the police when they arrived at the scene. The time between the initial call during which the husband states that his son had just shot his family members and himself and the time of police arrival was approximately 30 minutes. The coolness of the victim's body temperatures indicated that the victims had been dead for a longer period of time than could be concluded from the telephone call.

The bloodstain evidence in this case also provided additional criteria of an extended postmortem interval and supported the evidence provided by the coolness of the bodies and the presence of rigor mortis in the second son. The pool of clotted blood beneath the head of the infant son and the presence of dried, diffused serum stains on the left lateral aspect of his shirt indicated an extended period of elapsed time since bloodshed occurred. Clot retraction and expression of serum from quantities of blood much less than that observed beneath the head of the wife usually require in excess of 30 minutes to be produced. This evidence was inconsistent with the version of events given by the father, and indicated a significant lapse of extended time between the postmortem interval of the deaths when compared to the time the emergency call was made.

An experiment was conducted to determine the interval of time for similar serum diffusion and drying of blood on pajamas to occur. (See Chapter 4 for details of this experiment.) Experimental data indicated that up to five hours would be required for that amount of diffusion and drying of blood to occur under controlled conditions.

The husband was arrested and subsequently convicted of first-degree murder at trial. During the trial, it was revealed that the husband had a relationship with another woman whom he had wanted to marry. Additionally, a handwritten document identified as written by the husband was produced at trial which in part stated that the handgun was not an instrument of harm, but one of good. "It was a squirt gun. I used it to spray God's love on my wife and children, to give them peace and transform their bodies into sprays of flowers."

Gunshot Injuries: Case 7

A successful businessman was last seen alive by his family as he left for work in the morning in a northeastern state. He was located in his automobile in the early afternoon approximately four miles from his residence in a remote area of the countryside. The absence of fresh tire tracks in the snow other than those from the victim's vehicle, indicated his was the only vehicle in the area that day. The engine of the vehicle was running and the tape deck was playing. The windows were up and intact with the exception of the driver's side window which was broken, with glass and brain tissue on the ground beside the vehicle. The victim was found sitting in the driver's seat with massive head destruction (Figure 8.55). A hunting rifle was positioned in the vehicle with the stock to the right of the victim and the muzzle pointing upward towards the victim. The left hand of the victim was around the muzzle of the weapon and the right hand near the trigger mechanism (Figure 8.56). High-velocity blood spatter was present on the front of the rifle barrel and on the lateral and dorsal areas of the hands of the victim. Further examination of the vehicle revealed a projectile exit hole in the roof of the automobile above the head of the victim. The front passenger seat, rear seats, and interior window showed evidence of blood spatter and tissue on their surfaces (Figure 8.57).

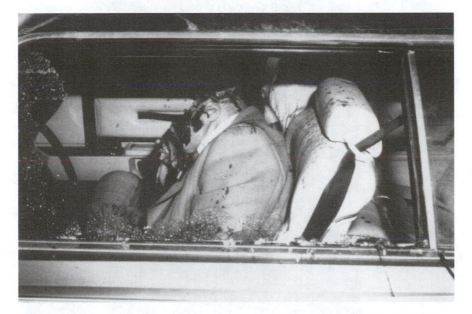

Figure 8.55 The victim, with massive head destruction, positioned in driver's seat of vehicle.

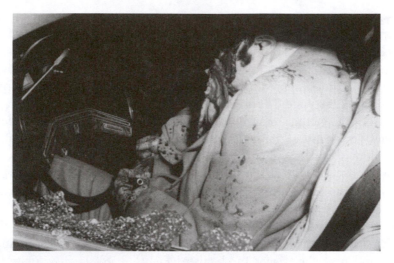

Figure 8.56   The barrel of the rifle was placed between the legs of the victim, with his left hand around the muzzle.

Figure 8.57   View of interior of vehicle showing tissue and blood spatters on front passenger seat.

Postmortem examination revealed that the firearm was discharged in the mouth of the victim producing massive damage to the head. The presence of high-velocity back spatter on the hands of the victim was consistent with the left hand being near the muzzle and the right hand at the trigger mechanism at the time of discharge (Figure 8.58). The location of bloodstains and spatter on the seats of the vehicle further demonstrated that no other person was in the vehicle at the time the firearm was discharged and that the doors and windows had been closed at that time. Subsequent investigation revealed that the victim had been despondent over the recent death of his mother, and that in fact her favorite music was playing on the tape deck in the vehicle at the time the victim was discovered. The manner of death was determined to be suicide although no suicide note was recovered.

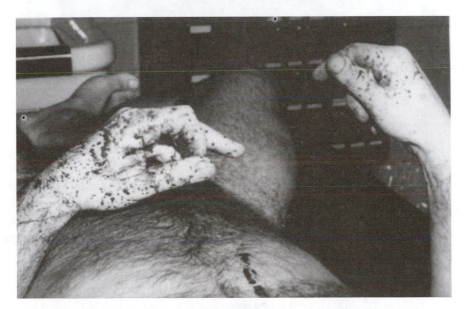

Figure 8.58 High-velocity impact blood spatter on dorsal lateral aspect of victim's left hand which was gripped around muzzle of rifle. Note high-velocity impact spatter on lateral aspect of right hand used to fire rifle.

Blunt-Force Injuries: Case 1

At approximately 2:00 AM police responded to the residence of a wealthy businessman with a report of a break-in and serious injury as reported by the 15-year old daughter. The victim, in this case a 45-year old white male, was found on his bed in the master bedroom of the residence having sustained massive blunt trauma to the head. His wife wearing a nightshirt stained with blood and brain tissue, was questioned by police and stated that she and her husband had gone to bed at approximately 11:30 PM. She was asleep with her

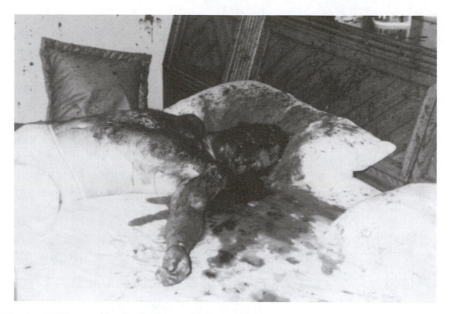

Figure 8.59 View of victim on bed with massive skull fracture and extrusion of brain tissue.

husband and was awakened by noise and thought the dog was jumping up and down on the bed. She then observed an unidentified person standing over her husband, striking him on the side of the bed where he lay asleep. This unidentified person came over to her, held her down, pushed a pillow over her face, and struck her in the stomach. The assailant then left and she saw that her husband was badly hurt. She rushed to her daughter's bedroom to check on her, and the daughter then called 911.

The postmortem examination of the victim revealed crush fractures of the right orbit, right temporal bone, anterior right parietal bone with extrusion of brain tissue, as well as fractures of the right mandible and maxilla with dislodgment of several teeth (Figures 8.59 and 8.60). The blunt object used to inflict injuries was not recovered at the scene nor in the surrounding area of the residence, but based upon the extent of the injuries, it was thought to be of considerable size and weight.

Examination of the scene and bloodstain evidence therein revealed extensive bloodshed and deposition of blood and brain tissue on the bed and headboard as well as other nearby surfaces (Figure 8.61). Blows struck while the victim was in his final position on the bed created an extensive radiating pattern of medium-velocity impact blood spatter as well as projected brain tissue extending above and behind the victim to the headboard shelf and mirror (Figures 8.62 and 8.63). The vacant side of the bed sheet to the left of the victim showed numerous areas of spattered, dripped, projected, and

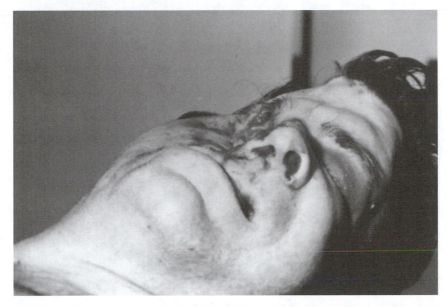

Figure 8.60 View of victim showing areas of fracture at right mandible and maxilla.

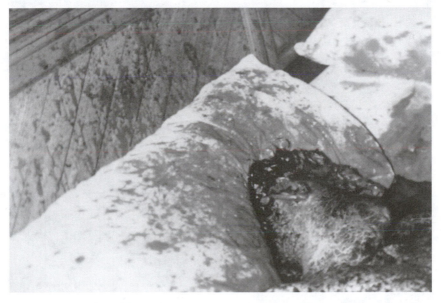

Figure 8.61 Radiating patterns of blood spatter and tissue on bed and headboard.

Figure 8.62 Projected brain tissue and blood spatter above and behind victim on headboard shelf and mirror.

Figure 8.63 Projected brain tissue and blood spatter above and behind victim on headboard shelf and mirror.

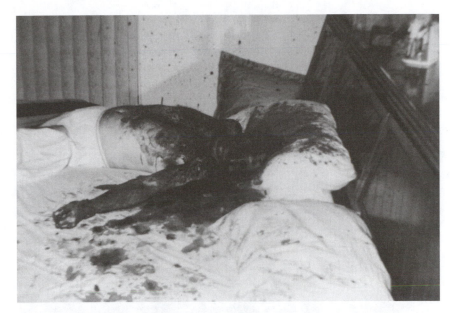

Figure 8.64   Note the vacant side of bed exhibits areas of bloodstaining.

transferred bloodstains (Figure 8.64). Some of the transfer bloodstains were created by a hand wet with blood. Dislodged teeth from the mouth of the victim were also present on the vacant side of the bed sheet (Figure 8.65 A and B). On the left edge of the vacant side of the bed sheet was a large contact bloodstain which was produced by a source of blood with sufficient volume to flow down the side of the bed (Figure 8.66). Cast-off bloodstains on the ceiling near the fan originated from an area above the vacant side of the bed (Figure 8.67). On the carpet to the left of the bed blood transfers are visible consisting of left- and right-handprints which appear to have been deposited and then wiped in an effort to clean the hands (Figure 8.68). These were not likely created by the victim.

Blood had spattered and projected onto the wall and cushion which rested against the wall to the right of the victim (Figures 8.69 and 8.70). Removal of the cushion revealed a void area which indicated that the cushion was in place at the time the blood was deposited on the cushion and adjacent wall (Figure 8.71).

Examination of the front of the nightgown worn by the wife showed extensive transfer staining of blood and brain tissue. There was a transfer pattern of rectangular shape that measured approximately 7 × 2 1/4 inches (Figure 8.72 A and B). There are also numerous circular to oval-shaped cast-off type bloodstains with diameters ranging from 0.3 to 10 mm. A trail of these cast-off bloodstains extended across the chest area from the lower right to the upper left of the nightshirt (Figure 8.73).

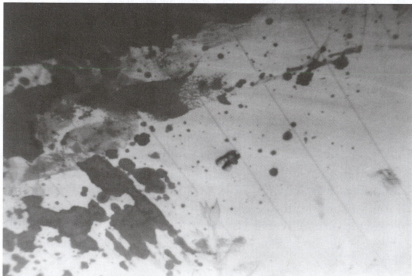

Figure 8.65 (A) Area on sheet of vacant side of bed with transfer handprint in blood. (B) Area on sheet of vacant side of bed with dislodged teeth and projected bloodstains.

Figure 8.66 Large contact stain on vacant side of bed with downward flow pattern.

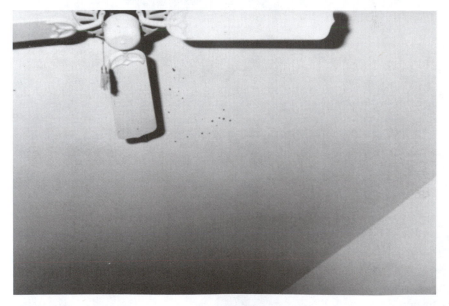

Figure 8.67 Cast-off bloodstains on ceiling near fan originating from vacant side of bed.

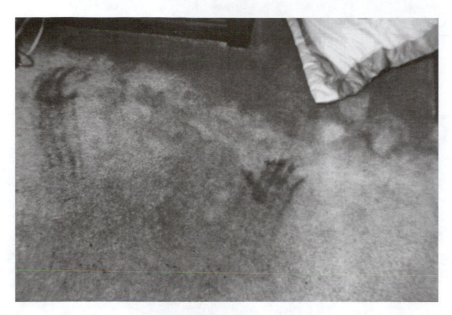

Figure 8.68 Blood transfers produced by left and right hand on carpet to the left of the bed.

Figure 8.69 Spattered and projected blood on wall and cushion against wall to right of victim.

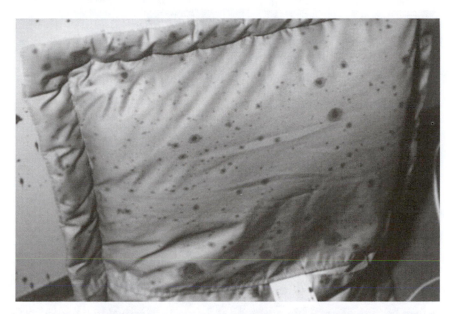

Figure 8.70   Close-up view of cushion against the wall showing blood spatters.

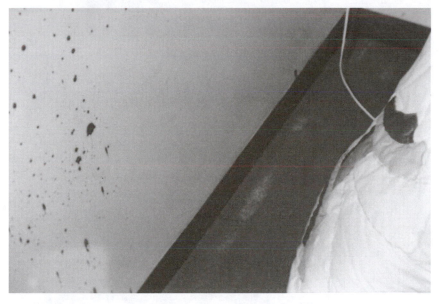

Figure 8.71   Void area behind cushion indicating cushion was in place at time of blood deposition.

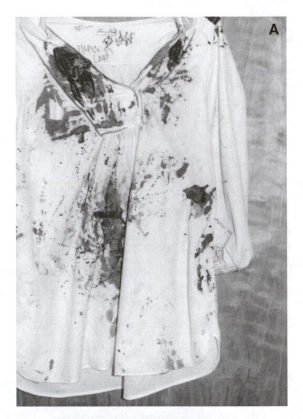

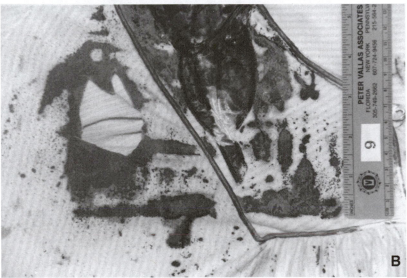

Figure 8.72 (A) Nightshirt worn by wife showing extensive areas of blood staining and brain tissue. (B) Closer view of rectangular transfer pattern.

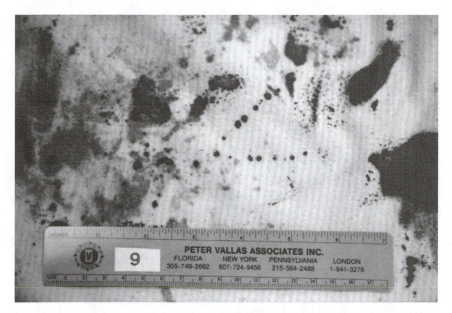

Figure 8.73 Cast-off blood stains across front chest area of nightshirt.

These findings showed serious inconsistencies with the version of events given by the wife. She could not have been in bed next to her husband at the time of bloodshed because there would have been a void on the vacant side next to the husband. The bloodstain evidence further indicated that the assault on the husband and initial bloodshed occurred on the side of the bed where the wife said she was sleeping. Furthermore, the assailant could not have been standing over the husband on his side of the bed since there was no void or interruption in the bloodstain patterns on the cushion and wall to the right of the husband. The bloodstains on the nightshirt of the wife are consistent with her being in proximity to an event involving blood being flung from an object as well as being in contact with an object containing wet blood and brain tissue. The bloodstains and tissue transfer are not consistent with her being asleep in bed during the administration of a beating of her husband lying next to her.

Police investigation indicated that there was no forced entry to the premises and no valuables were reported missing. The stepson of the victim and his girlfriend were questioned with the girlfriend finally giving a statement. She was at the residence the night of the homicide and witnessed the stepson coming out of the bedroom carrying a sledgehammer. She admitted that she assisted her boyfriend with the disposal of his bloodstained clothing in several dumpsters and led police to a river where the sledgehammer was submerged. Police divers recovered the weapon which was standing upright on the river bottom. The head was wrapped in foil and cloth and secured in a plastic bag (Figures 8.74 and 8.75). There was sufficient blood trapped in the plastic bag for DNA typing as the victim's blood.

Further police investigation revealed that the wife and victim were embroiled in a bitter divorce settlement agreement prior to his death and there was a large insurance policy which listed the wife as the beneficiary which was a possible motive for the homicide. The wife and stepson of the victim were arrested and charged with the homicide. They each accused the other of the homicide and eventually were tried separately. The stepson was convicted of being an accessory after the fact to murder but received a lengthy prison sentence for being a persistent felony offender. The wife was convicted of first-degree murder and sentenced to life in prison. During her trial, the tape of the 911 call was played for the jury. In the background of the 15-year old daughter's voice was heard the voice of the mother telling her daughter to "show feeling".

Blunt-Force Injuries: Case 2

A grounded and abandoned shrimp boat was located near Key West, Florida by area fishermen. Local law enforcement, including marine patrol, responded to the scene finding the vessel looted and partially salvaged by

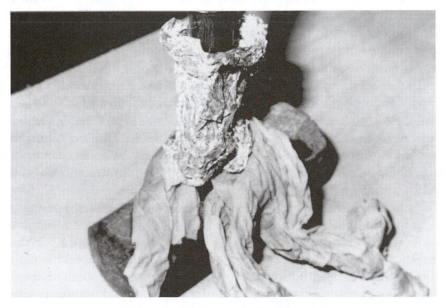

Figure 8.74 View of the sledgehammer wrapped in foil and cloth.

Figure 8.75 View of plastic bag with bloody water which was wrapped around sledgehammer when recovered from river.

scavengers (Figure 8.76). The captain, well known in the local shrimping industry, was missing and had not been seen since he and a newly hired mate set out the previous week for two weeks of shrimping. It was determined that the new mate was picked up from the shrimp boat after it went aground and taken to shore by a fishing boat. The mate offered several statements to these fishermen concerning the captain. He had fallen into the hold, broken his leg, and was airlifted to a hospital. Another statement referred to the captain as being transported to the hospital by another vessel after injuring himself. A third version of events indicated that the captain and he had gotten into a fight with a wrench and crow-bar before being transported to the hospital. A check with local medical facilities showed that the captain had not been seen by a doctor or treated for injuries at any local hospital. Law enforcement officials could not locate the new mate for further questioning but a criminal history check indicated that he used three names and three social security numbers. An APB was put out on this individual.

The examination of the boat revealed numerous bloodstains on the exterior and interior of the wheelhouse. On the right side exterior door casing near the top are numerous circular to oval shaped bloodstains with diameters ranging from 0.5 to 3.0 mm with some smaller and larger stains present (Figures 8.77 and 8.78). This pattern is consistent with medium-velocity impact blood spatter. Continuation of this type of blood spatter was seen on

Figure 8.76   View of the shrimp boat, aground and abandoned in shallow water.

Figure 8.77   Right-side entrance of wheelhouse at front of vessel.

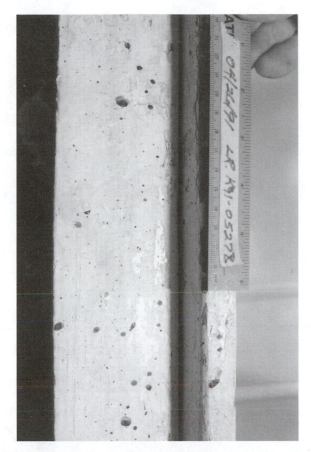

Figure 8.78 Medium-velocity impact blood spatter on right-side door casing of wheelhouse.

the surface of the brown wooden inner structure of the entranceway at approximately the same level (Figure 8.79). In this area some of the more elongated bloodstains exhibited a nearly horizontal directionality into the wheelhouse. Located on the underside of the upper horizontal structure of the wheelhouse entranceway was a projected bloodstain pattern consisting of large elongated stains approximately 5 to 6 mm in diameter with smaller and larger bloodstains present (Figure 8.80). The bloodstain pattern exhibited a directionality towards the interior of the wheelhouse. It wass likely associated with the physical activity which produced the medium-velocity impact blood spatter on the right door casing and inner wall structure.

The interior of the wheelhouse consisted of a forward main console with wheel and associated controls (Figure 8.81). To the right of the wheel, the lower edge of the console near the floor exhibited a medium-velocity impact

Figure 8.79   Continuation of blood spatter wooden entranceway to wheelhouse.

Figure 8.80   Projected bloodstain pattern on upper door jamb of wheelhouse entrance.

Figure 8.81 View of wheelhouse interior.

blood spatter pattern. These bloodstains are circular to oval in shape with many of the more elongated stains exhibiting an upward directionality in the shape of a radiating cone (Figure 8.82).

Beneath this area of the console was an additional medium-velocity impact blood spatter pattern concentrated on the exterior surface of a fire extinguisher and a metal panel box (Figure 8.83). On the wall behind the wheel and console were several stains consistent with cast-off bloodstains. These were likely associated with the physical activity which produced the medium-velocity impact blood spatter in the wheelhouse. The throttle cables passed through the floor in the area of these described bloodstains. These cables exhibited contact bloodstains with some blood clots and hair present (Figures 8.84 and 8.85). A videotape of the vessel interior showed that a considerable quantity of blood had flowed down the cables to an area below the main deck. Approximately 2 quarts of blood were found to have collected in a plastic bucket located below the floor cable opening.

On the rear outer deck near the center of the boat was a large irregularly shaped blood-soaked area (Figure 8.86). Some drip patterns may be associated with this area.

Representative blood samples were obtained from the described areas on the boat and found to be of human origin. DNA profiling of these samples compared to DNA profiles of samples of the wife and daughter of the captain

Figure 8.82 Medium-velocity impact blood spatter pattern on lower edge of the console to right of the wheel.

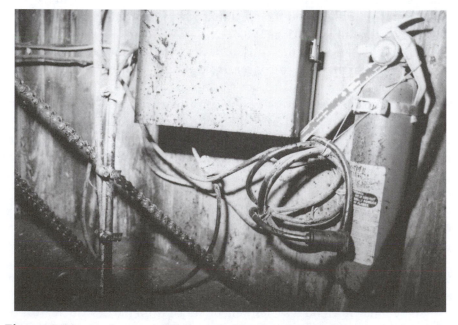

Figure 8.83 Medium-velocity impact blood spatter pattern on the fire extinguisher and the firebox beneath the console.

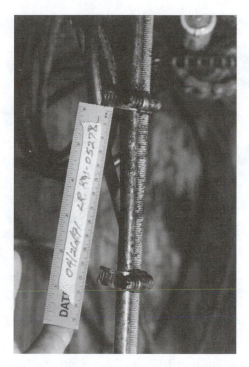

Figure 8.84 The throttle cable, routed through the floor of deck, with blood-stains and hair on its surface.

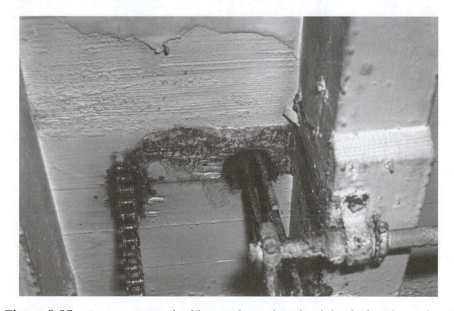

Figure 8.85 Continuation of cables on the underside of the deck to lower level showing evidence of blood flow.

Figure 8.86   The outer deck at center of boat, showing blood-soaked area below winches.

established convincingly that the bloodstains on the boat originated from the captain.

The bloodstain interpretation in this case indicates that the captain received at least two blows to the head likely with a blunt instrument while standing close to the right side entranceway to the wheelhouse. The assailant would have been positioned outside the wheelhouse striking at the victim in the direction of the wheelhouse. After the initial blows were struck, the captain sustained additional blunt force injuries inside the wheelhouse close to the floor. The head of the victim rested against the throttle cables and the hole in the floor for a sufficient period of time to permit drainage and flow of blood down the cables and into the bucket positioned below. The amount of blood recovered from the bucket was consistent with the victim sustaining severe if not fatal injuries. He was eventually removed from the wheelhouse in some manner. There was no evidence of drips of blood or drag patterns to indicate the victim crawled or walked out of the wheelhouse. There was blood evidence on the main deck to indicate that the victim was in contact with the center of the main deck. No evidence of medical assistance to the victim was noted. The nearby winch and cable may have been utilized to deposit the captain overboard. It was ascertained that some extra anchor chain was missing from the boat as well as a crowbar and the captain's rain gear. The body of the captain was never recovered.

The events of the case and the description of the missing mate were shown on "America's Most Wanted" TV program and he was soon apprehended in a neighboring state in a waterfront area. He subsequently pled guilty to a lesser charge and was sentenced to state prison.

Blunt-Force Injuries: Case 3

On the west coast of Florida an elderly deaf couple resided in a neighborhood populated mostly by hearing-impaired individuals. They were attacked in their home which was a single-story house where they slept in separate bedrooms. Police and paramedics responded to the scene after the victims were discovered by a neighbor. They found the wife to be deceased on the floor of her bedroom and the husband severely injured, but alive on the bed in his bedroom. He was admitted to a local hospital in critical condition and subsequently survived his injuries. Both victims sustained multiple blunt-force trauma to the head which was determined to have been inflicted by a hammer with a rounded striking surface (Figures 8.87 and 8.88).

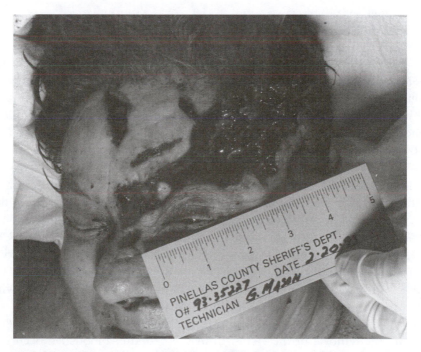

Figure 8.87 View of deceased wife with multiple blunt-force injuries to the head, inflicted with a hammer.

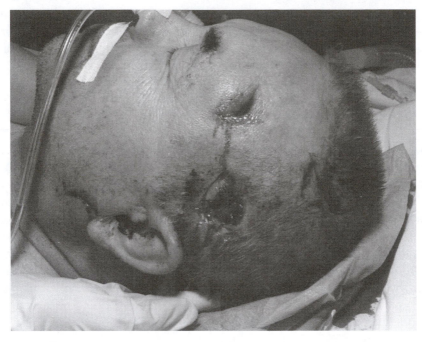

Figure 8.88 The severely injured husband with multiple blunt-force injuries to the head, inflicted with a hammer.

The female victim was located on the floor of her bedroom near the door clad in her nightgown which had been pulled up above her waist (Figure 8.89). Blood transfer stains including hair swipes were present on the lower portion of the wall and leading edge of the open bedroom door indicating contact with these surfaces prior to her final position (Figures 8.90 and 8.91).

The bed of the female victim was heavily bloodstained with large areas of clotted blood. Medium-velocity impact blood spatters were concentrated on the right side pillow as one viewed from the foot of the bed. Above this area on the wall behind the bed was a radiating pattern of medium-velocity blood spatter with an origin close to the pillows on the bed (Figures 8.92, 8.93, and 8.94). Cast-off bloodstain patterns were present above the bed to the right of the victim on the ceiling (Figure 8.95). It was concluded that the female victim received multiple blunt force blows to her head area while lying face up on the bed with her head close to the pillows. The assailant was positioned to her right while administering the blows. Blood drag patterns indicate the removal of the victim from the bed after bloodshed occurred. Within the drag patterns were blood swipes or transfers with the appearance of having been produced by hair or bristles (Figure 8.96). A broom showing the edges of the bloodstained bristles was located in the bedroom and likely

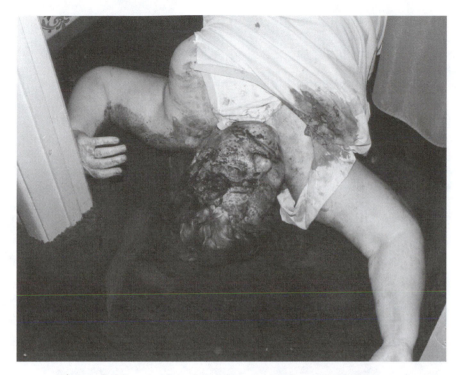

Figure 8.89   The female victim on the floor of the bedroom.

Figure 8.90   Transfer stains and hair swipes on the lower portion of the wall and edge of the open bedroom door near the female victim.

Figure 8.91 Close-up view of transfer stains and hair swipes on the lower portion of wall and edge of the open bedroom door near the female victim.

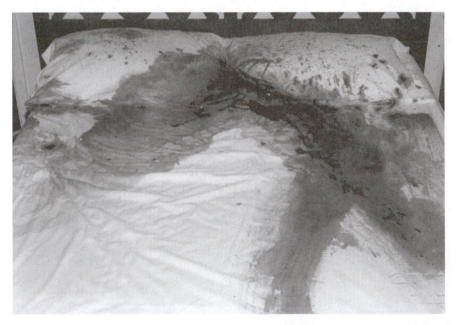

Figure 8.92 The heavily bloodstained bed of the female victim with large amount of clotted blood.

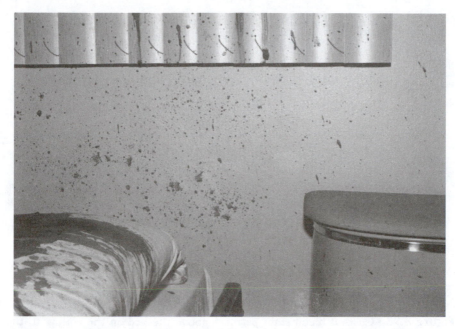

Figure 8.93 Radiating pattern of medium-velocity impact blood spatter on the wall above and behind the bed.

Figure 8.94 Continuation of radiating pattern of medium-velocity impact blood spatter on the vertical blinds.

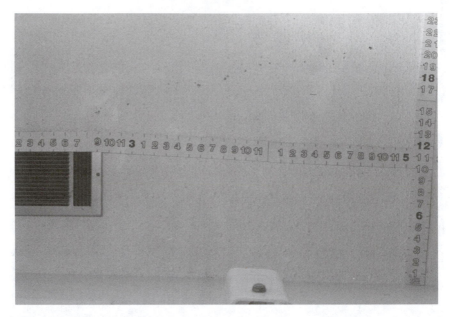

Figure 8.95 Cast-off blood stain patterns above the bed on the ceiling to the right of victim.

Figure 8.96 Transfer swipes appear to have been produced by hair or bristles.

utilized by the assailant to alter the bloodstains on the bed (Figure 8.97). A partial bloody footwear impression was located on the bloodstained sheet indicating the assailant was on the bed at some point in time after bloodshed occurred. This impression was identified as the sole of an Air Raid brand sport shoe that was subsequently matched with class and individual characteristics to a shoe belonging to the assailant (Figure 8.98).

Figure 8.97   Broom showing bloodstained bristles, found in bedroom.

Figure 8.98   (Left) Partial bloody footwear impression located on sheet; **(right)** sport shoe of suspect matched to the partial bloody shoeprint with class and individual characteristics.

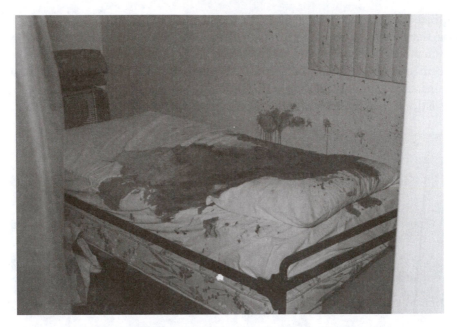

Figure 8.99 Heavily bloodstained bed of husband.

Examination of the bedroom of the husband showed a single bed which was heavily bloodstained. Some medium-velocity impact blood spatter was present on the upper edge of the bloodstained pillow with the majority of the blood spatter impacting on the wall and vertical blinds close to and to the right of the bed (Figures 8.99 and 8.100). Some of the medium-velocity impact blood spatters on the wall and vertical blinds contained clots of blood. A contact bloodstain pattern on the wall approximately midway on the bed indicates movement of the victim during bloodshed (Figure 8.101). The victim lay in this second position for a period of time allowing blood to flow down the wall to the floor and create a large blood drip pattern on the lower wall and baseboard (Figure 8.102). It was concluded that the male victim received multiple blunt force blows to the head while lying on the bed in two positions with the assailant positioned to the left of the victim. The clotted blood spatter indicates a time lapse during the beating. After the initial blows were struck, there was time for blood to commence clotting (at least 3–15 minutes) and the beating resumed which produced the clotted medium-velocity impact blood spatter. Some of this clotted blood spatter was over the contact transfer bloodstain as an indicator of the sequence of events.

The assailant was arrested not long after the homicide and assault on the couple. He had been in possession of their automobile. He too was a deaf individual living in the neighborhood and was known by the victims having

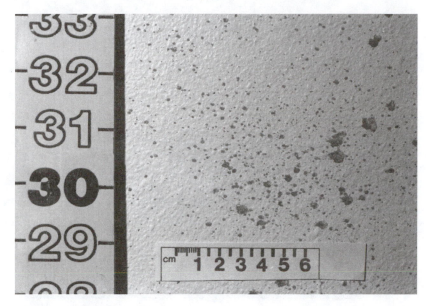

Figure 8.100 Medium-velocity impact bloodstain pattern on wall.

Figure 8.101 Medium-velocity impact bloodspatter and transfer bloodstains on wall with the continuation of bloodstain pattern on the vertical blinds adjacent to the bed.

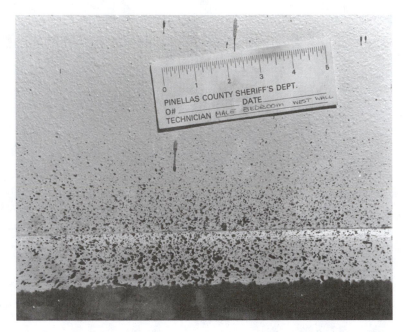

Figure 8.102 Large blood drip pattern with satellite spatter on lower wall and baseboard behind bed.

done odd jobs for them in the past. The clothing of the victim and the hammer used as the weapon were never recovered. However, the shoes of the victim proved to be a crucial piece of evidence connecting him to the scene. The defendant was tried and convicted of murder in the first degree and sentenced to death.

Blunt-Force Injuries: Case 4

In the early morning, a woman reported to the police that her live-in lesbian roommate was dead in the house that they shared. Police and paramedics responded to the scene and found the female roommate lying on a mattress in the living room of the residence having sustained blunt-force injuries to the head area. She was clad in only her underwear and was partially covered with a quilt (Figure 8.103 A and B). She was pronounced dead at the scene. Subsequent postmortem examination confirmed severe blunt-force injuries to the face and top of the head with the cause of death determined as aspiration of blood into the lungs. Additional findings included patterned linear contusions on the front chest area and the right upper arm. Fresh bruises were also present on both hands with flattening of a gold ring worn on the second finger of the right hand (Figures 8.104, 8.105, and 8.106).

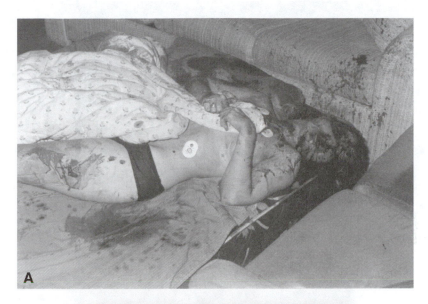

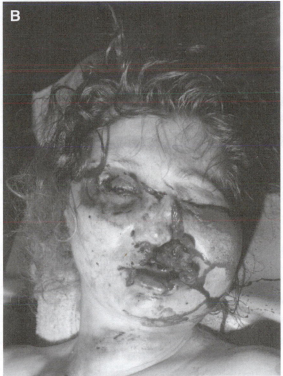

Figure 8.103 (A) View of the female victim on mattress in living room of residence; (B) crushing facial injuries sustained by the victim.

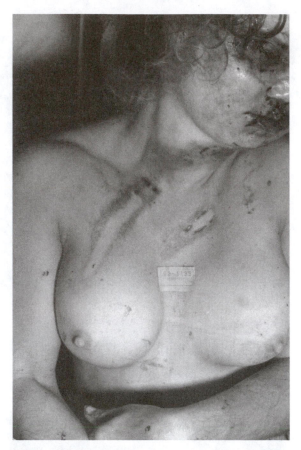

Figure 8.104   Patterned linear contusion on front chest of victim.

Further examination of the scene revealed the mattress on the living room floor to be situated adjacent to a couch behind it as well as to the left. The couch and wall including vertical blinds behind the couch and above the mattress showed a large pattern of medium-velocity impact blood spatter more heavily concentrated at the left edge of the couch (Figure 8.107 A and B). To the right of the body of the victim on the wall behind her, the pattern showed more elongated bloodstains. The origin of the blood spatters on this wall and couch below was the location of the victim's head in its final position as well as when it was elevated to the level of the cushions on the couch during the infliction of injuries. Some additional medium-velocity impact blood spatter as well as cast-off patterns of blood were present on the couch, wall, and vertical blinds which also confirmed the fact that the blows were administered to the victim while she was in a partially erect (sitting) position as well as supine on the mattress.

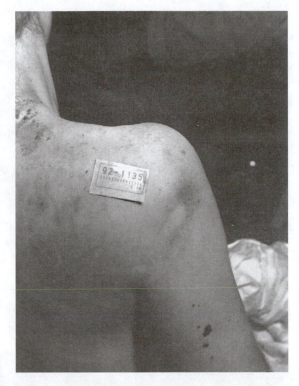

Figure 8.105 Patterned linear contusion onthe right upper arm of the victim.

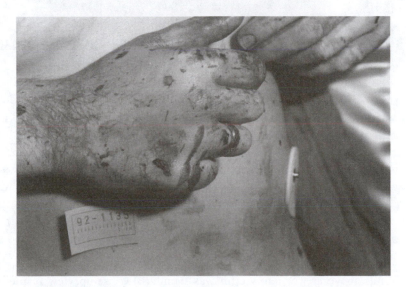

Figure 8.106 Bruising on the right hand of the victim. Note flattened ring on finger.

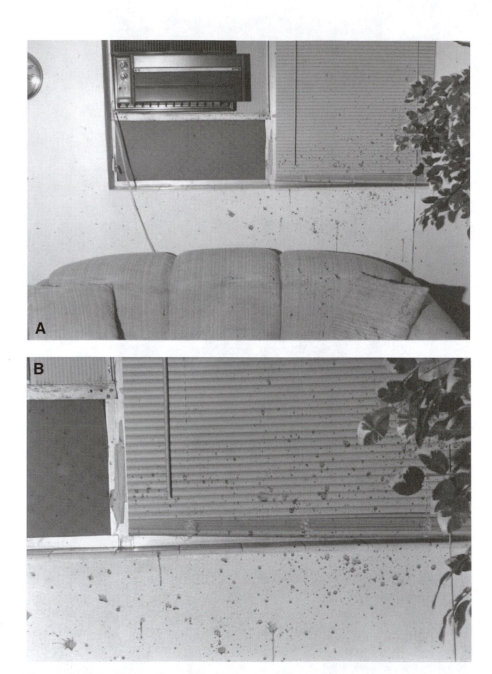

Figure 8.107 (**A**) Medium-velocity impact blood spatter on the couch, wall, and blinds above area where victim was found. (**B**) Close-up view of medium-velocity impact blood spatter on the couch, wall, and blinds.

Figure 8.108 Aluminum baseball bat, utilized as a blunt weapon, found in the bathroom.

An aluminum baseball bat, located in the bathroom, had dents and light reddish staining on the surface (Figure 8.108). The bathtub also showed evidence of light or diluted reddish stains and spatters on the surfaces near the faucet. The stains on the bat and the tub showed a positive reaction with the presumptive test for blood, phenolphthalein. This would indicate that an attempt was made to clean blood from the bat by rinsing it in the bathtub.

Upon further questioning of the roommate who reported the incident, it was noticed that there were bloodstains present on her clothing. An area of the left upper short sleeve and upper rear of her T-shirt showed several cast-off type bloodstains as well as a possible projected bloodstain on the right front leg of her shorts (Figure 8.109 A and B). Examination of her legs showed several small medium-velocity impact spatters of apparent blood. These stains, as well as those on her clothing, were confirmed to be consistent with the type of the victim. The roommate initially denied any involvement

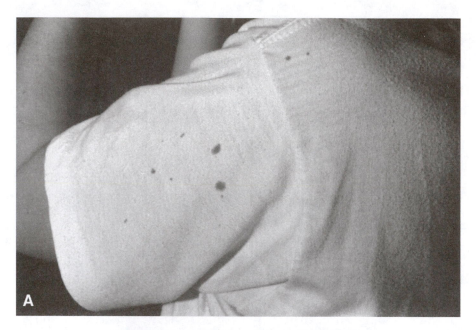

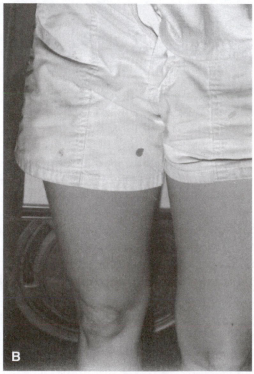

Figure 8.109 (A) Cast-off bloodstains on the upper left arm and sleeve of suspect's T-shirt; (B) small bloodstain on the right front leg of the suspect's shorts.

in the homicide of her lesbian girlfriend but then stated that all she remembered was standing over her supine body with a baseball bat in her hand. Investigation later revealed that the deceased had been out with other friends and had returned home late. Jealousy may have been a motive for the attack. This case is a good example of the relatively small quantity of blood spatter that may be present on the person and/or clothing of an assailant despite the large quantity of blood spatters on other surfaces at the scene. The directionality of the blows struck usually dictates the areas that will receive the largest quantity of blood spatter, In this case, the force of the blows was away from the assailant and thus little spatter was present on her person and clothing. The roommate was arrested and subsequently found guilty of the murder at trial.

Blunt-Force Trauma: Case 5

A 42-year old male was last seen alive leaving a topless bar at closing time with three young men in their early twenties. A short time later, a police officer on routine patrol noticed the interior light of a vehicle parked with the driver's door open in an area adjacent to a lake near the main highway, approximately three-quarters of a mile from the topless bar. The officer drove into the area to investigate and encountered two of the young men standing near the vehicle with the door open. A second empty vehicle was parked nearby. While questioning the men, the officer looked toward the frozen lake and saw the victim lying on the ice in a pool of blood (Figure 8.110). He had been beaten and stabbed. The two men were subsequently arrested and investigation led to the arrest of the third individual several days later.

Postmortem examination revealed that the victim had suffered two stab wounds to the back to the upper and lower right side and one in the front epigastric region (Figure 8.111). The right pleural cavity contained approximately 1500 ml of fluid and clotted blood; the peritoneal cavity contained approximately 800 ml of blood. There was evidence of bruising in the rear shoulder area. The victim also sustained massive head trauma including multiple skull fractures and underlying brain injuries. Death was attributed to severe brain injury due to blunt force and internal hemorrhage resulting in injury to right lung and liver due to stab wounds.

Examination of the scene of this homicide revealed irregular blood transfer patterns on the ground near the victim's vehicle produced by contact with a source of blood with a relatively flat surface and associated with some movement (Figures 8.112 and 8.113). The rear of the victim's jacket contained heavy bloodstaining with dirt and debris in the area of the stab wounds in the back and most likely represented the source of the blood that produced

Figure 8.110 Victim of the beating and stabbing on the frozen pond. Note dilution of the blood pool on the ice.

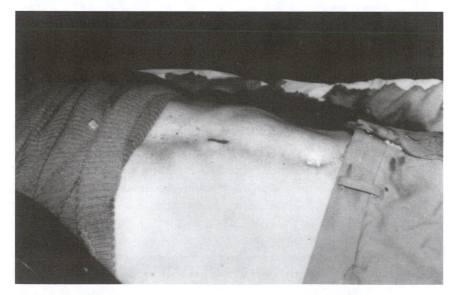

Figure 8.111 Stab wound in the epigastric region of the victim.

Figure 8.112   Blood transfer patterns on the ground near the victim's vehicle.

Figure 8.113   Close-up view of the blood transfer patterns.

Figure 8.114 Blood transfer patterns found on a rock on the embankment near the edge of the pond.

these transfer bloodstains on the ground. The severe head injuries sustained by the victim did not occur in this location. There was no appreciable trail of blood from this point to the edge of the bank of the lake. It is possible that the victim was carried over to this point and thrown over the bank onto the ice. Halfway down the bank there was an additional area of blood transfer where the victim likely made contact on the way down the bank (Figure 8.114). The blunt force injuries that produced the massive skull fractures, brain injuries, and heavy bleeding occurred while the victim was in a prone position on the ice. There was evidence of medium-velocity blood spatter on the shoulder of the victim, on the ice adjacent to the body, and on the edge of the nearby bank. There were, additionally present on the jacket of the victim and on the ice, fragments of brain tissue and skull. The blunt weapon in this case was an ax handle which was recovered from the defendant's vehicle. Evidence that this was the weapon involved is shown by the blood and tissue transfer pattern of the weapon on the jacket of the victim (Figure 8.115). Bloodstains consistent with the group and genetic marker profile of the victim were also demonstrated on the axe handle.

The three defendants offered differing versions of the homicide. They admitted to drinking with the victim in the bar and leaving with him at closing time with the promise of smoking marijuana. This apparently was a ploy to rob him and possibly steal his car, Mercedes-Benz. The defendants

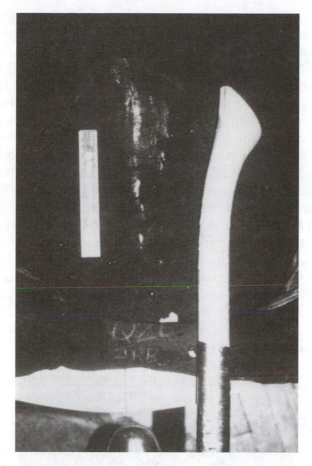

Figure 8.115 Blood and tissue transfer pattern of the ax handle to the victim's jacket.

agreed that the victim became involved in a fight with the defendants in the parking area near the lake. One defendant claimed to have seen the other two hit the victim with a stick and fists a few times and carry him over to the edge of the bank and throw him over. At this point, this defendant did not want to get involved and ran off leaving the other two defendants. The remaining two defendants differed in their accounts of the beating and stabbing of the victim with each implicating the other.

The examination of the clothing and footwear of each of the defendants was helpful to the reconstruction of this case, but did not provide all the answers. The defendant that had left the scene was apprehended days later. He had washed his clothes so that their examination did not provide additional information. His boots did not show evidence of bloodstains, but he had since walked through mud during a rainstorm which could have removed any remaining bloodstains. Had this defendant stabbed the victim initially as claimed by another defendant he may not have received bloodstains on his clothing. A second defendant showed minimal smearing of blood on his clothing which was consistent with carrying the victim. The third defendant admitted that he had stabbed the victim once and observed the other two beating the victim on the ice while he stood on the top of the bank. The top of the bank was approximately 50 feet away and 6 feet elevated from the location of the victim on the ice. This defendant's clothing and boots showed numerous small circular stains of medium-velocity impact blood spatter on the lower right leg and boot, and the upper left and right thighs, and on the left arm of his jacket (Figures 8.116, 8.117 and 8.118). This array of blood spatter indicated proximity to and possible participation in the beating of the victim. The right boot in the area of the heel showed some medium-velocity blood spatter, blood crusts, and hair consistent with scalp hair of the victim and was likely produced by kicking the victim in the head (Figure 8.119). The version of events offered by this defendant was certainly refuted by the bloodstaining evidence. This defendant was permitted to plead to a lesser charge of homicide and reduced sentence. He then testified for the prosecution against the other two defendants who were convicted and received life sentences in prison.

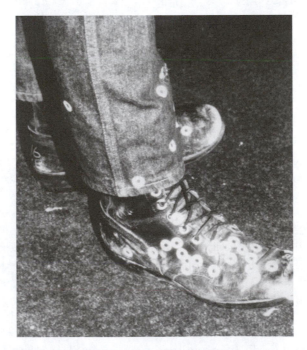

Figure 8.116 Medium-velocity impact blood spatter on the lower right leg of jeans and right boot of defendant.

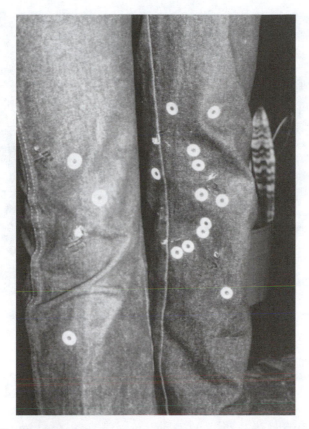

Figure 8.117 Medium-velocity impact blood spatter on the right knee and left upper thigh of jeans of defendant.

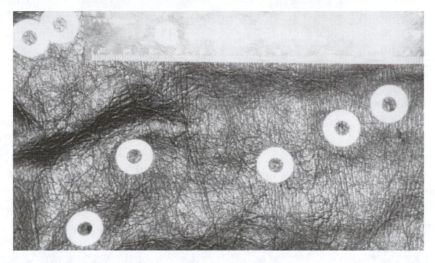

Figure 8.118 Medium-velocity blood spatter on left jacket sleeve of defendant.

Figure 8.119   Bloodstains on rear heel of right boot of defendant.

Blunt-Force Injuries: Case 6

Another instance in which the alertness and perception of a police officer on routine patrol resulted in the immediate apprehension of suspects in a homicide case occurred in Louisiana. Traveling on a two-lane highway parallel to a bayou canal, a police officer noticed two vehicles off the roadway near the bank of the canal. He stopped and noted that one vehicle was partially submerged in the water and the other was attempting to push it even farther into the water (Figure 8.120). The victim in this case was in the front passenger area of the first vehicle having sustained fatal head injuries. The wife of the victim and her male acquaintance were arrested and charged with the homicide. A second female was arrested in conjunction with this case but eventually not charged with homicide.

The postmortem examination of the victim revealed multiple lacerations of the forehead and left side of the head with a circular, depressed fracture in the left temporal region of the skull with underlying injury to the brain due to beating with a blunt instrument (Figures 8.121 and 8.122). The semicircular laceration and circular depressed fracture of the skull were consistent with the blunt instrument being a hammer. There were no defensive injuries or other trauma to the victim.

The reconstruction of this case was based upon evaluation of the scene where the victim was located and then the scene of the beating which was a

Figure 8.120 Scene at edge of a bayou canal with the defendant's vehicle on the muddy embankment.

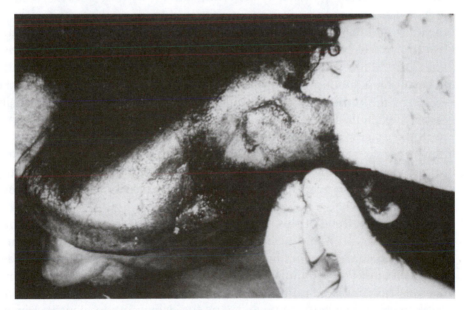

Figure 8.121 Semi-circular laceration in the left temporal region of the victim's head consistent with having been produced by a hammer.

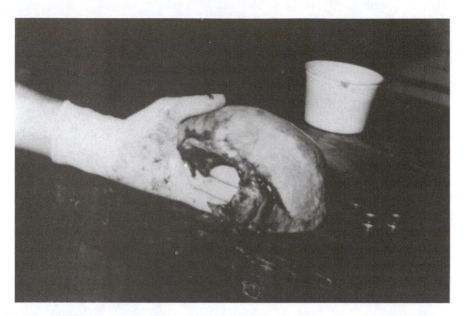

Figure 8.122 Circular depressed fracture in the left temporal region of the victim's skull, just below a semicircular laceration.

bedroom of a trailer occupied by the victim and his wife. At the canal scene it was apparent that there was an attempt to dispose of the victim in his vehicle by pushing it into the bayou canal with a second vehicle. The canal was estimated to be approximately 20 feet deep; thus had the vehicle been successfully submerged, the case may never have been solved. The bank of the canal was a soft, wet, grassy area which caused difficulty with traction and thus with pushing the vehicle into the water. This problem was compounded by the fact that the first vehicle with the victim in the front seat was in parked gear during the attempts to push it. The victim had sustained injury prior to being placed into the vehicle as evidenced by the blood transfers and smears on the left rear fender of the vehicle (Figure 8.123). He most likely made contact with this area as he was being transported into the front seat.

The primary scene of this homicide was the trailer bedroom shared by the deceased and his wife. The trailer was orderly, with no signs of a struggle. However, considerable effort had been taken to clean up the blood at the crime scene prior to the initial arrival of the investigators. The bed in the master bedroom was clean with fresh sheets and bedspread (Figure 8.124). No blood was visible in the room except on the ceiling. (An individual cleaning up a bloody crime scene often does not notice blood on ceilings.) Present in this case were two distinct cast-off bloodstain patterns on the ceiling. One pattern was located over the bed parallel to the wall at the head of the bed.

Figure 8.123 Bloodstain pattern on the left rear fender of the victim's vehicle.

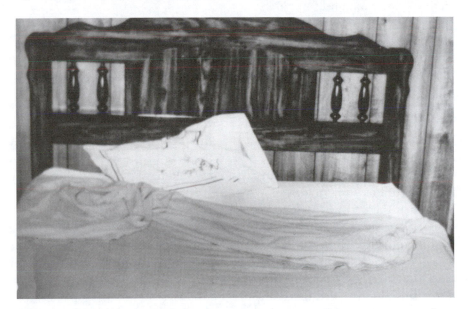

Figure 8.124 View of the bed in the master bedroom after the crime scene had been cleaned up.

Figure 8.125 Cast-off bloodstains on the ceiling above the bed to the left of victim's position on bed.

Circular cast-off bloodstains were observed on the ceiling above the right upper area of the bed which became more oval or elongated as the pattern extended in a northerly direction (Figure 8.125). An assailant would have produced this pattern with overhead swings of a weapon while positioned on the left side of the bed. The second cast-off bloodstain pattern on the ceiling was observed as circular bloodstains above the right upper area of the bed which became more oval or elongated as the pattern extended in an easterly direction towards the foot of the bed in the area of the overhead light and fan (Figures 8.126 and 8.127). An assailant would have produced this pattern with overhead swings of a weapon while positioned on the bed near the foot.

When the bed was stripped of the bedspread and clean sheets, and the mattress turned over, a large bloodstain was observed on the right upper area which coincided with the calculated position of the victim based on the location of the cast-off bloodstains on the ceiling (Figure 8.128). A further search of the crime scene produced a plastic bag which was found to contain numerous bloodstained items including a mattress cover, bottom sheet, pillows, and pillow cases in addition to bloodstained towels, bloodstained shower cap, and a bloodstained claw-type hammer.

The bed was made up with the sheets and pillows in their cases found in the bag. The major bloodstain on the sheet coincided with the bloodstain on the mattress (Figure 8.129). This bloodstain was associated with some

Figure 8.126 Cast-off bloodstains on the ceiling above the bed near the light fixture and fan.

medium-velocity blood spatter and arterial spurt patterns which extended onto a heavily bloodstained pillow. This reconstruction further verified the position of the victim to be in a prone position on the bed when he was struck by multiple blows with a blunt instrument. The second pillow was heavily bloodstained in conjunction with some brain tissue and was possibly placed over the head of the victim at some point after blood was shed.

The claw hammer and shower cap were interesting items of evidence in this case. The hammer was consistent in size and shape with the injuries sustained by the victim. A trace of blood was detected on the hammer but was too limited in quantity for further testing. A hand towel taken from the garbage bag was considerably bloodstained and showed a transfer pattern in blood produced by a hammer (Figure 8.130). The plastic shower cap was considerably bloodstained on the inside surface and contained fragments of brain tissue. There was a semicircular defect in the shower cap which was consistent with having been produced by the hammer. This would indicate that the victim was beaten while wearing the shower cap. This is an important feature of the case in that the shielding effect of the plastic shower cap would be expected to greatly reduce the quantity of medium-velocity spatter produced during the beating. Relatively little of this type of spatter was seen on the sheet and pillows of the bed. Yet sufficient blood could have accumulated on the hammer and been cast off the weapon during the back swing.

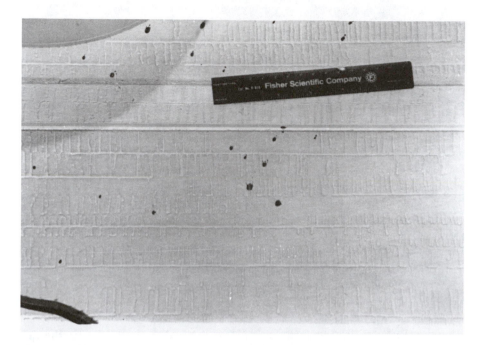

Figure 8.127 Close-up view of cast-off bloodstains on the ceiling above the bed near the light fixture.

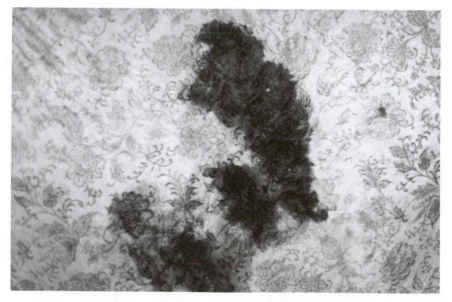

Figure 8.128 Large bloodstain on the underside of the mattress.

Figure 8.129 The victim's bed made up with the bloodstained sheets and pillows.

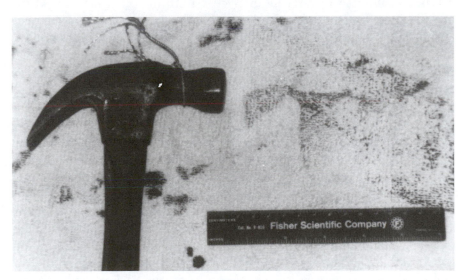

Figure 8.130 Blood transfer pattern on the towel compared to the hammer.

Figure 8.131 Front of the shirt worn by the male defendant showing the blood pattern on right shoulder area produced by his carrying of the victim from the scene.

The male defendant in this case denied any role in the beating of the victim. He admitted to carrying the victim from the bed to the car at the request of the victim's wife. Examination of the clothing worn by the male defendant did not show the presence of blood spatters or cast-off patterns. There were transfer bloodstain patterns in the area of the right shoulder of the shirt which were consistent with his having carried the victim over his shoulder as he described (Figures 8.131 and 8.132).

The clothing of the wife worn at the time of arrest did not show a trace of blood. It is possible that she changed her clothes. At the scene, in another bedroom, women's slacks and a blouse were located which contained several types of bloodstain patterns. The slacks showed scattered areas of spatter and drips of blood on the mid- to lower leg areas (Figure 8.133). On the blouse there was evidence of a small quantity of medium-velocity blood spatter on the left sleeve (Figure 8.134) with smearing of blood on the right sleeve. Scattered small smears of blood were present on the front of the blouse. The rear of the blouse showed several cast-off bloodstains in the mid-back region which exhibited a downward directionality (Figures 8.135 and 8.136). This type of bloodstain pattern is frequently seen on the back of an assailant's shirt resulting from blood cast off a weapon as it is raised over the head

Figure 8.132 Back of the shirt worn by the male defendant showing the blood pattern on right shoulder area produced by his carrying of the victim from the scene.

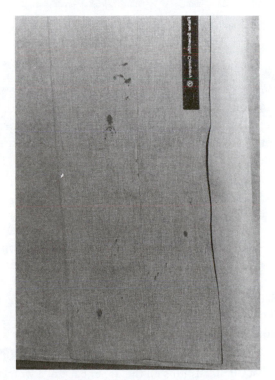

Figure 8.133 Blood spatter and drip pattern on the right lower leg area of women's slacks found at scene.

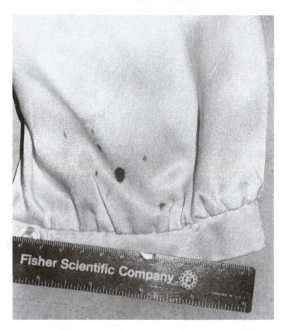

Figure 8.134 Blood spatter on left sleeve of a women's blouse found at scene.

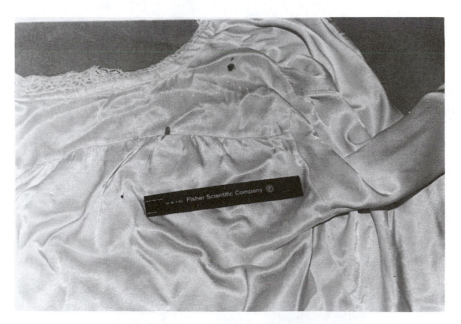

Figure 8.135 Cast-off bloodstains on the upper back of a women's blouse found at scene.

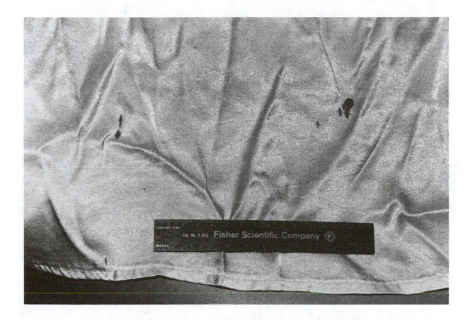

Figure 8.136 Cast-off bloodstains on the lower back hem of a women's blouse found at scene.

similar to the manner in which cast-off bloodstains are produced on ceilings. Some of the blood droplets do not possess the energy to reach the height of the ceiling and fall downward in an arc-like fashion. It was concluded that the wearer of the blouse either participated in the administration of the beating of the victim or was standing nearby with her back to the events taking place in order to receive the cast-off bloodstains on the rear of the shirt. The lack of medium-velocity blood spatter on the front of the blouse can be explained by the shielding effect of the shower cap worn by the victim. There was not an abundance of blood spatter on the sheets or pillow cases on the bed.

The wife of the victim in this case pleaded guilty to homicide prior to trial and is serving a life sentence in prison. Her male acquaintance later pled guilty to a lesser charge of manslaughter.

Blunt-Force Injuries: Case 7

A husband was charged with the murder of his wife who was found dead in the laundry room of their apartment building in the early evening hours. The husband stated that he had accompanied his wife to the laundry room and stayed with her until the wash cycle had started on the washing machine. He then returned to their apartment to watch television. When his wife did

Figure 8.137 The victim, as found by police on the floor of the laundry room upon arrival at scene.

not return to the apartment he grew concerned and returned to the laundry room and discovered his wife lying on her back on the floor in a pool of blood, her head crushed. The husband went on to state that he lifted the head of his wife, felt for a pulse, and realized that she was dead. In frustration he slammed his hands to the bloody floor, wiped them on his coat, and ran to a neighbor's apartment to summon the police. He returned to the laundry room with the neighbor and again attempted to pull his wife up by placing his hands behind her head. He was restrained by the neighbor who also placed a towel over the face of the victim prior to the arrival of the police (Figure 8.137).

At autopsy it was determined that the victim had sustained severe lacerations at the right frontal, parietal, and occipital areas of the scalp with underlying cerebral contusions (Figure 8.138). There was no evidence of skull fracture. A small laceration and bruising were noted bilaterally on the right forehead area. Bruising was also noted bilaterally in the submandibular region of the face and the central portion of the neck. Superficial lacerations were noted in the midline of the neck (Figure 8.139). Extensive areas of hemorrhage were noted in the soft tissues of the neck and upper sternal area with no evidence of fractures. Fractures were noted in the left second and fifth ribs. The immediate cause of death was attributed to respiratory failure due to manual strangulation. There was no evidence of sexual assault associated with this homicide.

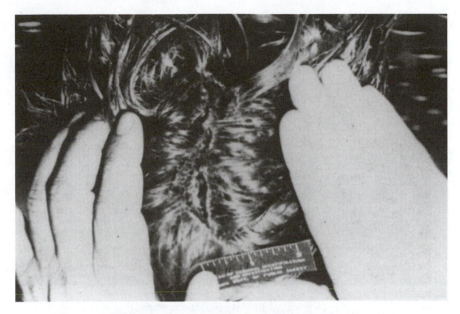

Figure 8.138 Severe scalp laceration sustained by the victim.

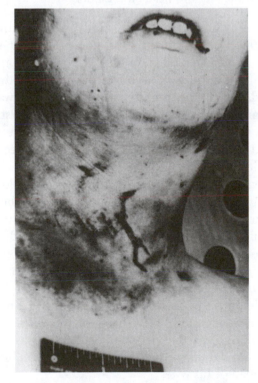

Figure 8.139 Bruises and superficial lacerations on the neck of the victim.

Figure 8.140 Medium-velocity bloodstain pattern impacting on the wall a short distance above floor in a radial or spoke-like pattern. The origin of these bloodstains is the area of the victim's head on the floor.

The scene of this homicide was a laundry room with three washing machines along one wall and two dryers along the other with the victim positioned in the center area of the room. The radiating medium-velocity bloodstain pattern showed a point of convergence at the victim's head (Figure 8.140). This bloodstain pattern impacted on the floor, wall, washing machine, and the dryer nearest to the head of the victim. The bloodstains within this radiating pattern were confined to a short distance above the level of the floor and resulted from repeated impact of the victim's head with the floor while in that position.

Bloodstains which resulted from free-falling drops of blood impacted on top of the washing machine (Figure 8.141). It is likely that the victim received initial injury to the head while standing at the washing machine. This resulted in blood drops falling to the washing machine surface. Additional drops of blood fell to the top surface of the dryers and garbage can top on the opposite side of the room which are consistent with bleeding from the head of the victim while standing. A blood swipe pattern was present on a dryer which likely represented contact by the bloody hand of the victim prior to falling to her final position (Figure 8.142). There was no evidence of bloodstain patterns on the floor near the victim that could be associated with the statement of the husband that he had slapped his hands in blood on the floor after raising the head of his wife.

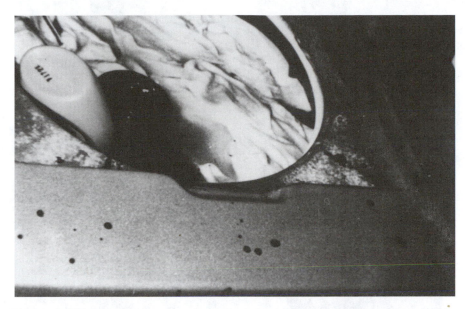

Figure 8.141 Bloodstains on the top of the washing machine resulting from dripping from above.

Figure 8.142 Blood transfer patterns on clothes dryer.

Figure 8.143   Shoeprints in blood on floor of laundry room.

There were numerous bloody shoeprints on the floor of the laundry room which were found to be consistent with having been produced by a sole pattern similar to shoes worn by the husband. He had previously stated that he had entered the premises on two occasions after blood had been shed. The directionality of the shoeprints shows them to be erratic in movement rather than simply in and out of the room (Figure 8.143). More important to the reconstruction of this case was the examination of close-up photographs of the bloody shoe prints near the body. There was medium-velocity blood spatter superimposed over several of the shoeprints (Figure 8.144).The formation of the bloody shoeprint likely preceded the production of the medium-velocity spatter. It was concluded that the person wearing the shoes that produced that shoeprint in blood was present in the laundry room near or at the time of the struggle that produced bloodshed. This observation was not consistent with the version of events given by the husband.

The jacket worn by the husband contained considerable blood staining which was determined to be the type of his wife. Bloodstains consistent with medium-velocity impact spatter were located on the right sleeve and chest.

Figure 8.144 Medium-velocity blood spatter impacted on top of shoeprint in blood.

Extending over the right shoulder area and down the back of the jacket were cast-off bloodstains which are typically produced during a beating and not by slapping one's hands in blood on the floor (Figure 8.145). On the right sleeve of the husband's jacket was a palmar transfer pattern in blood which was produced by a relatively small hand (Figure 8.146). This was likely produced by the victim as she attempted to defend herself during the course of the struggle in the laundry room.

The husband was convicted of the homicide of his wife. This case provides an excellent demonstration of the value of bloodstain evidence that clearly refuted the version of events described by the accused and provided strong physical evidence for the prosecution at trial.

Cutting/Stabbing Injuries: Case 1

The victim in this case, was last seen alive leaving a gay bar with an unknown white male whom he had met that evening for the first time according to friends of the victim. The following morning when a neighbor saw blood near the apartment door of the victim and did not get any response to knocking, he called the police.

The victim was located in the southwest corner of his bedroom in a sitting position on top of a brown plastic clothes hamper. He was clad in white socks but otherwise nude. He faced the foot of a waterbed with an overturned bicycle on the floor between himself and the bed. The body was heavily bloodstained

Figure 8.145   Jacket of husband with blood spatter on front surface.

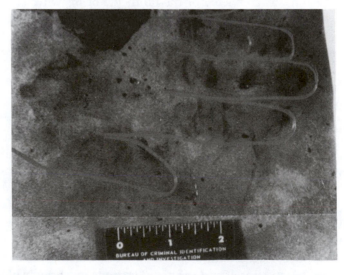

Figure 8.146   Palmar transfer pattern in blood on sleeve of husband's jacket.

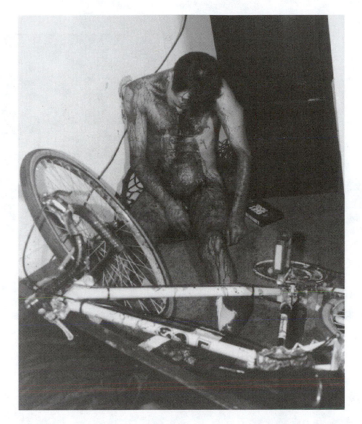

Figure 8.147 View of victim on floor of bedroom in front of waterbed and bicycle.

(Figure 8.147). The victim had sustained a fatal incised wound to the right side of the neck which severed the trachea and the right carotid artery. No other injuries were present according to the autopsy report (Figure 8.148).

The waterbed was situated forward of the victim and approximately centered in the bedroom against the east wall of the room. The pillow situated on the right side of the bed (as one would lie in bed) showed downward dripping of blood and areas of projected bloodstains. The left side pillow showd a large contact bloodstain as well as some drip patterns and projected bloodstains. The wall and window sill behind the bed exhibited patterns of small circular bloodstains likely produced as the result of arterial spurting and exhalation of blood from the severed trachea and right carotid artery (Figure 8.149).

The wall in the southeast corner of the bedroom showed additional arterial spurt patterns and the cradle of a telephone on a nightstand in the corner showed a large contact bloodstain on the top surface. The wire to the receiver had been cut (Figure 8.150).

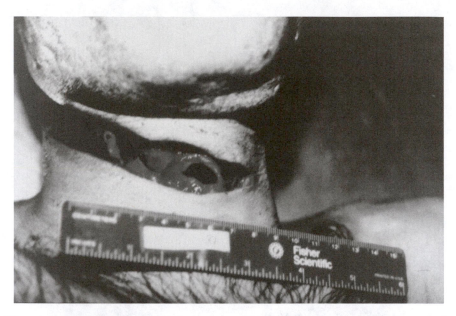

Figure 8.148 Fatal incised wound to right side of neck which severed the trachea and right carotid artery.

Figure 8.149 Projected and contact bloodstains on waterbed pillows with continuation of projected bloodstains on wall and window sill.

Figure 8.150 Arterial spurt pattern on wall near nightstand containing blood-stained telephone.

The south wall showed evidence of additional arterial spurting as well as contact transfer bloodstains consistent with the victim moving towards his final position. The large transfer bloodstain appeared to be feathered in a direction back towards the east wall opposite to the ultimate direction taken by the victim. This altering of direction may well have been the result of the unsteady victim as he was rapidly losing blood (Figure 8.151). On the floor in this area were numerous drip patterns of blood.

The west wall, and the inside of the entrance door to the apartment, exhibited a large classic arterial spurt pattern with characteristic downward flow patterns present. This was consistent with the victim still in a somewhat standing position close to this area before falling to his final position (Figure 8.152). On the floor of the hallway outside the entrance door were numerous transfers of blood, some of which were identified as having been produced by

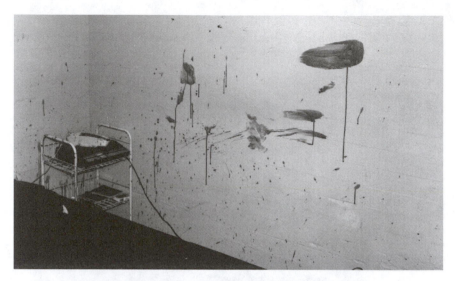

Figure 8.151 Transfer bloodstains on east wall near the telephone.

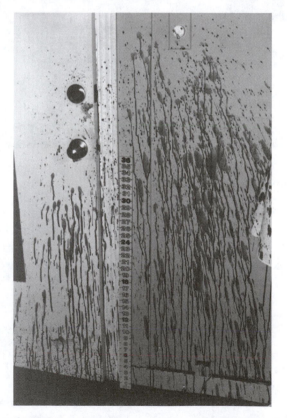

Figure 8.152 Arterial spurt pattern on bedroom door.

feet other than those of the victim since he was clad in socks. These bloody footprints continued down the hall toward the rear door of the house and left identifiable impressions with sufficient ridge detail for a positive identification of a suspect.

Based upon the bloodstain evidence, it was concluded that the victim sustained the incised wound to the right side of the neck while somewhat prone on the bed with his head near the pillows. Despite the severity of his wound he was able to exit the bed and managed to reach the area of the entrance door before collapsing into the sitting position in which he was found.

Subsequently, a suspect was arrested for this homicide and confessed that he was engaged in anal intercourse with the victim while on the bed. The victim was on his hands and knees facing the pillows. The assailant was behind and above him when he grabbed a knife with his right hand from the nightstand to the left of the bed. As he was about to have an orgasm the assailant cut the victim's throat. He then cut the phone line, left the bedroom and held the doorknob from the outside as the victim tried to get out of the room. When he heard the victim collapse, he reentered the bedroom to retrieve his clothing and left through the rear door of the residence. He stated that he knew that he was tracking blood with his bare feet. The defendant pled guilty to murder prior to trial.

Cutting/Stabbing Injuries: Case 2

The body of a man in his early twenties was discovered near railroad tracks in a northern city during the early morning hours by children on their way to school (Figure 8.153). It was first assumed that he was the victim of a pedestrian-train accident because of the severe damage to his neck. Closer examination revealed that the victim had suffered a severely slashed throat and multiple stab wounds to the chest, abdomen, and back (Figure 8.154). Autopsy revealed a total of eight stab wounds in addition to the large incised wound of the throat and some minor defensive wounds to the fingers and hands. Death was attributed to massive internal bleeding due to perforation of the heart and liver.

A police officer who had been called to the scene recognized the victim as one of three people in a vehicle that he had stopped the previous evening for speeding. A check of the ticket records led to the identification of the vehicle and two brothers were arrested as a result of this investigation. The three individuals had been drinking together the previous evening at several bars and had decided to continue drinking in a remote area near the railroad tracks where the victim was found. At this point each brother blamed the other for the fatal stabbing which was the result of an argument.

Figure 8.153 The victim of a multiple stabbing on the ground near railroad tracks.

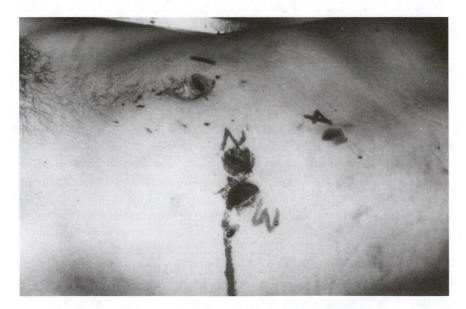

Figure 8.154 Location of the four stab wounds in the lower front chest and abdomen of the victim.

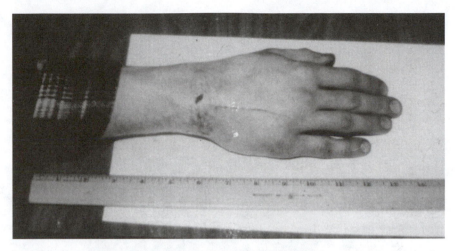

Figure 8.155 Right hand of the defendant showing a cut on the dorsal surface.

Examination of the scene revealed the presence of some bloodstains and smearing on the railroad track where the altercation most likely began. Only a trace of blood was seen in the snow in the area of drag marks on the ground between the tracks and the final location of the body where a large pooling of blood was present beneath and around the victim.

It was interesting to note in this case that neither defendant showed evidence on their clothing and shoes of the victim's blood which was group O. However, one brother showed blood smearing on the front of his trousers that was consistent with his own blood which was group A. This brother had sustained a moderately severe cut on his right hand which was bandaged when he was apprehended a day after the incident (Figure 8.155). This would explain the blood on his trousers that matched his own group A.

The blue jeans worn by the victim in this case became a key item of evidence linking an assailant to the victim. The victim's blue jeans exhibited moderate bloodstaining in the front midsection and thigh areas, some of which was consistent with bleeding by the victim (Figure 8.156). There were additional scattered round- and oval-shaped spots of blood present on the right front and rear leg surface of the blue jeans representing dripping of blood and some medium-velocity blood spatter. These bloodstains were produced by droplets of blood traveling towards the victim from a source either above, in front of, or in back of the victim depending upon his posture at the time. Based upon the location and physical characteristics of the bloodstains, they did not appear consistent with having been produced by blood from the wounds of the victim. Nine of these bloodstains were removed and subjected to blood-grouping tests and were found to be blood group A. Two additional stains were found to be group O. The group A bloodstains

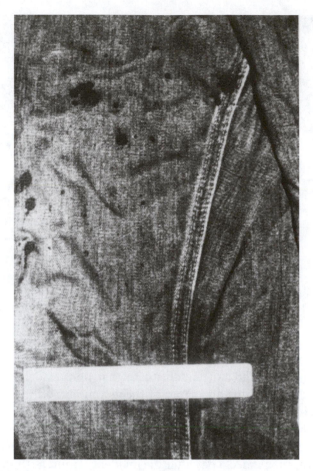

Figure 8.156 Bloodstains on the right front leg of the victim's blue jeans, deposited by the defendant with the cut hand.

were consistent with the blood of the brother with the cut hands who was a group A and provided strong evidence of his proximity to the assault at a time when he was bleeding actively from his hand. The second brother possessed group O blood similar to the victim but had no visible injury. The second brother was convicted of homicide despite these findings. The brother with the cut hand later pleaded guilty prior to his trial. Both received life sentences for the homicide.

This case emphasizes the importance of careful examination of the victim's clothing as well as that of a suspect or suspects during an investigation. In this particular case the victim's clothing was bagged after autopsy and was actually examined for the first time by the expert for the defense of the brother whose blood was not on the victim's clothing. Potentially exculpatory evidence was never subjected to any examination or analysis by the medical examiner nor investigating agency. As it turned out the jury did decide that the second brother was at least contributory to the homicide despite the bloodstain evidence.

Another interesting feature of this case is the lack of blood from the victim on both of the suspects despite the multiple stab wounds and throat slashing sustained by the victim. In cutting and stabbing cases, the assailant wielding the weapon does not always receive significant bloodstaining from the victim. Often, the most serious bleeding of the victim is internal. Externally, clothing and other apparel worn by the victim will saturate with blood from wounds. Blood spatter may be minimal since it requires impact with an exposed source of the blood to be produced. In cutting and stabbing cases, the severance of an artery may produce sizable arterial spurt patterns on the assailant and nearby surfaces depending upon their locations. In those cases where the assailant slashes the throat of a victim from a position behind, he may be shielded from impact of the arterial spurting. Sometimes, the severance of a neck artery may occur as a final act or coup de grace subsequent to previous injuries to the victim and arterial pressures may be minimal or absent during the agonal period. In those situations, arterial spurting would not be expected to occur.

Cutting/Stabbing Injuries: Case 3

The importance of careful examination of the scene and clothing of the victim for evidence of bloodstains that may represent injury of an assailant has been previously demonstrated. This case represents one in which all the bloodstains at the scene and on the victim were deposited by the assailant. In upstate New York, police responded to a vehicular-pedestrian accident. The driver of the vehicle claimed that a male pedestrian ran into his path and the collision was unavoidable. The victim was taken to a local hospital and was treated for minor injuries. The attending physician questioned the victim concerning a slashed wrist, which required suturing but did not appear to be related to the vehicular accident. The individual was reluctant to offer an explanation to the physician, but later gave a statement to the police officer investigating the accident saying that his live-in girlfriend had slashed his wrist during an argument. He then grabbed her by the throat and pushed her away, and she fell to the floor unconscious. The boyfriend panicked, became depressed, and attempted suicide in several ways. He first attempted to electrocute himself with the cord from a coffeemaker and then drank a glass of cleaning solution. He then drove away from the house in his truck, and a few miles down the road purposely crashed his vehicle into a tree. Still alive, and relatively uninjured, the boyfriend then ran in front of an oncoming vehicle—which he also survived (Figure 8.157).

Figure 8.157   Medium-velocity blood spatter on the left front-end of the vehicle resulting from impact with previously injured boyfriend attempting to commit suicide.

The 16-year-old girlfriend was found on the floor in the kitchen of the house shared by the couple (Figure 8.158). Postmortem examination revealed the cause of death to be asphyxiation. The pathologist determined that marks on the neck of the victim had been produced by sustained pressure on the neckline of the sweater utilized as a ligature. The front of the sweater and blue jeans of the victim were considerably bloodstained with transfer patterns of blood (Figure 8.159). A bloodstained towel was near her right shoulder. Several knives were scattered on the kitchen floor as well as numerous blood-stained paper towels. On the kitchen counter near the sink a coffeemaker was found with the cord cut, but still in the electrical outlet. A metal fork was nearby (Figure 8.160). Circular spots of blood on the countertop represented bleeding from a source above the counter. A nearly empty glass containing a cleaning solution was found on the opposite side of the sink (Figure 8.161). All the bloodstains at the scene including those on the victim were found to be the type of the boyfriend. The girl sustained no blood-producing injuries. Examination of the scene did indicate that the boyfriend may have attempted suicide in the manners in which he claimed. However, he was convicted of homicide after a jury trial. The verdict in the first trial was appealed and eventually overturned. A new trial was ordered approximately

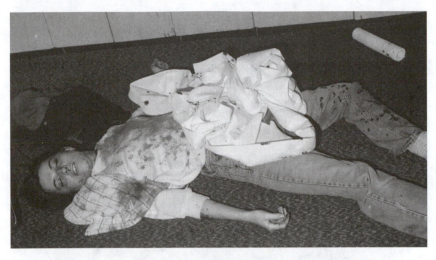

Figure 8.158 Victim with bloodstained shirt on the kitchen floor partially covered with paper towels.

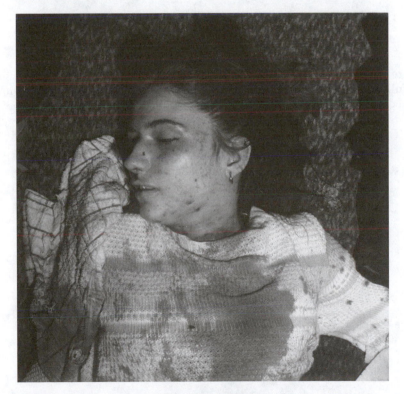

Figure 8.159 Closer view of blood transfer patterns on the front of the victim's shirt that were determined to be the blood type of the boyfriend and not that of the victim.

Figure 8.160 Severed electrical cord and fork utilized by boyfriend to unsuccessfully electrocute himself. Note blood drips on countertop from previously slashed wrist.

Figure 8.161 Glass on the counter top containing a cleaning fluid that boyfriend attempted to drink with additional blood drips nearby.

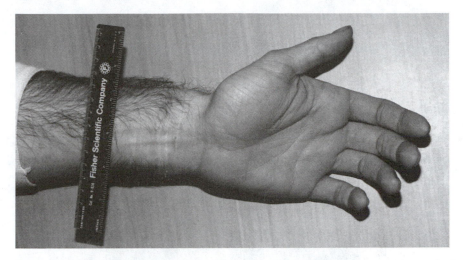

Figure 8.162 Healed scars of left wrist of boyfriend showing major wrist slash and parallel, healed hesitation wounds.

two years later. The defense at this time requested a reevaluation of the physical evidence and bloodstain pattern interpretation. As part of this rein-vestigation, a request was made to examine the wrist of the defendant who was still in custody. The healed scar representing the wrist slash incurred two years previously was well defined. However, parallel to this major healed scar on the wrist were several superficial healed scars representing additional incised wounds (Figure 8.162). The presence of these classical hesitation wounds provided strong evidence that the wrist slash sustained by the defen-dant was self-inflicted. The location of the wrist slash was not in a typical location to be classified as a defensive wound. The defendant was convicted a second time by a jury without the benefit of testimony concerning the wrist or bloodstain pattern interpretation since the defense attorney chose not to offer the testimony of his expert.

Cutting/Stabbing Injuries: Case 4

A white male in his early fifties from the Middle East was found dead in his jewelry-designing and manufacturing shop in the downtown area of a large city. He was lying on his back in a large pool of blood near some gas cylinders (Figure 8.163). The body was found by family members after the deceased did not arrive home for dinner and did not respond to telephone calls to the place of business. The door to the premises was locked with no sign of forced entry. The family members admitted themselves with their own set of keys.

Death was considered to be due to massive external bleeding related to slash wounds of the wrists and backs of the knees (Figures 8.164 and 8.165).

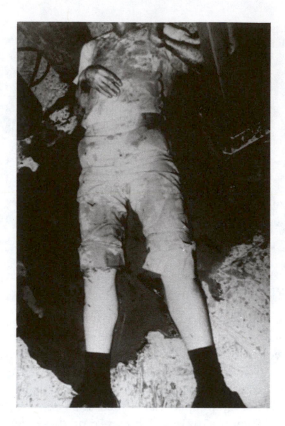

Figure 8.163 Victim as found lying in pool of blood in jewelry manufacturing shop. Note that trouser legs are rolled up.

The deep wounds extended to the bone in each area and severed tendons, arteries, veins, and nerves in the wrists and behind the knees. At each location there was a single deep slash with no evidence of superficial hesitation cuts. The postmortem examination did not reveal any additional injuries to the victim nor evidence of restraint. Toxicology studies gave negative results.

Review of the scene photographs did not reveal evidence of the occurrence of a fight or struggle. The large pool of blood beneath and around the victim was relatively undisturbed. There were numerous bloody shoeprints on the floor leading away from the body (Figure 8.166). However, prior to the photographs having been taken the scene was accessible to the family, EMT personnel, and police investigators who likely tracked blood on the floor after approaching the body. There was an absence of blood on the shoes of the victim. The trouser legs of the victim were pulled up above the knees which would have exposed the site of injuries to the back of the knees. The slashes to these areas did not involve damage to the trousers. A scalpel with a plastic handle and number 11 blade was located between the legs of the

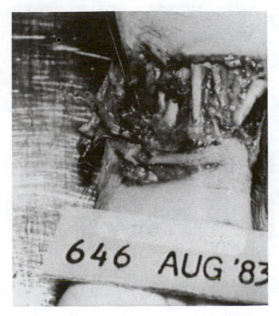

Figure 8.164 Deep, incised wound in right wrist of victim.

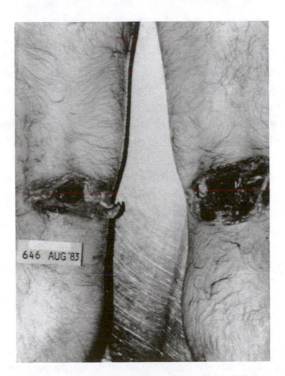

Figure 8.165 Deep, incised wounds behind both knees of victim.

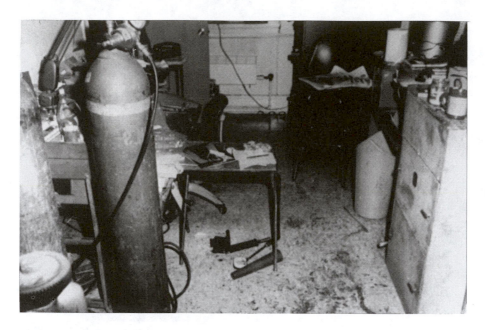

Figure 8.166   Shoeprints in blood on floor leading away from victim.

victim at the level of the knees (Figures 8.167 and 8.168). The front of the victim's shirt was smeared with blood and evidence of blood spatter with cast-off bloodstains in the area of the front shoulders, extending onto the face of the victim (Figure 8.169). Blood flow and drip patterns on the floor to the left of the victim's left leg and waist were observed in conjunction with some apparent arterial spurt patterns on an adjacent table leg. These bloodstains would be consistent with the victim sitting on the floor in that area prior to falling backward to his final position.

The history of the victim indicated some evidence of despondency and previous visits to a psychiatrist. An overdose of aspirin had been ingested approximately three weeks prior to his death. Although there was no evidence of a suicide note at the scene, this case was eventually classified as a suicide. Many aspects of the investigation support this conclusion. It is recognized that only 15 to 20% of suicide victims leave notes. Prior attempts at self-destruction are not uncommon. The areas of injury to the victim were accessible for him to inflict injury.

Exposure of the back of the knees by raising the trouser legs prior to slashing is consistent with self-infliction. The absence of hesitation cuts is an unusual aspect of this case but, on the other hand, there was no evidence of any of the injuries that were defensive in nature. The fact that both wrists and rear of both knees were deeply slashed severing tendons and nerves as well as arteries and veins would tend to cast doubt that the victim could have

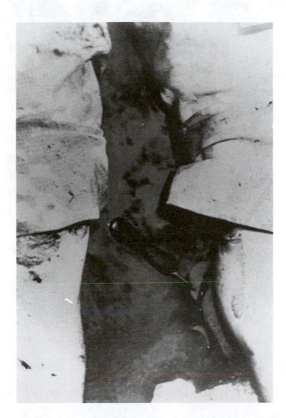

Figure 8.167   Scalpel located on the floor between the legs of the victim.

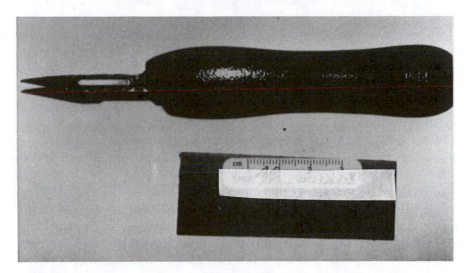

Figure 8.168   View of the scalpel with a thick handle and a #11 blade.

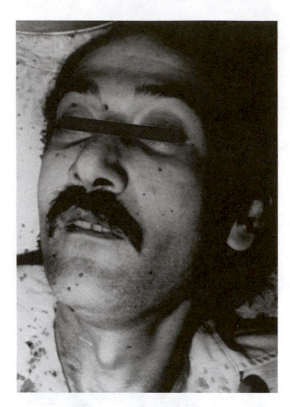

Figure 8.169   Victim's face showing distribution of blood spatter.

inflicted these injuries to the four locations himself. It was the opinion of some physicians that the victim could have self inflicted the knee injuries and one wrist injury but not cut both wrists and knees in that fashion. How would he have been able to hold the scalpel in a hand that sustained severe tendon and nerve damage? There exist two possibilities that would be consistent with the bloodstains on the face of the victim. The scalpel could have been supported between the knees of the victim or held in the mouth and the blade then drawn across the wrist. Either scenario would account for the location of the scalpel between the legs of the victim. Neither the clothing nor the weapon was available for examination to further support these possibilities. An unusual blood transfer pattern on the left calf of the victim may have been associated with the scalpel handle but unfortunately was not clearly resolved in the photographs made available for review.

A search of the forensic literature did not reveal a similar case of deep, bilateral slashing of the wrists and knees in the absence of hesitation cuts and thus this case is considered highly unusual. A theory that the victim declined to resist or was incapacitated by a drug or chemical means prior to being slashed methodically by an unknown assailant was not substantiated by the postmortem examination nor the physical evidence.

Litigation in this case involved denial by an insurance company of a claim by the family for death benefits because of a suicide clause in the policy. The case was ultimately settled just prior to trial in civil court.

Glossary

Angle of impact   The acute or internal angle formed between the direction of a blood drop and the plane of the surface it strikes.

Arterial spurting (or gushing) pattern   Bloodstain patterns resulting from blood exiting the body under pressure from a breached artery.

Back spatter   Blood directed back towards the source of energy or force that caused the spatter. Back spatter is often associated with gunshot wounds of entrance.

Bloodstain   The resulting transfer when liquid blood has come into contact with a surface or when a moist or wet surface comes into contact with dried blood.

Bubble rings   Rings in blood that result when blood containing air bubbles dries and retains the bubble's circular configuration as a dried outline.

Cast-off pattern   A bloodstain pattern created when blood is released or thrown from a blood bearing object in motion.

Clot   A gelatinous mass formed as a result of a complex mechanism involving red blood cells, fibrinogen, platelets and other clotting factors. Over time, the blood clot retracts, resulting in a clear separation of the mass from the more fluid, yellowish blood serum which remains at the periphery of the stain. (*See* serum stain.)

Directionality   The directionality of a bloodstain or pattern which indicates the direction the blood was traveling when it impacted the target surface. Directionality of a blood drop's flight can usually be established from the geometric shape of its bloodstain.

Directionality angle   The angle between the long axis of a bloodstain and a predetermined line on the plane of the target surface which represents $0°$.

Direction of flight   The trajectory or flight directionality of a blood drop which can be established by its angle of impact and directionality angle.

Drawback effect   The presence of blood in the barrel of a firearm that has been drawn backward into the muzzle.

Drip pattern   A bloodstain pattern which results from blood dripping into blood.

Expirated or exhaled blood   Blood that is blown out of the nose, mouth or a wound as a result of air pressure and/or air flow which is the propelling force.

Flight path   The path of the blood drop as it moves through space from the impact site to the target.

Flow pattern   A change in the shape and direction of a wet bloodstain due to the influence of gravity or movement of an object.

Forward spatter   Blood which travels in the same direction as the source of energy or force causing the spatter. Forward spatter is often associated with gunshot wounds of exit.

High-velocity impact spatter   A bloodstain pattern caused by a high-velocity force impact/force of approximately 100 feet per second or greater such as that produced by a gunshot or high speed machinery. It must be emphasized that blood does not spatter at the same velocity as the velocity of the wounding agent. This pattern is characterized by a mist-like dispersion which, due to the high surface area of small droplets can only travel a short horizontal distance in their flight. The preponderance of individual spots of blood produced by these mist-like blood droplets are usually 0.1 mm, or smaller, in diameter although some larger spots are also always produced.

Impact pattern   Bloodstain pattern created when blood receives a blow or force resulting in the random dispersion of smaller drops of blood.

Impact site   The point on a bloody object or body which receives a blow. Often, impact site is used interchangeably with point of origin. Impact site may also refer to areas on the surface of a target which is struck by blood in motion.

Low-velocity impact spatter   Bloodstains produced on a surface when the blood source has been subjected to a low-velocity force approximately 5 feet per second or less to a blood source.

Medium-velocity impact spatter   Bloodstains produced on a surface when the blood source has been subjected to a medium-velocity force between approximately 5 and 25 feet per second to a blood source. A beating typically causes this type of spatter. The preponderance of individual spots of blood produced in this manner are usually 1 to 3 mm in diameter but larger and smaller spots also occur.

Misting   Blood which has been reduced to a fine spray as the result of the energy or force applied to it.

Parent drop   A drop of blood from which a wave cast-off or satellite spatter originates.

Point or area of convergence   A point or area to which a bloodstain pattern can be projected on a two-dimensional surface. This point is determined by tracing the long axis of well-defined bloodstains within the pattern back to a common point or area.

Point or area of origin   The three-dimensional point or area from which the blood that produced a bloodstain originated. This is determined by projecting angles of impact of well-defined bloodstains back to an axis constructed through the point or area of convergence.

Projected blood pattern   A pattern created when blood is projected or released as the result of force.

Ricochet or secondary splash   The deflection of large volumes of blood after impact with a target surface that results in staining of a second surface. Ricochet does not occur when small drops of blood strike a surface.

Satellite spatter   Small droplets of blood that are projected around or beside a drop of blood upon impact with a surface. A wave cast-off is also considered a form of satellite spatter.

Scallop Pattern   A bloodstain produced by a single drop which is characterized by a wave-like, scalloped edge.

Serum stain   A clear, yellowish stain with a shiny surface often appearing around a bloodstain after the blood has retracted due to clotting. This separation is affected by temperature, humidity, substrate, and/or air movement.

Skeletonized bloodstain   A bloodstain that consists only of its outer periphery, the central area having been removed by wiping after liquid blood has partially dried. A skeletonized bloodstain is also produced by the flaking away of the central portion of a completely dried stain.

Smear   A relatively large volume of blood, usually 0.5 ml or more, that has been distorted to such a degree that further classification is not possible. A smear is similar to a smudge, but a smear is a stain produced by a larger volume of blood.

Smudge   A bloodstain that has been distorted to a degree so that further classification is not possible.

Spatter   The dispersion of small blood droplets due to the forceful projection of blood.

Spine   The pointed edge characteristics that radiate away from the center of a bloodstain. Their formation depends upon impact velocity and surface texture.

Splash   A stain pattern created by a low-velocity impact upon a quantity of blood approximately 1.0 ml or greater striking a surface.

Swipe   The transfer of blood onto a surface not already contaminated with blood. One edge is usually feathered which may indicate the direction of travel.

Target   A surface upon which blood has been deposited.

Terminal velocity   The maximum speed to which a free-falling drop of blood can accelerate in air which is approximately 25.1 feet per second.

Transfer pattern   A contact bloodstain created when a wet, bloody surface contacts a second surface as the result of compression or lateral movement. A recognizable mirror image or at least a recognizable portion of the original surface may be transferred to the second surface.

Void or shadow   Absence of bloodstain in an otherwise continuous bloodstain pattern. Often the geometry of the void will suggest an outline of the object which has intercepted the blood; such as a shoe, furniture, person, etc.

Wave cast-off   A small blood droplet that originates from a parent drop of blood due to the wave-like action of the liquid in conjunction with striking a surface at an angle less than 90 degrees.

Wipe   A bloodstain pattern created when an object moves through an existing bloodstain removing blood from the original stain and altering its appearance.

This glossary has been adapted from terminology compiled by the Terminology Committee of the International Association of Bloodstain Pattern Analysts. The suggested list of the Committee was proposed in 1996. This glossary is offered as a guideline and is not designed to be all encompassing. However, these terms have been carefully studied and represent definitions that will be useful in communication within the discipline of bloodstain pattern interpretation. Input was also received from many individuals throughout the forensic community both in the United States and Canada. It should be recognized that the terminology utilized in this text is not all-inclusive and variations may exist in different texts and other sources. It is felt that the terminology presented here does represent a significant agreement and consensus of opinion of many individuals. There is a need for consistent and uniform terminology in order to avoid confusion and misleading interpretation in the evaluation of written conclusions and oral testimony in court.

The definition of angle of impact or angle of incidence of a blood drop as the internal angle at which it strikes a surface relative to the horizontal plane of that impacting surface is widely but not universally used. DeForest, Gaensslen and Lee, in their text *Forensic Science—An Introduction to Criminalistics* prefer to define angle of impact as the angle of incidence conforming to the optical reflection and refraction of light rays. They measure the angle of incidence relative to the "normal" of the impacting surface rather than the horizontal plane of the surface itself. The "normal" of a surface is an imaginary line perpendicular (90 degrees) to the horizontal plane of the surface. A straight-on impact of a blood drop along the normal to a surface would be said to have an angle of incidence of 0 degrees rather than a 90-degree angle of impact. A 10-degree angle of incidence relative to the normal in this system would correspond to an 80-degree angle of impact relative to the plane of the horizontal surface. To determine angle of incidence relative to the normal from the width to length ratio, the cosine function must be utilized rather than the sine function. To convert the angle of incidence relative to the normal to the more universal angle of impact relative to the horizontal plane of the surface, it must be subtracted from 90 degrees. It is very important to realize which system is being utilized in a bloodstain interpretation to avoid confusion. Perhaps it is better in this instance to maintain the classical definition of angle of impact relative to the horizontal plane of the impacting surface, which is more familiar to investigators as a means of maintaining consistency and uniformity.

Appendix 1: Trigonometric Tables

Trigonometric Tables—Sine and Tangent Functions

Degrees	Sine	Tangent	Degrees	Sine	Tangent
0.0	.0000	.0000	46.0	.7193	1.036
1.0	.0175	.0175	47.0	.7314	1.072
2.0	.0349	.0349	48.0	.7431	1.111
3.0	.0523	.0524	49.0	.7547	1.150
4.0	.0698	.0699	50.0	.7660	1.192
5.0	.0872	.0875	51.0	.7771	1.235
6.0	.1045	.1051	52.0	.7880	1.280
7.0	.1219	.1228	53.0	.7986	1.327
8.0	.1392	.1405	54.0	.8090	1.376
9.0	.1564	.1584	55.0	.8192	1.428
10.0	.1736	.1763	56.0	.8290	1.483
11.0	.1908	.1944	57.0	.8387	1.540
12.0	.2079	.2126	58.0	.8480	1.600
13.0	.2250	.2309	59.0	.8572	1.664
14.0	.2419	.2493	60.0	.8660	1.732
15.0	.2588	.2679	61.0	.8746	1.804
16.0	.2756	.2867	62.0	.8829	1.881
17.0	.2924	.3057	63.0	.8910	1.963
18.0	.3090	.3249	64.0	.8988	2.050
19.0	.3256	.3443	65.0	.9063	2.145
20.0	.3420	.3640	66.0	.9135	2.246
21.0	.3584	.3839	67.0	.9205	2.356
22.0	.3746	.4040	68.0	.9272	2.475
23.0	.3907	.4245	69.0	.9336	2.605
24.0	.4067	.4452	70.0	.9397	2.748
25.0	.4226	.4663	71.0	.9455	2.904
26.0	.4384	.4877	72.0	.9511	3.078
27.0	.4540	.5095	73.0	.9563	3.271
28.0	.4695	.5317	74.0	.9613	3.487
29.0	.4848	.5543	75.0	.9659	3.732
30.0	.5000	.5774	76.0	.9703	4.011
31.0	.5150	.6009	77.0	.9744	4.332
32.0	.5299	.6249	78.0	.9781	4.705
33.0	.5446	.6494	79.0	.9816	5.145

Trigonometric Tables—Sine and Tangent Functions (continued)

Degrees	Sine	Tangent	Degrees	Sine	Tangent
34.0	.5592	.6745	80.0	.9848	5.671
35.0	.5736	.7002	81.0	.9877	6.314
36.0	.5878	.7265	82.0	.9903	7.115
37.0	.6018	.7536	83.0	.9925	8.144
38.0	.6157	.7813	84.0	.9945	9.514
39.0	.6293	.8098	85.0	.9962	11.43
40.0	.6428	.8391	86.0	.9976	14.30
41.0	.6561	.8693	87.0	.9986	19.08
42.0	.6691	.9004	88.0	.9994	28.64
43.0	.6820	.9325	89.0	.9998	57.29
44.0	.6947	.9657	90.0	1.000	0.000
45.0	.7071	1.000			

Appendix 2: Precautions for Infectious Diseases: AIDS and Hepatitis B and C

HENRY C. LEE, PhD

The widespread apprehension and controversy over exposure to various infectious diseases, such as AIDS and hepatitis B, have resulted in the development of guidelines and precautions for law enforcement personnel. Today, with AIDS and hepatitis B infections virtually epidemic, police officers, crime scene investigators, and forensic laboratory examiners are more likely than ever before to encounter these infectious blood or other body fluids during routine activities.

Acquired immunodeficiency syndrome (AIDS) has a variety of manifestations that range from asymptomatic, and signs of AIDS-related complex (ARC), to severe immunodeficiency and life-threatening secondary infections. The virus that causes the disease is known by several names. In nontechnical literature, it is frequently referred to as the human immunodeficiency virus (HIV). In scientific literature, it is usually identified as HTLV-III/LAV, which stands for "human T-lymphotropic virus type III/lymphadenopathy-associated virus." The virus is a "retrovirus" which invades the victim's immunity system, destroys it, and causes the patient to become highly susceptible to secondary infections. The AIDS virus has been isolated from blood, bone marrow, saliva, lymph nodes, brain tissue, semen, plasma, vaginal fluids, cervical secretions, tears, and human milk. The mode of transmission generally involves direct contact of contaminated blood and body fluids with open cuts, wounds, lesions, or mucous membranes. There is currently no cure for AIDS.

Hepatitis B and C are infectious diseases of the liver. They are types of serum hepatitis that will result in jaundice, cirrhosis, and sometimes cancer of the liver. The virus may be found in human blood, urine, semen, cerebrospinal fluid, saliva, and vaginal fluid. Injection into the bloodstream, droplet exposure of mucous membranes, and contact with broken skin are the primary hazards.

The following guidelines are established based on the current scientific and medical knowledge. By practicing these precautions, laboratory examiners and police officers may perform their duties as required by law, while minimizing the risk of accidental infection, whether administering cardiopulmonary resuscitation (CPR) at the scene of an accident, collecting evidence at crime scenes, examining physical evidence at the laboratory, or dealing with individuals who are high-risk carriers.

Precautionary Measures

The precautions specified below should be enforced routinely, regardless of whether the persons involved are known to be AIDS or hepatitis B infected.

1. All blood and body fluids are to be considered infectious whether wet or dry.
2. All needles, syringes, blades, razor blades, knives, and sharp instruments should be handled with caution and placed in puncture-resistant containers.
3. Good personal hygiene is the best protection against infectious diseases. Wash hands with soap and water after each assignment.
4. Know your skin integrity. Keep all wounds carefully bandaged while on duty. Use a bandage that provides a complete impermeable 360 degree coverage. Change the bandage if it becomes soiled or dirty.
5. Latex gloves should be worn when handling blood specimens, body fluids, materials, and objects exposed to contamination. Dispose of gloves after one use.
6. Gowns, masks, and eye protectors should be worn when clothing may be soiled by blood or body fluids or when procedures are being performed that may involve extensive exposure to blood or potentially infectious body fluids (such as the transport of the victim's body, laboratory examination specimens, postmortem examinations).
7. Avoid all hand-to-face contact including eating, smoking, and drinking where the possibility of transmission exists.
8. Hands and skin area must be washed immediately and thoroughly if they accidentally become contaminated with blood or body fluids.
9. Contaminated surfaces and objects should be cleaned up with a one (1) part household bleach to nine (9) parts water (1:10 dilution). An alcohol pad or soap and water can be used as a subsequent cleaning solution and to remove the odor of bleach.
10. Constantly be alert for sharp objects. When handling hypodermic needles, knives, razors, broken glass, nails, broken metal, or any other

sharp object bearing blood, use the utmost care to prevent a cut or puncture of the skin.

Specific Guidelines for the Laboratory Examiner

1. When handling and examining contaminated blood or body fluids, the examiner shall wear double latex gloves, lab coat, mask, and eye coverings.
2. Cover the lab bench with a protective sheet and remove instruments from the lab bench before examining any blood or body fluids.
3. Sharp instruments, such as needles, knives, scalpels, blades, broken glass, broken metal, auto lens, nails and other objects shall be handled by the examiner with deliberate care to prevent infection from accidental cuts or punctures.
4. After completing the examination:
   a. Any sharp objects should be packaged carefully and properly.
   b. Any liquid blood and body fluids should be diluted with equal amounts of sodium hypochlorite solution and disposed of properly.
   c. The lab bench should be cleaned with 1:10 sodium hypochlorite solution and rinsed with soap and water.
5. Hands must be washed after removing gloves, gowns and masks before leaving the examination area.
6. Any spills should be cleaned promptly with soap and water, or household detergent.

Specific Guidelines for the Crime Scene Investigator

1. Crime scene investigators should wear latex gloves and coverall gowns when conducting crime scene searches.
2. Surgical masks should be worn when aerosol or airborne particles may be encountered, for example, blood droplets, dried blood particles, and so forth.
3. Double latex gloves, surgical masks, and protective eyewear should be used when collecting or handling liquid blood, body fluids, dried blood particles, blood-contaminated evidence, or bodies of the deceased.
4. Latex gloves, eye-coverings, surgical masks, and a gown should be worn when attending an autopsy.
5. When processing the crime scene, constantly be alert for sharp objects and broken objects or surfaces.
6. Do not place your hands in areas where you are unable to see when conducting a search.

7. Under no circumstances should anyone at the crime scene be allowed to smoke, eat, or drink.
8. When liquid blood and body fluids are collected in bottles or glass vials, these containers must be labeled prominently "Blood Precautions."
9. Blood and body fluid-stained clothing and objects must be dried and packaged in double bags and labeled properly. If evidence collected from a possibly infected person, the package should be labeled "Caution Potential AIDS (Hepatitis) Case."
10. If practical, use only disposable items at a crime scene where infectious blood is present. All nondisposable items must be decontaminated after each use.
11. Any reports, labels, or evidence tags splashed with blood should be destroyed with the information copied on clean forms.
12. After completing the search of a scene, investigators should clean their hands with diluted household bleach solution and with soap and water solution. Any contaminated clothing and footwear should be disposed of properly.

Specific Guidelines for the Police Officer

1. Whenever the slightest possibility of exposure exists, the officer should wear latex gloves, protective gown, and face mask.
2. In addition to latex gloves, disposable footwear protection should be worn at motor vehicle accidents where the possibility of contamination exists.
3. Special masks are to be used when administering cardiopulmonary resuscitation (CPR). It is the officer's responsibility to see that the mask is disinfected after each use.
4. Precautionary measures should always be applied to avoid being bitten or assaulted during arrests or questioning witnesses or suspects.
5. When searching areas that are not clearly visible, a flashlight or baton should be used to illuminate the area. Do not place your hands between car seats or under car seats.
6. When searching a suspect, a cautionary pat search should be conducted. If possible, the suspect should be directed to empty his pockets and socks.
7. Physical evidence containing blood or body fluids should be marked and handled using the same guidelines as previously described.
8. Any contamination of exposed skin should be immediately washed with 1:10 bleach solution and rinsed well with soap and water.

9. Any contaminated clothing and gloves should be discarded properly. Other nondisposable material should be decontaminated with bleach solution and washed thoroughly.
10. If an accidental exposure occurs, the incident is to be reported immediately to the supervisor or proper authority, and physician.

Index

A

Abdominal cavity, 116–118, 119
Abdominal wounds, case studies, 257, 288
Abrasions, 106, 118
Absorption elution, 165
Adenosine deaminase (ADA), 165
Adenylate kinase (AK), 165
Age
    of bloodstains, 94–96, 159, 164
    of the victim, 105
AIDS, precautions for, 311–315
Albrecht Mechanism, 156, 157, 158
American Journal of Forensic Medicine and Pathology, 10
3-Aminophthalate, 158
3-Aminophthalhydrazide. *See* Luminol
Amputation, 112, 113
Anal orifice, 118
Angle of impact
    definition, 303, 307
    determination of origin and, 36, 38–40, 129
    ellipse of bloodstain and, 27, 29–34
    of free-falling droplets onto nonhorizontal surfaces, 27–34
    length to width ratio and, 31–34
    produced by horizontal motion, 40–41, 43–44
Angular considerations, low-velocity impacts, 19–58
Area of convergence, 35–36, 37, 129, 305
Arterial spurting (gushing), 17, 42, 45, 283, 284, 285, 303
Artifacts, creation of, 128, 143
Asphyxial deaths, 1, 2, 114, 115, 276, 292
Aspiration of blood, 250

Assailant
    bloodstains from, 289–290
    bloodstains on, 61–62, 143–145, 146, 147
    evidence for activity of, 129
    movement of, 125, 144, 172, 173
Automobiles. *See* Vehicular trauma
Autopsies, 10, 126

B

Back spatter, 303
    from gunshot trauma, 68, 72, 73, 79, 110
    in case studies, 181, 186–187, 189
    reasons for absence of, 201–202
Balthazard, Victor, 5–6
Basic Bloodstain Institutes, 8, 9
Basophils, 12, 13
Beating. *See* Blunt-force trauma; Medium-velocity impact
Biological properties of blood, 12–13
Bleach, 98
Blood. *See also* specific patterns
    biological properties of, 12–13
    clotting of, 87–90
        definition, 303
        effects of disease and medications on, 105
        time, and estimation of blood loss, 120, 248
    decomposition of, 140, 154
    degradation experiments, 94–96
    dripping into blood. *See* Satellite spatter
    drying of
        timeframe, 85–87, 90–93, 120, 130, 218
        on various surfaces, 90–93
        weight loss from, 122
    external forces that alter, 15–17
    major vessel disruption, 112–119

physical properties of, 14–15
specific gravity of, 14
viscosity of, 14
volume
    crime scene estimation of, 122, 123, 124
    of droplet, 19–20
    in human body, 120, 121
    in pericardial cavity, 116
Blood droplets. *See also* Blood spatter; Cast-
    off or splashed blood
    direction of flight, 303
    drying process in, 86, 191
    flicking of, 64, 65
    free-falling, 278. *See also* Cast-off or
        splashed blood
        horizontal motion and, 40–41
        onto horizontal surfaces, 19–27
        onto nonhorizontal surfaces, 27–34
        point or area of convergence, 35–36,
            129
        point or area of origin, 36–40
        terminal velocity of, 21, 306
    oscillations within, 19
    shape of, 19, 31–34
    size of
        from high-velocity impacts, 68, 69, 70
        from medium-velocity impacts, 59
    surface tension forces in, 14–15, 19, 20
    volume, 19–20
Blood group antigens, 165
Blood grouping, 1, 139, 140, 165, 169, 217,
    289–290
Blood loss evidence, 119–121
Blood spatter. *See also* Cast-off or splashed
    blood
    blood dripping into blood. *See* Satellite
        spatter
    from blunt-force trauma, 222–225, 228,
        235–238, 242, 245, 248, 249–250,
        252, 254, 260, 262–264, 272–275,
        280–282
    definition, 305
    directionality of, 11, 129, 303
    distance from source, 10, 22–24
    external forces that alter, 15–17
    from gunshot trauma, 68–84, 181,
        187–188, 189, 191, 192, 202, 208. *See
        also* Back spatter
    from high-velocity impact, 67–74

from medium-velocity impact, 59–67
from sharp-force trauma, 298, 300
*Bloodstain Analysis With an Introduction to
    Crime Scene Reconstruction,* 10
Bloodstain Pattern Analysis in Violent Crimes,
    10
*Bloodstain Pattern Analysis - Theory and
    Practice,* 9
Bloodstain Patterns, 9, 59, 97
Bloodstains. *See also* individual patterns
    absence of, on assailant, 62–63, 291
    aging of, 94–96, 159, 164
    correlation with autopsy and laboratory
        reports, 126
    definition, 303
    diameter of, from free-falling blood
        droplet, 21
    dilution of, 96, 97, 98, 101, 130, 258
    dried, flaking of, 86, 128
    effects of luminol on subsequent analysis
        of, 165–166
    ellipse of
        and horizontal motion, 41, 43–44
        and impact angle, 27, 29–34
    examination of clothing, 142–149
    integration with other physical evidence,
        125
    multiple, 47, 53, 55, 61, 62
    radial patterns on, 61–62
    transfer patterns. *See* Blood transfer
        patterns
Blood transfer patterns, 17, 50, 52–53, 55, 58,
    99–100, 144
    case studies
        blunt-object trauma, 225, 228,
            242–244, 246, 259–260, 271, 279, 282
        gunshot trauma, 182–184, 186–187,
            197
        sharp-force trauma, 285–287, 292, 293,
            300
    definition, 306
Blunt-force trauma, 1
    case studies, 232–281
    cast-off blood from swing of weapon, 42,
        46–47, 272, 275
    contusions from, 2, 106, 107, 250, 252, 253
    two-handed or backhanded delivery, 47
    types of wounds, 106–108
    velocities of, 17

Boat, blunt-force trauma case study on, 232–241
Bone fractures, 106, 112–113
Brain tissue, 112
    blunt-force trauma and, 222
    gunshot trauma and, 110, 113, 114
    oxygen to, 116
Bruises, 2, 106, 107, 250, 252, 253
Bubble rings, definition, 303

C

Camps, Francis, 5
Capillary action, on cloth, 90
Carotid artery, 116, 119, 283, 284, 285
Cars. See Vehicular trauma
Case studies
    in bloodstain pattern interpretation, 177–301
    blunt-force trauma, 232–281, 282
    gunshot, 177–232
    sharp-force trauma, 281–301
    use of luminol, 169–173
Cast-off or splashed blood, 17, 42–48.
        See also Blood spatter
    case studies
        blunt-force trauma, 237, 242, 246, 255, 266–268, 270, 272–275
        gunshot trauma, 225, 227, 231
        sharp-force trauma, 298
    definition, 303, 305, 306
    from parent droplet (wave cast-off), 27, 28, 306
    from swing of weapon, 42, 46–47, 144, 272, 275
Chemiluminescence, 153, 158. See also Luminol
Chest wounds, 116, 119, 120, 192–193, 257, 288
Clean up activities, 98, 129, 162, 166, 168, 171, 266. See also Dilution
Cloth. See Surface texture
Clothing, 63–64, 119–120, 121
    evidence preservation, 140, 141, 143, 144
    examination of, 127, 142–149
    fibers from, 199, 200–201
    pockets of, 144

protective
    for luminol use, 160–161
    as precaution for infectious diseases, 312–314
Clot retraction, 88
Clotting. See Blood, clotting of
Color of blood
    aging and alterations in hemoglobin, 94–96
    oxygenation and, 12, 42
Computer programs for crime scene diagrams, 133, 134–136
Concerning the Origin, Shape, Direction, and Distribution of the Bloodstains Following Head Wounds Caused by Blows, 4
Contusions, 2, 106, 107, 250, 252, 253
Convergence
    definition, 305
    determination of point or area of, 35–36, 37, 129
Coomassie Blue, 166
Coughed blood. See Exhaled or expirated blood
Crime scene
    diagrams of, 132–139, 194
    methodology for search patterns, 131–132
    outdoor, 130–131
    photographs of, 127, 130
    precautions for infectious diseases, 313–315
    preliminary activities for evidence collection, 126
    in public places, 127
Cutting. See Sharp-force trauma

D

Dense zone, 87
Diagrams of crime scene, 132–139, 194
Diffusion, surface texture and blood drying time, 90–93, 130
Dilution
    of bloodstains, 96, 97, 98, 101, 130, 258
    of luminol, sensitivity and, 164
Directionality
    of blood flow, 48–49, 129, 189, 210
    of blood spatter, 11, 129, 303
    definitions, 303

Distance from source, 10, 22–24
DNA analysis, 139, 140, 145, 166, 232, 237
Documentation
    of evidence, 126, 127, 128, 130, 139
    incorporation of luminol data, 168
Dominant hand, 6
Drag patterns, 50, 51, 122, 123, 242
Drawback effect, 79–80, 83, 304
Dried bloodstains, 85–87
Drip pattern, 17, 25–27, 64, 65, 304
Droplets. See Blood droplets
Dry cleaning, effects on bloodstains, 98, 101
Drying of blood. See Blood, drying of

E

Economic aspects, grants, 7
Electrophoresis, 165
Emergency medical team, 128
Environmental conditions, 130
    blood loss and, 120
    drying time and, 85, 120
Enzyme typing, 165
Eosinophils, 12, 13
Erythrocytes, 12, 13, 87
Erythrocytic acid phosphatase, 165
Esterase D (ESD), 165
Evidence
    authority for collection of, 142
    blood loss, 119–121
    bloostained clothing, 142–149
    collection of, 125, 127–129, 130–132, 140–142, 164. See also Luminol
    documentation of, 126, 127, 128, 130, 139
    evaluation of, 126, 128, 129, 130, 132–139, 140–142
    labeling, 140
    preservation of, 139, 140, 141, 144, 164
Exhaled or expired blood, 17, 64, 66, 90
    in case studies, 196, 197, 206–208
    definition, 304
Experiments
    blood degradation, 94–96
    diffusion and drying time, 90–93
    to duplicate patterns, 11
    with firearms, 74–80
Experiments and Practical Exercises in Bloodstain Pattern Analysis, 9, 85

Expired blood. See Exhaled or expired blood
Explosions, velocity of, 17
External forces that alter blood, 15–17

F

Fading of bloodstains, 98
Femoral arteries and veins, 118
Fibrin, 87
Fibrinogen, 87
Filters, in luminescence photography, 168
Fingerprints and handprints, 52, 55, 125, 129, 170, 226, 282
Fire, effects on bloodstains, 96–98, 99–100
Firearms. See Guns
Fire Investigation, 98
Flash photography, 167–168
Flies, 64, 66, 67, 96
Flight Characteristics of Human Blood and Stain Patterns, 7, 8
Flight path, of blood droplet, 304
Flow pattern
    on board fishing vessel, 237, 239
    definition, 304
    directionality of, 48–49, 129, 189, 210
Footprints. See Shoeprints
Forensic Science - An Introduction to Criminalistics, 307
Forward spatter, 72, 304
Fractures, 106, 112–113
Free-falling blood. See Blood droplets, free-falling
Furrowing wound, 72

G

Genetic markers, 139, 140, 165
Ghosting effect, 98
Glossary, 303–307
Glyoxalase (GLO), 165
Gouging, 98
Gravitational forces, 87. See also Blood droplets, free-falling
Gunpowder, 78, 82, 143, 194
Guns, blood in the barrel of, 80–83, 110
Gunshot trauma, 70, 71
    case studies, 177–232
    penetrating vs. perforating, 110, 180

self-inflicted, 70–72, 73, 74, 110, 112, 113
  behavioral patterns of, 189, 210
  in case studies, 189, 219–221
simulated head for experiments with,
  74–80
size of droplets from, 67–74
soot from, 98, 178, 179, 204, 205, 210
types of wounds, 110–112
velocity of blood spatter from, 17, 59

H

Hair, effects on gunshot trauma, 79, 80
Hair transfer bloodstain patterns (swipes),
  17, 50, 53, 246, 306
Handedness, 6, 47
Handprints. *See* Fingerprints and handprints
Head, simulated, 74–80
Heat, effects on bloodstains, 96–98, 99–100,
  128, 140
Hematin, 154
Heme, 155–156, 158–159, 164
Hemin, 158
Hemoglobin, 94, 155–156, 165
Hemorrhages, of the eye, 2
Hepatitis B and C, precautions for, 311–315
High-velocity impact, 16, 17
  blood spatter from, 67–74
  definition, 304
  experiments with firearms, and use of
    simulated head, 74–80
Historical background, 3–10, 153–155
HIV, precautions for, 311–315
Horizontal motion, effects of pattern, 40–41
Horizontal surfaces, pattern of free-falling
    droplets onto, 19–27
Hospital records, 10
Humidity. *See* Environmental conditions
Hydrochloric acid, 164
Hydrogen peroxide, 154, 155, 158, 159
Hypochlorites, 154

I

Ice, bloodstains on, 96, 130, 258
Impact pattern, definition, 304
Impacts. *See* Angle of impact; High-velocity
    impact; Low-velocity impact;
    Medium-velocity impact

Impact site, definition, 304
Impressions. *See* Blood transfer patterns
Incised wounds, 108, 109, 110. *See also*
    Sharp-force trauma
Indazolon-4-carboxylic acid, 155
Infectious diseases, precautions for, 311–315
Injuries. *See* specific anatomical sites
International Association of Bloodstain
    Pattern Analysts, 306
*Interpretation of Bloodstain Evidence at Crime
    Scenes*, 9, 98, 177
Interpretation of evidence
  goals, 11
  luminol luminescence patterns, 162–163
  objectives, 10–11
Intoxication, 112–113, 120
Iron, 156, 158–159

J

Jeserich, Paul, 5
Journal of Forensic Identification, 10, 62
Journal of Forensic Sciences, 10
*Journal of the Canadian Society of Forensic
    Science*, 10
Journals, 10
Jugular vein, 116

K

Kidney wounds, 118
Kirk, Paul, 5, 7
Knife wounds. *See* Sharp-force trauma

L

*Laboratory Manual on the Geometric
    Interpretation of Human Bloodstain
    Evidence*, 7–8
Laboratory methods
  ability and scope of, 140
  precautions for infectious diseases, 313
  reports, 126
Lacerations, 106, 107, 108, 112, 277,
    297–298, 300. *See also* Sharp-force
    trauma
Left-handedness, 6
Legal aspects, 80, 105–124, 168
Legal Medicine Annual, 80

Length/width ratio of blood droplets, 31–34
Leucomalachite green reagent, 128, 145
Leukocytes, 12, 13
Liver wounds, 117–118
Livor mortis, 1, 3
Low-velocity impact. *See also* Blood droplets,
    free falling; Cast-off or splashed blood
  angular considerations, 19–58
  definition, 304
  external forces and, 15–16, 17
  patterns associated with, 48–58
Luminescence. *See* Luminol
Luminol
  blood detection with, 98, 101, 129,
    153–173
  interpretation of luminescence, 161–163
  preparation of, 155, 159–161
  reaction, 155–159
  toxicity, 160
Lung wounds, 116
Lymphocytes, 12, 13

M

MacDonnel, Herbert Leon, 7–9, 62, 122
Machinery trauma
  size of droplets from, 69, 70
  velocity of, 17
Mannequin, use of, 143, 145
Martial arts weapons, 59
Medical and medicolegal aspects, 105–124
Medications taken by victim, 105
Medium-velocity impact, 16, 17
  blood spatter from, 59–67
  definition, 304
Menstrual blood flow, 118
Mesenteric artery, 118
Metals, luminescence with luminol, 161
Methodologies
  crime scene diagrams, 132–139
  crime scene search patterns, 131–132
  preparation of luminol, 155, 159–161
Mist-like dispersion, 68, 69, 70, 305
Models
  trigonometric relationship of bloodstain
    ellipse and angle of impact, 27,
    29–34, 309–310
  trigonomic analysis for point or area of
    origin, 36, 38–40, 309–310

Monocytes, 12, 13
Mouth and tongue, 114, 115, 119
Movement, of the assailant, 125. *See also*
    Shoeprints
Movement of the victim, 11, 50, 90, 119, 122,
    123
  in case studies, 194, 195–196, 206, 272
  crime scene evaluation and, 127–128
Multiple cast-off patterns, 47, 53, 55, 61, 62
Multiple wounds, 40, 112, 116
Muscle mass of victim, 105
Muzzle. *See* Guns

N

Neck wounds, 116, 119
Neutrophils, 12, 13
Ninhydrin, 165
Nonhorizontal surfaces
  luminol patterns on, 163
  pattern of free-falling droplets onto, 27–34
Nose and sinuses, 114, 115, 119

O

Occupational health
  precautions for infectious diseases,
    311–315
  protection equipment for luminol use,
    160–161
Origin. *See* Source of blood
Oxygen, color of blood and, 12, 42

P

Parent droplet, 27, 28, 305
PCR (polymerase chain reaction), 166
Pelvic area, 116, 118
Petechial hemorrhages, of the eye, 2
Phenolphthalein, 128, 145, 162, 200, 255
Phosphoglucomutase typing (PGM), 165
Photography
  autopsy, 10, 126
  of crime scene, 127, 130, 143
  of luminol luminescence patterns, 164,
    166–168
  use in crime scene diagrams, 133
Physical properties of blood, 14–15
Piotrowski, Eduard, 4–5

Plasma, 12
Platelets, 13, 87
Point of convergence, 35–36, 37, 129,
    305
Polymerase chain reaction (PCR), 166
Pools of blood, 48, 127
Porphin, 156
Postmortem lividity, 1, 3
Potassium oxalate, 140
Projected blood. *See* Cast-off or splashed
    blood
Prosthetic group of proteins, 155

Q

Quadrant zone method for crime scene
    search, 131–132

R

Rectangular plotting method, 133, 137
Red blood cells (RBC), 12, 13, 87
Reference texts, 4–10
Research on Blood Spatter, 5–6
Restriction fragment length polymorphism
    (RFLP), 166
Rh factor. *See* Blood grouping
Ricochet of blood, 42, 305
Right-handedness, 6
Roads, surface texture of, 130

S

Saliva, 161
Satellite spatter, 17, 25–27, 64, 65, 304
    case studies, 178, 180, 184
    definition, 305
Scallop pattern, 305
Secondary splashing, 42, 305
Semen, 161, 166
Serum, 87, 88, 91, 92, 218, 305
Shadow. *See* Void areas
Sharp-force trauma, 17
    case studies, 257–264, 281–301
        use of luminol, 172–173
    incised wounds, 108, 109, 110
    stabbing trauma, 17, 59, 106, 108, 109,
        116, 117
    types of wounds, 108–110

Shock, percent blood loss with, 120
Shoeprints, 52, 125, 144, 172, 173, 247, 280,
    296, 298
Shoes, 63, 64, 172, 173, 262. *See also*
    Shoeprints
Shoring wound, 72
Simulated head, for experiments with
    firearms, 74–80
Sine functions, 30
Skeletonized bloodstain, 86, 305
Skull fractures, 112–113
Smear, definition, 305. *See also* Swipes
Smoke and soot, effects on bloodstains,
    96–98, 99–100
Smudges, definitions, 48, 50, 305
Sneezed blood. *See* Exhaled or expirated
    blood
Snow, bloodstains on, 96, 130
Sodium carbonate, 159
Sodium fluoride, 140
Sodium hydroxide, 160
Sodium perborate, 159
Soil, bloodstains on, 130
Soot
    effects on bloodstains, 96–98, 99–100
    from gunshot trauma, 98, 178, 179, 204,
        205, 210
Sourcebook, 153
Source of blood
    determination of point or area of, 36,
        37–40
    distance from, 10
    multiple, 40, 112, 116
    point or area of origin, definition,
        305
Specific gravity of blood, 14
Spinal fluid, 96, 97
Spine, definition, 306
Splashed blood. *See* Cast-off or splashed
    blood; Ricochet of blood
Spleen wounds, 118
Stabbing. *See* Sharp-force trauma
State of Ohio v. Samuel Sheppard,
    5, 7
Stereomicroscope, 145
Strangulation. *See* Asphyxial deaths
Substrate. *See* Clothing; Horizontal surfaces;
    Nonhorizontal surfaces; Surface
    texture

Suicide, behavior prior to, 291–295, 298. *See also* Gunshot trauma, self-inflicted
Surface tension on blood droplet, 14–15, 19, 20
Surface texture
  blood drying and, 85, 90–93
  effect on bloodstain characteristics, 22–24, 27, 130
  effect on luminol luminescence patterns, 163–164
  of roads, 130
Survival time, post-injury, 119
Suspect, support/contradiction of statements by, 11
Swipes, 17, 50, 53, 246, 306

T

Takayama confirmatory test, 165
Target, definition, 306
Temperature. *See* Environmental conditions
Terminal velocity, 21, 306
Tetramethylbenzidine, 162
Thrombocytes (platelets), 13, 87
o-Tolidine, 162
Trachea, 283, 284
Transecting baseline plotting method, 134, 139
Transfer bloodstain patterns. *See* Blood transfer patterns
Triangulation plotting method, 133, 138
Trigonometric tables, 309–310
Tripods, 167

U

Urethral orifice, 118

V

Vaginal orifice, 118
Vehicles
  blunt-force trauma case studies and, 257–267
  gunshot trauma within, 219–221

Vehicular trauma, 118
  bloodstain patterns with, 56, 58, 292
  evidence collection, 130–131, 140
  impact from, 90
Velocity
  of explosions, 17
  of gunshot trauma, 17, 59
  of impacts. *See* High-velocity impact; Low-velocity impact; Medium-velocity impact
  terminal, 21, 306
Vertical surfaces. *See* Nonhorizontal surfaces
Victim
  age of, 105
  estimation of time of death, 96, 218
  health of, 105
  movement of. *See* Movement of the victim
  muscularity of, 105
Viscosity of blood, 14
Void areas, 50, 53–55, 56, 57, 146, 147
  in case studies, 180, 181, 231
  definition, 306
Volume. *See* Blood, volume
Vomiting of blood, 67

W

Walls, radial patterns on, 61–62. *See also* Cast-off or splashed blood
Washing, effects on bloodstains, 98, 101–102
Wave cast-off, 27, 28, 306
Weather, 96, 130
White binder reinforcements, 144, 146
White blood cells (WBC), 12, 13
Wind, 130
Wipe patterns, 50–52, 129
  definition, 306
  on skeletonized bloodstain, 86, 305
Witnesses, support/contradiction of statements by, 11
Wounds, major vessel disruption and, 112–119

Z

Zone method for crime scene search, 131–132